THE GREAT INDIAN FRAUD

THE GREAT INDIAN FRAUD

Serious Frauds which Shook the Economy

Smarak Swain

BLOOMSBURY
NEW DELHI • LONDON • OXFORD • NEW YORK • SYDNEY

BLOOMSBURY INDIA
Bloomsbury Publishing India Pvt. Ltd
Second Floor, LSC Building No. 4, DDA Complex, Pocket C – 6 & 7,
Vasant Kunj, New Delhi 110070

BLOOMSBURY, BLOOMSBURY INDIA and the Diana logo are
trademarks of Bloomsbury Publishing Plc

This edition published in 2020

ISBN: PB: 978-9-3898-6722-0; eBook: 978-9-3898-6724-4
2 4 6 8 10 9 7 5 3 1

Typeset in Manipal Technologies Limited
Printed and bound in India by Gopsons Papers Pvt. Ltd., Noida

Bloomsbury Publishing Plc makes every effort to ensure that the papers used in the manufacture of our books are natural, recyclable products made from wood grown in well-managed forests. Our manufacturing processes conform to the environmental regulations of the country of origin

FSC www.fsc.org MIX Paper | Supporting responsible forestry FSC® C191020

To find out more about our authors and books visit www.bloomsbury.com and sign up for our newsletters

To
My lovely grandmothers,
Late Banija Swain
and
Late Jamuni Jena

CONTENTS

ACKNOWLEDGEMENTS

It is difficult to recall the exact moment, but the idea to study financial frauds and to write a book on it crystallised while I was delivering a lecture at the Indian Institute of Management (IIM), Indore. Satyasai Rath, my senior colleague in the Indian Revenue Service (IRS), had been the inspiration behind the initiative. He had prodded me to research on motives behind creative accounting practices. The lengthy discussions I had with him on creative accounting practices helped me develop competence on this topic. Later, he referred me to Professor Saumya Ranjan Dash and Professor Mehul Raithatha at IIM Indore, who arranged the lecture on creative accounting practices in February 2019. The debates I had with Professor Raithatha and his students helped me develop a cogent narrative style on this topic.

I got important insights on bank frauds from batchmate and colleague Pradeep Singh Gautam, who had just returned from the UK, where he had researched the Insolvency and Bankruptcy Code (IBC) of India. Another batchmate, Rupesh Agarwal, now posted in the Serious Fraud Investigation Office (SFIO), gave critical insights on company law in India. Yet another batchmate, Lalit Mohan Jindal, now on deputation at the Central Bureau of Investigation (CBI), helped me with understanding the law on economic crimes.

For assistance on origin frauds, I reached out to Md Moin Afaque, an old classmate from Indian Institute of Technology (IIT), Kharagpur, who is now working for the Indian Trade Service (ITS). He shared many case studies on anti-dumping duties and circumvention, which helped me form a calibrated perspective on India's trade defence measures.

I am greatly indebted to chartered accountants I have met professionally and my colleagues in the Income Tax department and the Department of Revenue. My understanding of accounts and finance has deeply been shaped by tax professionals and tax officers I have interacted with in the course of my work.

I did not have to go too far for help on export-import and Goods and Services Tax (GST) frauds. My wife Ashima, who has worked for many years in the Customs department, also happens to be a master trainer on GST. I am grateful to Ashima for many other reasons. She suffered through my many contemplative phases, in which I only read and wrote, in the middle of a lockdown forced upon us by the COVID-19 pandemic. For the record, I had offered to help her with household chores during the lockdown.

Gangadhar Patil and Hemant Gairola of 101reporters.com read the book and shared important feedback on the narration and pace. Praveen Tiwari of Bloomsbury Publishing motivated me through the entire process of writing. Shreya Chakraborti, Bhaswati Mukhopadhyay and Nitin Valecha, part of the editorial team at Bloomsbury Publishing, did fantastic fact-check and flawless editing of the book.

PROLOGUE

Serious frauds are a result of failures that challenge free markets and disrupt economic processes in ways more profound than the fraud itself. Such fraudulent acts create ripples that undermine the economic security of liberal democracies like India.

The free market economy is based on the idea that when individuals are left to themselves, they take decisions in self-interest that automatically leads to order. Order comes from uncoordinated behaviour of individuals, almost like a miracle. Economist Adam Smith, who introduced us to this miracle in 1759, described it as an 'invisible hand' of the market. Smith said by pursuing self-interest, an individual 'frequently promotes that of the society more effectually than when he really intends to promote it'.[1]

Austrian-British economist Friedrich Hayek saw the invisible hand of the market as a spontaneous order, which comes in a free market and results in better allocation of resources, than any planning could achieve. It is now widely accepted that an ideal free market economy, where every individual is free to act selfishly, is much more efficient than any alternative system in which the State intervenes. The State has no role in a free market economy.

However, an ideal market is possible only when every market participant follows the rules and does not game the system. When participants try to game the market, 'market failure' happens. Free markets yield poor outcomes whenever market failure happens. This is where the State plays a role: preventing and curing market failure.

Market failures are broadly of four types: Externalities, asymmetric information, market power and public goods.[2] Financial frauds are a form of market failure through 'asymmetric information' and may be the severest of all forms of market failure. The 2008 sub-prime mortgage crisis in the US, which became a worldwide economic crisis, is often quoted by critics of the free market system to prophesize that free market economics has failed. The sub-prime crisis was the result of financial frauds perpetrated at multiple levels. Banks and other lending institutions aggressively gave home loans to individuals with sub-prime credit rating at prime lending rates. This was brokered by mortgage intermediaries, who were eager to get more and more customers so that they could get brokerage. Banks, in turn, securitised these sub-prime loans by declaring them as prime loans. Investment banks misrepresented the characteristics of these securities and sold them to institutional investors. When homebuyers defaulted on their loans en masse, the securities turned stale and afflicted the entire chain. There was fraud committed at multiple levels.

Financial frauds are cheat codes that can undermine a free market economy. Small and stray frauds such as credit card fraud or phishing affect some people, but serious frauds in the financial system of an economy affect the entire economy. First, it affects the level of trust people have in the market. In a way, serious frauds can be equated to epidemics and pandemics. After the COVID-19 pandemic, workers and managers went into a lockdown mode. There was widespread fear in the market and the global economy came to a near standstill. COVID-19 infected a number of people, but the fear of contracting it affected economic behaviour of many more. Similarly, whenever a serious fraud hits the news, people lose their confidence on the entire market. The market's integrity is questioned.

Critics jump in and cry foul. They write away the free market economy and call for more government interference and control. Many a time, serious frauds generate public opinion against keeping the market free. Instead of demanding laws against market failure, they demand laws against the free market itself.

A second consequence is that it undermines the level of trust within the market. Individual and institutional investors withdraw their investments from the market, thus affecting the market's efficiency. The call for greater regulation translates into reactive rules that require more stringent documentation and due diligence. This, too, affects the market's efficiency.

A third consequence, which happens in the case of widely-prevalent frauds, is economic rupture.

Hence, preventing serious frauds is one of the prime responsibilities of the government that believes in free market economy. Ironically, given the complexity of the financial world of our times, it is very difficult for any State or regulator to prevent financial frauds.

What Are Serious Frauds

This book seeks to profile serious frauds, their modus operandi and their impact on economic institutions. The book goes on to show that the modus operandi followed in serious frauds are derived from elementary mathematics and logic. Modus operandi of most serious frauds we have read about in recent years are similar to the ones detected decades ago. That indicates, the modus operandi of serious frauds has not actually changed over time. The complexity of the system has changed, which has helped serious frauds to recur and perpetuate the system.

A few definitions are warranted to put terms, used in this book, in perspective. Economic crime or white-collar crime includes any kind of criminal behaviour or infringement that leads to unlawful economic advantage to the person committing it. It is a broad definition that includes many financial and non-financial crimes. Financial crimes are a subset of economic crimes that include tax crimes, corruption, terror financing, money laundering, etc.

'Fraud', itself being a generic word, is often used to describe financial as well as some non-financial crimes. For instance, elaborate schemes to fool the taxman are also referred to as tax fraud. However, the phrase 'financial fraud' has a specific definition in relation to the market. For the purpose of this book, financial fraud is defined as 'acts and statements through which financial market participants misinform or mislead other participants in the market by deliberately or recklessly providing them with false, incomplete or manipulative information related to financial goods, services or investment opportunities'[3] in a way that violates the law.

A serious fraud needs to be understood by its colloquial meaning. It is a financial fraud of enormous proportions. There are some exceptions though. Some serious frauds are not financial frauds. For instance, the Comptroller and Auditor General (CAG) of India and the CBI have, at various times, levelled allegations of corruption in procurements and resource allocation that involve malfeasance of billions, even trillions, of rupees. However, such scams do not directly affect the economy, although they directly affect government finances. It is a different story for another time.

Serious frauds discussed in this book are large financial frauds that harm the economy. And then again, not all financial frauds take the form of serious frauds. Only those financial frauds that can trigger a vicious cycle of fraud, siphoning and profiteering, become serious frauds. Such frauds grow in size in each cycle and manage to take on such gigantic form that they instill trust and confidence in people. It is only when the bubble bursts that people get to know the reality. However, by then, the fraud would have been committed and the money siphoned off.

The bubble usually bursts when a gatekeeper is not impressed by the halo of success created by the fraudsters. Gatekeepers are intermediaries who are supposed to provide necessary checks and balances, including independent directors, external auditors, attorneys, credit rating agencies and regulators such as the Securities and Exchange Board of India (SEBI) and the Reserve Bank of India (RBI).

There is a general consensus among scholars that financial frauds are linked to economic cycles.[4] In its April 2020 issue, *The Economist* observed that booms 'help fraudsters paper over cracks in their accounts, from fictitious investment returns to exaggerated sales. Slowdowns rip the covering off'.[5] It claimed that many big book-cooking scandals of the past 20 years emerged during economic downturns. As star investor Warren Buffett once said: 'You only find out who is swimming naked when the tide goes out.'[6] Economic crises lead to a general credit crunch, which strains fraudulent schemes. Many of them fall apart as a consequence. An economic crisis also instills pessimism and caution in the heart of auditors and creditors and they start asking hard questions, which they otherwise would not. This, of course, helps detect frauds.

While downturns expose frauds, fraudsters gnaw at the market at all times and have become quite pervasive in recent times. Frauds in financial statement, for example, often occur.[7] The line between creative accounting and accounting fraud has always been blurred, but the frequency of accounting scandals has been so high in recent years that they are now often seen as being hidden in the nook and cranny of corporate life.[8] In a global banking fraud survey conducted by KPMG in 2019, more than 50 per cent of respondents globally said they experienced an increase in fraud value.[9] Investment scams, such as ponzi schemes, have become so rampant that they 'seem to have reached the proportion of an epidemic'.[10] A study conducted by the Canadian Securities Administration in 2007, found that one in twenty Canadians were victims of investment frauds.[11]

Why are there so many global financial frauds? This is a question we shall be asking time and again in this book. At an elementary level, every fraud is a problem of control. Wherever control fails, fraudsters abuse the loophole, but the problem of recurring financial frauds is more than just a problem of control. Every serious fraud is dealt with by tightening norms and disclosure requirements. And yet, financial frauds recur. The reason behind this is the increasing complexity of financial transactions. New technologies, coupled with innovative financial tools, have introduced many a jargon in the world of finance and make it less comprehensible.[12] A wide array of financial instruments and legal structures are readily available to help the corporates structure their business in ways that hide liabilities and conceal sham transactions.

Take, for example, the case that most scholars studying accounting frauds consider an archetype–Enron. Enron used Special Purpose Vehicles (SPVs) to effect sophisticated off-balance sheet accounting to hide its rising debts, which helped it paint a better picture than the reality. It had set up more than 3,000 SPVs, of which 800 were based in tax havens. Tax havens provide a conducive ecosystem for fraudsters in the form of stringent banking secrecy laws and facilities to run shell companies while hiding their control over such companies.

Regulation fails repeatedly because the regulatory cycle–the time in which legal regulation catches up with a deviant innovation–is ruptured. Step 1 involves introduction of new technological and financial innovations. Rules to control abuse of such innovations are still not drafted. Scamsters smell new ways of committing fraud using these innovations. In Step 2, the scamsters commit the actual fraud. Regulators realise the misuse of new loopholes and try to bring new rules to institute control in Step 3. Then another innovation again takes us to Step 1 and the regulatory cycle continues. A healthy regulatory cycle is one where the time gap between Step 1 and Step 3 is low, maybe a couple of years. In recent years, we have seen situations where the regulatory cycle is ruptured. Regulators take years to detect frauds because of the increasing complexity of frauds. Innovations are being introduced at break-neck pace. Step 2 runs for extended periods. By the time regulators plug a loophole in the cycle, a new innovation would have already started a new cycle.

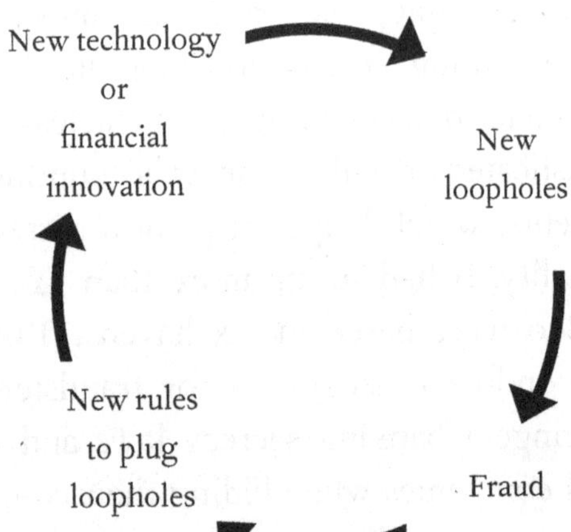

FIGURE 1: *The Regulatory Cycle*

Source: Author

This book seeks to simplify questionable schemes of our times that appear incomprehensible. There are only a handful of modus operandi that lead to serious frauds and they are derived from basic mathematics and logic. The age-old modus is being operated behind veils of complex corporate structures and exotic financial instruments. The first chapter on Bank Frauds narrates the incredible story of how fraudulent loans are taken and then siphoned off. Fraudsters, who manage to set up a vicious cycle of availing loans, perpetuate the biggest frauds against lending institutions. The second chapter gives an overview of unfair trade practices in the stock market and talks about how some of these securities frauds assume serious proportions by perpetuating vicious cycles. Chapter three shows how mispricing in international trade is used to rotate funds and commit EXIM frauds. Other interesting modus operandi, involving GST frauds and circumvention of anti-dumping duties, are also discussed in this chapter. The fourth chapter discusses a few of the many types of corporate frauds that involve creative accounting practices.

Creative accounting and manipulative bookkeeping are core to the cases discussed in the first four chapters. The fifth chapter discusses pyramid and ponzi schemes that are closer to the ordinary meaning of swindling.

Chapter six discusses shell companies, mailbox companies and secrecy jurisdictions that facilitate and catalyse fraudulent acts. In a way, they constitute a favourable ecosystem that fraudsters utilise and rely on.

A disclaimer on the narrative is due at this time. At times, the book talks to the reader when explaining modus operandi, which the reader may mistake for a how-to-commit-fraud guide. The author considers himself a crusader against serious frauds and at no time intends to educate the reader about how to commit frauds. The narration keeps shifting to enliven the chronicle. Portrayal of some of the greatest fraudsters of our time is adulatory, at times, and it is so because they are not just another hustler. They are financial wizards who used their intelligence to follow the wrong path. The author is reverential towards their ingenuity, not their conduct. Their conduct is clearly deplorable.

The book discusses many convicted fraudsters. It also discusses some live cases wherein law enforcement authorities have levelled serious allegations, but the matter has not yet reached a finality in judicial forums. In such cases, the author merely discusses the allegations levied by law enforcement agencies, without drawing any conclusion on culpability. The discussion is based on material available in the public domain and does not derive from any information that may have come to the author's knowledge in the course of his discharge of official duties as investigator or assessor in the Income Tax department.

The views expressed by the author in this book are personal and do not reflect the opinion of the Government of India or the Income Tax department in any way.

1

The Perfect Bank Heist: Loan Fraud

The British royalty is known for its wealth and opulence. The magnificent Buckingham Palace, the London abode of the British royalty, is a fine example of this opulence. Each and every corner of this palace is intricately designed with the costliest of fixtures. The Royal Mews, that takes care of the road travel arrangements for the Queen and members of the Royal Family, boasts of a number of Rolls Royce, Jaguars and Bentleys as well as the finest horses in all of England. For special occasions at the Buckingham Palace, golden plates and antique golden cutlery are taken out for the royal guests. And just three miles from all this opulence and grandeur is Regent's Park, where stands the mansion of another king, Dr Vijay Mallya. Mallya, the fugitive Indian liquor baron who is wanted on alleged fraud and money laundering charges, had controlling stakes in United Spirits Ltd and United Breweries Ltd. He was also the founder and owner of the now defunct Kingfisher Airlines. Known for his flamboyant lifestyle, Mallya was the self-proclaimed 'King of Good Times'.

Mallya can not only match, but also exceed Buckingham's penchant for opulence. If the Queen sometimes eats out of gold plates, the King of Good Times often poops on a commode made out of gold.[1]

It has been more than a decade since the global financial crisis of 2008, and yet India still remains plagued by cases of bank loan frauds. The fraud purportedly pulled off by Mallya is considered the most infamous of such cases. Mallya, the promoter of liquor-cum-fertiliser conglomerate United Breweries Holdings Limited (UB Group), entered the airline industry with Kingfisher Airlines in May 2005. Owing to a series of unwise business decisions, the airlines accumulated heavy losses by the end of 2011. By early 2012, half of its fleet was grounded, its employees were on strike for non-payment of salary and the Income Tax department had attached its bank accounts for not depositing tax deducted at source (TDS) from its employees' salaries. The airline had to completely stop operations by October 2012.

By 2014, Kingfisher Airlines' debts accounted for most of the non-performing assets (NPAs) of India's public sector banks (PSBs). It is not that Mallya did not have the wherewithal to pay. In an acquisition deal that started in 2012, London-based multinational alcoholic beverage company, Diageo, bought majority shares in United Spirits Limited, a UB Group company, from Mallya. It paid Mallya ₹3,635 crore for his 19.3 per cent stake in United Spirits. Over the next few years, Diageo paid significant sums to various companies of the UB Group for acquiring majority stake in United Spirits. The deal went through despite Karnataka High Court's instructions to Mallya not to alienate his shares in United Spirits.[2] So Mallya clearly had the means to pay back creditors of Kingfisher Airlines. It was his moral and legal duty to clear the debt. After all, he had given his personal guarantee for the loans and UB Group's holding company had given a corporate guarantee.

Diageo made the payments to Mallya's offshore accounts.[3] Since the company was headquartered in the UK and Mallya himself was a non-resident Indian, there was nothing much the Indian authorities could do to recover the defaulted loan. By the time India's PSBs could take legal action for recovery of their loans, Mallya had escaped to the UK. He now shuttles between his English country estate and his mansion in Regent's Park.

The kind of fraud that Mallya committed only begets other frauds of a similar nature. When a person escapes the long hands of law after committing a serious fraud, he tends to trigger similar proclivities in a whole generation of imposters and swindlers. In Mallya's case, what's worse is that he was already an icon for many. In his good times, he ruled over all that our mothers considered vice and we cherished in our teenage: wine, women and other worldly pleasures. He had his stud firm in Bengaluru, the Kingfisher calendar that featured models in exotic locations, a yacht, a Formula 1 racing team, a cricket team in the Indian Premier League and the sword of Tipu Sultan, which he had bought at an auction to remind everyone that he was indeed the emperor of good times.

Even when he escaped from India, he did so with elan. On 2 March 2016, he attended the Parliament, picked his then girlfriend, seven pieces of luggage, flashed his diplomatic passport at immigration and boarded a Jet Airways flight to London.

However, Mallya's is not a typical case of loan fraud. Yes, he is a willful defaulter. It has been alleged that he has siphoned off funds from his firms through shell companies registered in tax havens. However, it cannot be denied that he was principally an entrepreneur who took up unwise and risky ventures. His case is unlike other loan frauds that surfaced in the decade starting 2009.

Trail of Loan Frauds

It, however, looks like Mallya's bank default was not as big as many other loan frauds seen through the decade. His default was to the tune of ₹9,091 crore, including interest (as on November 30, 2015). Add to that the income tax and service tax of ₹1,215 crore that he owed. In comparison, the one allegedly perpetuated by Infrastructure Leasing & Financial Services Limited (IL&FS) involved a loan default of ₹90,000 crore. The Bhushan Steel case involved a loan default of ₹45,818 crore. These two cases dealt a huge structural jolt to their respective sectors as well as to the economy.

Brij Bhushan Singal, the patriarch of Bhushan Group, was a self-made man. He started by making hinges and fasteners for railway tracks in Chandigarh. Along with his sons Neeraj Singal and Sanjay Singal, he acquired an ailing steel factory in Sahibabad in 1987. That marked the quick rise of the Bhushan Group.[4] The group split in 2011 after a family dispute. Brij Bhushan and Neeraj retained Bhushan Steel and Bhushan Energy, while

Sanjay took control of a third company called Bhushan Power and Steel.

In 2005, Brij Bhushan and Neeraj started construction of an integrated steel plant in Odisha. Those were heady times for the steel industry in India. The demand from the automobile sector was robust. China had a huge import appetite due to the upcoming 2008 Summer Olympics in Beijing. However, the sector faced a slowdown after the Olympics. Steel prices peaked in 2008 at $1,265 per tonne and quickly fell to $300 per tonne by 2012.

Loans started piling up while the revenue sources tapered. Interestingly, Bhushan Steel managed to secure more loans even as the industry was experiencing a slowdown. Its long-term loans increased from ₹15,528 crore in March 2012 to ₹21,664 crore in March 2013. By March 2015, the company's long-term loans swelled to ₹31,477 crore. Profits kept dwindling in this period and the company clocked a loss of ₹1,255 crore in 2014–15.

Signs of default were evident as early as August 2014, when the CBI alleged that Bhushan Steel had defaulted on a ₹100-crore loan repayment to Syndicate Bank, but bribed the bank chairman for a credit extension. Neeraj Singal was arrested on 7 August 2014, and later released on bail.

The key question here is: How did Bhushan Steel manage to raise so many loans from banks? The SFIO made a detailed forensic audit of its affairs in 2017, and filed a charge sheet subsequently. Their audit 'revealed that... Brij Bhushan Singal and Neeraj Singal... used a web of 155 companies, which were directly or indirectly controlled by the Singals, to siphon off money from Bhushan Steel and Bhushan Energy'.[5]

The SFIO divided the companies into four categories due to the complexity of transactions involving shell companies. The four categories were: A, B, C and D. Category A consisted of Bhushan Steel and Bhushan Energy, the operating companies. Category B included 62 companies that were directly under the control of Brij Bhushan Singal and Neeraj Singal. The Singals were shareholders and directors in these companies. Category C consisted of 85 companies in which employees of Bhushan Steel were made directors from time to time. The SFIO alleged that while some of these companies provided manpower to Bhushan Steel, others were involved in fund diversion. Category D comprised eight companies that were run by entry operators. Entry operators are professional syndicates that operate shell companies and provide services for laundering of funds.

The SFIO alleged in the charge sheet that banks granted loans to Category A companies and these companies gave loan funds to Category B shell companies as advances. Funds were layered through Category B companies and supplied to Category C companies. Category C companies then gave the funds back to the promoters. The promoters used the funds to acquire assets. A part of the funds were infused back into Category A companies as promoters' share. Such rotation of borrowed money ended up projecting loan funds as promoters' contribution in the accounts. Banks inferred that if promoters were putting in more money on a project, they could also advance more money.

Between 2009–10 and 2010–11, Bhushan Steel and Bhushan Energy transferred ₹1,770 crore as 'capital advance' to 32 Category B companies. It is an advance given for transfer of a capital asset (such as land, machinery or constructed space). Out of this, ₹1,150 crore was transferred to 19 Category C companies. These Category C companies transferred the funds to the bank accounts of Uma Singal, wife of Brij Bhushan Singal. She then infused these funds into Bhushan Steel as promoter contribution.

The SFIO, in its report, mentioned some very apparent instances of layering by these shell companies. In one instance, Bhushan Steel made an advance payment of ₹27 crore to KNK Traders, an unrelated party, supposedly for providing some service. KNK Traders transferred the amount on the same day to KBN Infra, a company controlled by Brij Bhushan Singal and Neeraj Singal.

When you approach a bank for project finance, bankers are ready to finance 70 per cent of the project if the promoters infuse 30 per cent of their money. Bankers insist on a promoters' contribution, which varies between 15 per cent and 40 per cent on a case-by-case basis.[6] If the SFIO's allegations are proven in the court, it would imply that the money infused by promoters into Bhushan Steel was actually siphoned from earlier loans and was not their own money. It created a false perception that the promoters were capable of bearing the cost of new projects.

The 32 Category B companies, being shell entities, never did any business activity. If large advances given to any entity lie in the balance sheet for a long time, auditors start asking questions such as: Why don't you recover it? Why lock up so much funds in giving advances? And, probably to avoid such queries, the company made accounting entries in 2013–14 and 2014–15, whereby the capital advances were shown as 'capital work in progress'. Capital work in progress in this sector usually implies construction activity for developing a new factory or machinery. However, Category B shell companies, the SFIO charge sheet alleged, remained true to their name and were never involved in developing any new asset. The SFIO also claimed in its charge sheet that the Singals acquired personal assets of ₹3,500 crore in India and elsewhere with the borrowed loans.

Meanwhile, Sanjay, Brij Bhushan's son, who had parted ways with his father and brother in 2011, was also facing similar issues in his business. In April 2019, the CBI alleged that Sanjay's company Bhushan Power & Steel Ltd diverted about ₹2,348 crore of loans from various banks into the accounts of more than 200 shell companies without any obvious purpose. On 5 July 2019, Punjab National Bank (PNB) filed a report with the RBI, alleging that Bhushan Power and Steel had defrauded it of ₹3,805 crore that were granted as loans. The bank's share price tumbled 8 per cent in a single day after the reporting. A week later, Allahabad Bank reported to the RBI that the company had defrauded it of ₹1,774 crore. With this news, shares of the bank plunged 15 per cent.[7]

Decade of Defaults and Derangements

Banks play an important role in economic development. They collect savings from people and lend them to businesses, thus stimulating commercial activity. However, banks themselves run a tight ship. They charge interest on loans and use it to pay interest on deposits made by retail customers. The difference of the two is what accounts for a bank's profit. There is always the risk that a borrower will default on its loans, in which case the loans become a loss for the bank (the technical term for this is NPAs).

To manage risks, banks evaluate borrowers. They call for their financials details and analyse their creditworthiness before approving the loan. Banks also ask for some assets as collateral. If they deem a business too risky, they refuse to grant a loan. A loan fraud happens when the borrower deceives the bank into adjudging a business venture as less risky than it actually is. This may happen with or without the complicity of the bank's employees.

The rise and fall of loan fraud scams roughly correspond to the economic boom and bust cycles. Bankers are in a bull rush to offer loans during periods of boom. Frauds ride on the general positive sentiment towards a specific sector during boom period and loans get sanctioned easily. Once they become 'too big to fail', they take new loans to pay off old ones. Repayment of old loans reinforces the faith of bankers and investors in their business. Matters spiral out of control once the sector faces a slowdown. Banks start showing reluctance to advance new loans. Servicing of old loans becomes tough and then, all of a sudden, the whole edifice crumbles.

This is what happened in India in the aftermath of the economic slowdown of 2008. The buzz in real estate had fizzled out. Infrastructure, power and steel sectors, all cyclical in nature, faced a period of stagnation. International markets were reeling under recession. Loan fraud cases rolled out like skeletons concealed in a small attic.

As per the data released by the RBI, in the 11 years between FY 2008–09 and FY 2018–19, a total of 53,334 bank fraud cases were detected, involving ₹2.05 lakh crore ($28.72 billion). This is almost equal to Nepal's GDP for FY 2018–19, $28.92 billion, and a little more than 10 per cent of Pakistan's GDP for the same year, $282 billion.

Interestingly, the number of bank frauds has increased over the years. More than 6,800 cases were reported in FY 2018–19, involving ₹71,500 crore, whereas 5,916 cases were detected in FY 2017–18 (₹41,167 crore).

The loan fraud cases of the two Bhushan factions have had a significant impact on the business ecosystem of the country. Other loan fraud cases that shook the system were the IL&FS scam, the Punjab & Maharashtra Co-operative (PMC) bank fiasco, the Sterling Biotech case, the Rotomac pen case and the Kanishk Gold case. Such frauds and scams had several severe impact on the economy.

The loss from NPAs is ultimately borne by the people of India. PSBs have taken the maximum hit from the frauds. As the PSBs are state owned, their loss is government's loss. Secondly, banks have become overly cautious in lending to sectors with a long gestation period. A third problem is that when faced with NPAs, banks have to increase their lending rates. Banks sustain their business on the difference between interest on loans they give and interest they give on deposits. When a bank takes a haircut, it has to make up for the loss by increasing its lending rate.

That apart, the fourth challenge is that such frauds increase the cost of raising a loan for a genuine businessman. There is no litmus test to find out if a firm is doing genuine business or is a suspect case. The RBI has prescribed a framework for detecting early warning signals (EWS) to warn bankers about possible frauds. Stringent due diligence norms have been proposed. RBI Deputy Governor M.K. Jain underlined in a microfinance conference in November 2019 that 'banks need to focus on repayment capacity of borrowers at the appraisal stage and monitor the loans through their lifecycle much more closely'.[8] However, the more the due diligence, the more the time needed to release loans and the higher the cost of raising a loan for the borrower.

Fifth, and most importantly, such large fraud cases vitiate the general atmosphere of trust between lenders and borrowers. Wherever trust is high, transaction cost is low. In a hypothetical situation where trust is 100 per cent, the borrower and lender do not even have to enter into an agreement and, thus, the cost of transaction remains low. As trust decreases, documentation and legal fees increase. Litigation also increases. The lower the trust in an ecosystem, the lower the efficiency of doing business. And consequently, lower the productivity of that economy.

Bankers face a trilemma of sorts in these times. They need to approve loans as they are in the very business of giving loans. They need to give loans and earn interest to meet their expenses and make a decent profit. However, given the spate of fraud cases, they now need to conduct more stringent due diligence. They also need to conduct regular reviews and inspections to catch what the RBI calls EWS. This increases their cost as well as borrowers' cost, leading to a no-win situation. Borrowers are deterred by the time-consuming processes.

Since bankers need to give loans and prospective borrowers are discouraged by the lengthy processes, such situation actually encourages fraudsters to apply for loans. Mind you, this conclusion is counter-intuitive to the perception that more due diligence weeds out fraudulent applicants. Due diligence is a subjective process and there is no clear formula for separating wheat from the chaff. Loan frauds have been following similar modus operandi for ages. Yet, they keep happening. So, why do banks commit the same mistakes that lead to fraudulent loans? Why does due diligence fail?

Before addressing these questions, it is important to understand how simple it is to pull off a loan fraud. Although deceptively simple for the culprit, it is difficult for banks to tell it apart from a genuine business requiring loans. The modus operandi of loan frauds is simple because the logic derives from elementary mathematics. Accounting helps shroud it in a veil of legitimate business activity.

The Mathematics of Bank Scams

You may approach the bank for a wide variety of reasons. When you approach banks for funds to start a new project, they usually first check your credit worthiness. They examine the cash flow of your existing businesses, how your business is doing, how other businesses in the same segment are functioning, etc. Then they ask the promoters to contribute about 30 per cent of the project's capital requirements. The banks chip in with a loan for the remaining 70 per cent. Banks also require promoters to provide some collateral. Usually, the assets planned to be purchased for the project are placed as collateral. Many a time, promoters also provide personal guarantee as a measure of comfort for the bank.

In a loan fraud of primitive complexity, the promoters would open a new company and pump in, say, ₹30 lakh as capital. The bank would then finance the company to the extent of ₹70 lakh. The promoters, on their part, would then try to siphon off their capital as well as bank loan from the company.

There are many ways of siphoning funds. Say, the company can purchase a junk software from a conduit at ₹100 lakh. The conduit then withdraws the money in cash and gives it back to the promoters. It is usually difficult to find the right price of a software, so a junk software can easily be passed off (on paper) as a valuable software and purchased. When siphoning funds, it is always beneficial for the promoters to do so outside the country. For, the banks would come for them once they realise they have been swindled. So, an alternative method of siphoning is to purchase a software or a patent (or any other intangible asset) from a foreign firm. The company would pay ₹100 lakh to the foreign firm. The foreign firm then wire transfers the funds to the promoters' offshore bank account.

This is a common modus operandi used for siphoning funds. Intangible assets such as software, patent, technical design, brand, etc., are preferred over tangible assets as it is difficult to ascertain the legitimate valuation of intangibles. No two intangible assets are similar. Judging the commercial viability of a patent, for instance, is a subjective exercise. In a survey conducted among inventors in the US, it was found that only about 60 per cent of patents awarded are commercialised.[9] Because patents are filed on niche technical innovations, bank auditors usually cannot judge their usability for a company that intends to purchase it. They merely go through the documentation. If the documentation is extensive and is certified by subject matter experts (experts rarely give independent opinion because the company hires such an expert who would validate its opinion), auditors do not raise any red flags on the purchase. Once the entire money is siphoned off, the borrowing company defaults in monthly instalment payments to the bank.

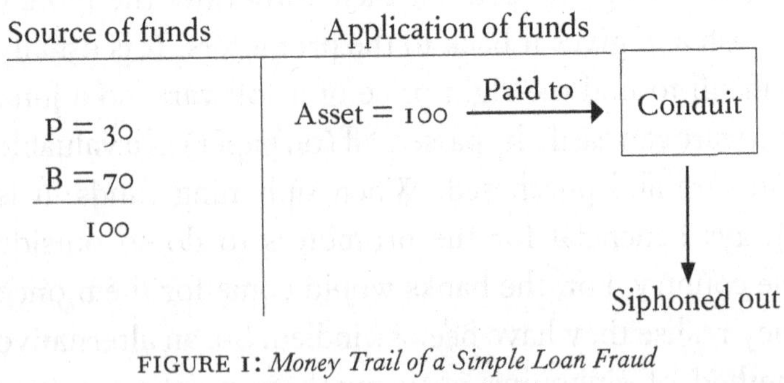

FIGURE 1: *Money Trail of a Simple Loan Fraud (P = promoters; B = bank)*

Source: Author

When the company defaults, the bank tries to recover the loaned amount from the assets hypothecated to the bank as collateral. In most cases, the project assets are hypothecated to the bank. Since the asset in above case is a worthless software/patent,[10] it will have no buyer.

We have discussed a typical case here. In a few cases, the company committing fraud does purchase some physical assets, but at a highly inflated price. The company may purchase a building or land from a relative of the promoter. The valuation is boosted by getting a report from a certified valuation engineer. The bank remains under the perception that the land is worth the amount paid for it. When the company defaults, the bank tries to auction the property, only to realise that the land is worth a small fraction of the price it was bought for.

According to the Indian Banking Fraud Survey[11] conducted by Deloitte, 10 per cent of all bank frauds are a result of overvaluation or non-existence of collaterals. About 9 per cent bank frauds are due to siphoning off or diversion of funds and 15 per cent frauds are attributed to fraudulent documentation. A typical loan fraud is usually a combination of these three.

However, there is an upper limit to how much money can thus be swindled. If the promoters contribute ₹30 lakh, the maximum they can make from the bank is ₹70 lakh. For instance, if the promoters want to net ₹700 crore, they would need to contribute a capital of ₹300 crore. One is not likely to have so much spare capital lying around, especially if one is not solvent enough.

How then did all these loan frauds, involving huge amounts, happen? We will discuss a new trick in the next section, an accounting trick that allows one to keep multiplying their money on paper even when they do not possess any real money.

When I was a kid, my parents had a familiar refrain that 'money does not grow on trees'. Probably all parents use such phrases to make children understand the value of money. It was only when I grew up and learnt accounting that I realised that money, in fact, can and does grow on paper.

Simple Loan Fraud with Window-dressing

So, how do you multiply your money on paper when you don't have much cash? It is pretty simple. When A gives money to B, it is recorded in the accounts of both. When B gives the money to C, it is recorded in the accounts of both. When C gives the same money to A, it is recorded in the accounts of both. Every time you rotate the same money between A, B and C, you generate extra money on paper. This practice is variously called circular transaction, round tripping, and *pudia ghumao* (Hindi phrase for 'pass the paper'). Circular transactions should always raise red flags as they try to show figures on paper that do not actually exist.

In the above example, say A invests ₹100 in B. It is reported in A's account as a debit entry and in B's account as a credit entry. Then B invests the same money in C's business. It is reported in B's account as a debit entry and in C's account as a credit entry. Then C invests the same amount in A. It is reported in C's account as debit and in A's as credit. Table 1 shows the mathematics behind this.

TABLE 1: *Generating Money through Circular Transactions*

Round 1 INR 100	*A credited*	*A debited*	*B credited*	*B debited*	*C credited*	*C debited*
	100	100	100	100	100	100
Round 2	100	100	100	100	100	100
Round 3	100	100	100	100	100	100
Total	300	300	300	300	300	300

Source: Author

In this illustrative circular transaction, *n* rounds of ₹100 investment will result in *n* times ₹100 in the balance sheet of A. B will also have ₹100*n* of investment on paper. C will also have ₹100*n* investment on paper. When a person studies the accounts of A, B or C, they will find 100*n* share capital in each company. This, when the real money behind the 300*n* funds (100n for each of the three) is only ₹100.

Now, let us design a scheme for committing a sizeable fraud. You start a company with seed capital of ₹30 lakh. You submit your business idea, cash flow projections and estimated profits to the bank. You convince the bank to invest in your company. The bank invests ₹70 lakh (industry standard being a ratio between promoter contribution and lender contribution of 3:7). You purchase computer hardware worth ₹1 lakh from a shell company for ₹100 lakh. On paper, the computer hardware is worth ₹100 lakh. The shell company layers the funds through many other shell companies and places ₹99 lakh back at your disposal. You invest ₹99 lakh back into the company as your capital.

Against the new capital infusion, you request an additional bank loan of ₹231 lakh (share of fund infusion by promoter and lender is 3:7). Once the bank grants the loan, you now have ₹330 lakh (₹99 lakh + ₹231 lakh) at your disposal. You use it to run the facade of running a business, pay EMI to the bank, buy cars (when easy money comes, you tend to develop a 'lifestyle' and penchant for luxury vehicles) and invest in more bogus machinery. You pay ₹300 lakh to a shell company to get hardware worth ₹3 lakh. The shell company again layers your funds and gives you ₹297 lakh.

In the third round, you make fresh investment of ₹297 lakh. Banks are impressed. When you pump in so much money, you are definitely bullish. If you are bullish, your bankers also become confident about your business. If you manage to bring in the investment as Foreign Direct Investment (FDI), bankers are all the more happy. They pitch in with ₹693 lakh (297:693 is 3:7). Now, you have ₹990 lakh at your disposal.

Table 2 shows an estimate of loans you can get by 'rotating' just ₹30 lakh.

You started with a meager capital of ₹30 lakh. By rotating it in 10 rounds, you have managed to get loans of ₹3,592,113 lakh (about ₹36,000 crore).

Now, this is a legendary fraud.

Of course, the above example makes the scam look like a cakewalk. Also, it portrays bankers as dumb onlookers. One will have to try harder to fool banks ten times over. The mathematics only shows the potential of loan frauds. Swindling is, after all, an art. As the size of a fraud increases, one has to keep up the semblances. For this, one needs to be a

TABLE 2: *Simulation of Loan Frauds by Rotating Funds*

Round (all figures in INR lakh)	*Promoter capital*	*Bank loan*	*Total funds*	*Reserve—for running the façade of business*	*Net available for purchase of assets*	*Actual value of assets*	*Funds rotated back to promoter*
	A	B = A*(7/3)	C = A + B	D	E = C – D	F	G = E – F
R1	30	70	100	0	100	1	99
R2	99	231	330	30	300	3	297
R3	297	693	990	30	960	9	951
R4	951	2,219	3,170	60	3,110	20	3,090
R5	3,090	7,210	10,300	120	10,180	70	10,110
R6	10,110	23,590	33,700	300	33,400	400	33,000
R7	33,000	77,000	100,000	1,000	99,000	900	98,100
R8	98,100	228,900	327,000	2,000	325,000	2,200	322,800
R9	322,800	753,200	1,076,000	6,000	1,070,000	5,000	1,071,000
R10	1,071,000	2,499,000	3,570,000	12,000	3,558,000	8,000	3,550,000
Total		3,592,113					

Source: Author

showman. Your pretense business can get some initial loan on the strength of fraudulent documentation alone. However, when the figures grow, many other bank checks come into play. To make the business look credible to the banker, it will help to rope in a renowned investment banker or a star entrepreneur as a minority shareholder.

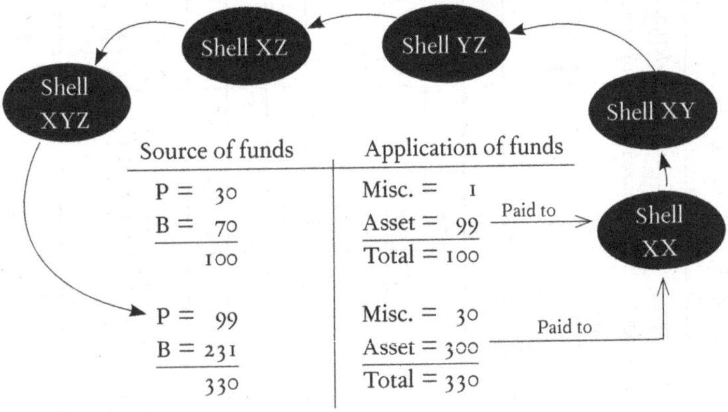

FIGURE 2: *Money Trail of a Loan Fraud Involving Round Tripping*

Source: Author

Shell companies play a key role in this scheme. These companies may be domestic or based in tax havens that provide the facility to open 'mailbox companies' online. Millions of dollars from shady deals flow every day through shell companies around the world. Shell companies are managed by semi-criminal syndicates, comprising advocates and chartered accountants who could not resist the lure of easy money. They are principally used for tax evasion, but can be used to meet other laundering needs.

Since operation of shell companies is a long story in itself, it is dealt in a separate chapter.

Shady Deals of Shadow Banks

The basic aim of a welfare state is economic development, which happens when there is a spurt in economic activity. Economic activities include making, providing, purchasing or selling of goods and services and it cannot happen without sufficient cash in the market. Cash (liquidity) is to market what electric current is to a house. Electric current luminates the lights in the house, air-conditioners during the summer and heaters during winter. If your house is in smog-and-pollutant wrapped Delhi, you need electricity to power air purifiers too. Power from the sub-stations run your house. In just the same way, liquidity, provided by commercial banks as well as financial intermediaries, drives economic activities in a country. Commercial banks operate under the regulatory purview of the RBI because they utilise money raised from public deposits to advance loans. Thus, they are constrained in giving loans to risky projects. This gap in supplying liquidity to the economy is filled by financial intermediaries such as non-banking financial companies (NBFCs), housing finance companies (HFCs) and cooperative banks. Together, they are called shadow banks.

Shadow banks do not raise money from public deposits. They raise funds from institutional investors, mutual funds, provident funds, pension funds, investment banks, etc. They also raise money from the market by issuing bonds. As they are not bound by the kind of regulations that govern commercial banks, they can advance risky loans too.

Shadow banks in India advance loans to infrastructure projects, real estate developers, logistics projects and retail consumers. In India, NBFCs have funded between 55 per cent and 60 per cent of commercial vehicle purchases, 30 per cent passenger car purchases and nearly 65 per cent of two-wheelers in recent times.[12]

When shadow banks default, a key source of the economy's liquidity gets disrupted. This is exactly what happened in India in 2019, according to some industry leaders. IL&FS, one of the largest shadow banks of the country, allegedly committed a fraud and defaulted on its loan repayments in September 2018. This triggered a domino effect, which led to a slowdown in the entire country's economy and ultimately resulted in a sub-5 per cent GDP growth rate in the first half of FY 2019–20.

The Risky Side of Mutual Funds

T.V. Mohandas Pai, former chief financial officer (CFO) of Infosys, is considered an industry leader in developing business ecosystems in India. He is also the most awarded CFO in the country due to his strategic role in transforming Infosys into one of the most respected and well-known software service providers in the world. In an article for a business daily, Pai explained that before the IL&FS scandal, 25 per cent to 30 per cent of NBFCs' funding would come from mutual funds. Mutual funds would buy commercial papers from NBFCs for short periods (90–120 days) and then used them to roll over the advance. This helped the NBFCs to obtain short-term loans and allowed them to roll over the loans upon maturity.

They used these loans to give long-term advances to their customers. Many of their customers, such as infrastructure and real estate developers, have long gestation periods and need long-term advances. 'Forty per cent of the incremental consumer financing (in 2018) was done by the NBFCs, not banks', explained Pai. 'Around 95 per cent of vehicles may have been financed by the NBFCs or by agents', he contended. 'Real estate companies were getting money largely from the NBFCs because they were not getting any lending from the banks. The NBFCs were giving these companies funds to start new projects, construction, financing, etc.'

After Real Estate Regulatory Authority (RERA) was appointed to regulate the real estate sector, 'they could not divert the money given by house owners. Hence, they depended on NBFCs even for their working capital requirements', Pai noted.[13]

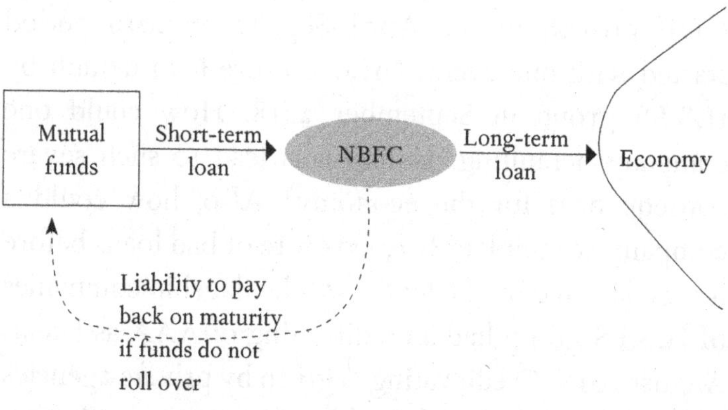

FIGURE 3: *NBFCs' Fund Management System during IL&FS Scam.*
Source: Author

Mutual funds panicked when IL&FS defaulted. 'Because mutual funds like DSP, HDFC and others were hit by the IL&FS scam, they stopped their funding to the NBFCs. When they stopped funding, the NBFCs had to release the money to pay back whatever is maturing', Pai reasoned. As a result, NBFCs withdrew liquidity from the market. The IL&FS scam was detected in September 2018 and mutual funds withdrew their investment in NBFCs in the October–December 2018 quarter.[14]

Pai said this reduced consumption in the economy and, thus, GDP growth rate came down to 5.6 per cent in the next quarter (January–March 2019). Pai estimated that in the 12 months post September 2018, NBFCs had withdrawn ₹3 lakh crore from the market to pay back to the mutual funds that refused to renew their short-term loans on maturity. This resulted in a liquidity squeeze, which, in turn, led to a 'lack of purchase of cars and autos, purchase of real estate and construction by real estate companies'.[15]

This chain reaction culminating in a sub-5 per cent GDP growth in the April–September 2019 period started with one event: ₹91,000 crore loan default by IL&FS group in September 2018. How could one company defaulting on its loans lead to such severe consequences for the economy? Also, how could a company accumulate ₹91,000 crore of bad loans before it was detected by the lenders? The flagship companies of IL&FS group had a credit rating of AAA as late as August 2018. Credit rating is given by private agencies and indicates financial health of a company. Rating of AAA is the gold standard of financial health. But then, IL&FS group collapsed like a house of cards in September 2018.

Bankers will be hot on your heels to recover their thousands of rupees if you splurge money from your credit card on that pricey Gucci bag or the Tissot watch you know you can't afford. How then could the lenders not know until IL&FS piled up ₹91,000 crore in bad debt?

Scam Begets Scam

The IL&FS scam is more of a case of corporate fraud than loan fraud. The top management of IL&FS group allegedly committed a corporate fraud to hide the loan fraud that was committed on it by its borrowers.

To understand the scam, consider a hypothetical case in which you are made the Managing Director (MD) of a large shadow bank. Let's call it Shadow Bank Group or SBG. Majority shareholders of the SBG are institutional investors, say, Life Insurance Corporation (LIC), State Bank of India (SBI) and Abu Dhabi Investment Authority (ADIA). There is no individual promoter who would be directly affected by what happens in the shadow bank. What happens in the SBG affects the individuals who take insurance policies from LIC and the individuals who have a savings account in SBI, but indirectly. Their exposure to the SBG is limited. Nor is it feasible for them to supervise the functioning of the SBG.

The SBG is professionally managed and you head the professional management as the MD of the group. The only supervision over the SBG is by other professional managers appointed by LIC, SBI and ADIA. They, too, do not have any direct stake in the shadow bank. The SBG takes loans from mutual funds, pension funds and other sources in the money market. It advances loans to infrastructure companies, builders and retail customers.

One fine day, you realise that a large quantum of loans advanced by the SBG have gone bad. What do you do? You recognise the bad loans or 'provision' it in your books. However, this provisioning creates many problems. Lenders may stop lending further money. Existing lenders will demand payback. The professionals appointed by majority shareholders will ask you for an explanation. They will fire you and appoint a new management to right-track the company.

However, if you do not recognise bad loans, no one is asking any questions. You keep enjoying the perks of being the chief of a huge financial corporation. You enjoy enormous power and privileges. You draw a hefty salary from the company and oversee so many employees, offices and operations. Your borrowers pamper you. You wield power and control over your borrowers, which include some of the top infrastructure and real estate companies of the country. You are, in effect, a small satrap.

There is no ethical dilemma in this situation. You must recognise the bad loans in your books and present the true state of affairs to investors and lenders. However, if you do not want to make that tough choice for whatsoever reason, be it fear or greed, you will choose not to recognise the bad loans. You decide to fudge your books to show false profits and false repayments.

You do know you cannot hoodwink the parties concerned forever. The longer the con job stays a secret, the larger and murkier will it get. The SBG will keep taking loans and keep burning money. What you are doing is hiding a small default and feeding it, till it becomes a monster default. But hey, it's not your money! You are not the promoter of the company. It is Other People's Money (OPM). So, you make hay till the sun shines.

You cannot do this all by yourself. You will have to keep taking fresh loans. To gain confidence of your lenders, you need to co-opt credit rating agencies. Essentially, granting favours to curry favours. You use your position as the MD of the company to give more contracts to the credit rating agencies and they feel obliged. You also need to divert the loans to finance your subsidiaries that are defaulting. However, the RBI knows that this is what a defaulting group would do. So, the central bank has placed a limit on the amount you can give to your subsidiaries. To circumvent RBI regulations, you need to co-opt your audit committee and statutory auditors. They are watchdogs to ensure that you do not fudge your books but if they are on the same page, you can cook your accounts as you wish, adding spices as you please, where you please. To bring the auditors on the same page, you give them more work: tax audits, statutory filings, advisory work, etc. Auditors also need to run their business and do not want to lose a 'valuable' client.

This still does not solve your problems. Your bad loans are real and they show on your balance sheet. So, you need to co-opt your borrowers. These are the same borrowers who are not repaying money they have taken from you. To run the facade, you need them. With their cooperation, you make book entries that hide the bad loans. Of course, they are eager to cooperate as long as you don't squeeze out the money they borrowed from the SBG.

Last but not the least, you need the support of others in your management team. You share the privileges of running such a huge finance business with them: good salary, stock options and luxurious perks. None of this is your money. It's OPM. So, why not share the loot with your coterie! This way, you co-opt your colleagues.

According to the SFIO, something similar happened in the case of the IL&FS group. IL&FS was founded in 1987, with HDFC, Unit Trust of India and Central Bank of India as the key shareholders. As the organisation grew, other investors such as LIC, ADIA and ORIX were brought on board. Just before it went bust, IL&FS had 302 subsidiaries that provided financial solutions to a host of sectors.

Ravi Parthasarathy was the founder and chief executive officer (CEO) of IL&FS. He remained the group's chairman until July 2018, when he resigned on health grounds. Incidentally, IL&FS' troubles began in July 2018, when two of its subsidiaries could not pay back loans they owed to external lenders. And then, in September 2018, IL&FS could not repay a short-term loan of ₹1,000 crore to Small Industries Development Bank of India (SIDBI). And then, the edifice crumbled. The group's outstanding loan, upon its default, totalled ₹91,000 crore.

The SFIO's forensic audit of the IL&FS group revealed that when subsidiaries faced a cash crunch (due to advances gone bad), the flagship company IL&FS Financial Services (IFIN) pumped money into the subsidiaries as inter-corporate loan. However, the RBI placed a cap on the percentage of funds an NBFC could lend to its related parties. To subvert the RBI's directive, IFIN advanced loans to other IL&FS subsidiaries through external parties. The SFIO identified ₹2,300 crore of funds fraudulently diverted by IFIN to sister concerns through external parties.

For instance, IFIN extended ₹270 crore in three tranches over three days to an external party called New India Structures in March 2018. New India Structures loaned the entire amount to IL&FS Transport Network (ITNL) within an hour of receiving the loan.[16]

In another instance, IFIN granted a loan of ₹205 crore to Vistaar Financial Services, an NBFC with a net worth of ₹5 crore, in March 2008, based on a referral letter by SREI Infrastructure. Vistaar wired ₹185 crore from the funds it received from IFIN to SREI Infrastructure. Using the funds from Vistaar, SREI Infrastructure extended a ₹200 crore loan to Fagane Songadh Expressway, an IL&FS company.[17]

Transactions such as these are called circuitous transactions. Funds that could have moved from A to Z directly (A -> Z) are moved through a circuitous route (A -> B -> Y -> Z) without any apparent commercial meaning. NBFCs are required to declare their transactions with related parties in their quarterly and annual audit reports. Loan payments to sister concerns beyond the limit prescribed by the RBI would raise suspicion of investors. That's why external parties are used as intermediaries.

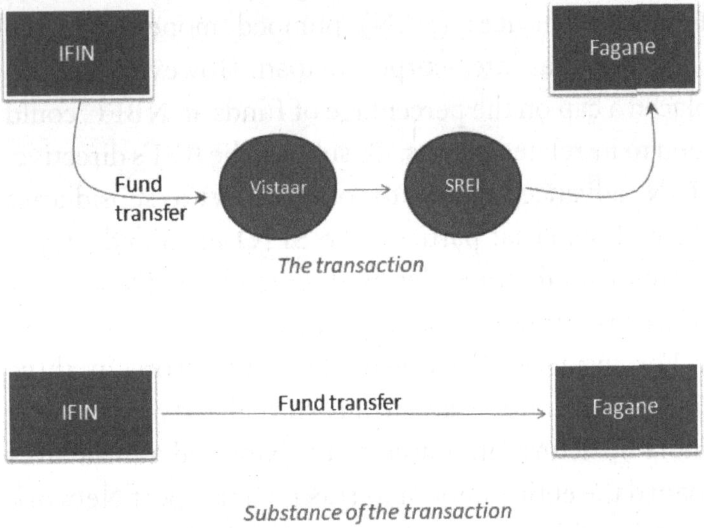

FIGURE 4: *Circuitous Transactions Explained*

Source: Author

The manipulations, quite simple in nature, normally get detected during the audit process. What is the purpose for which Vistaar took the loan from IFIN? Why did IFIN advance a loan of ₹205 crore when Vistaar's net worth is just ₹5 crore? What collateral did Vistaar give IFIN? How did Vistaar use the funds it received from IFIN? These are basic questions that the dreaded auditor is likely to ask any company during the audit process.

Apparently, the circuitous transactions went undetected during statutory audit. The SFIO levelled allegations of abetting the fraud on Deloitte and KPMG, the auditors for the IL&FS group companies at different times.[18]

This routing of money solves one problem: taking care of financing needs of the subsidiaries. However, the major problem is the mountain of bad loans sitting in books. Bad loans cannot be easily hidden by accounting jugglery. A creditworthy customer will regularly pay their instalments. If the customer fails to pay their monthly instalment for three consecutive months, the loan needs to be recognised as a stressed asset.

To solve this problem, the management at IL&FS allegedly came up with an ingenious scheme. The scheme is quite similar to the one I adopted during my college days. My father had granted me a loan of ₹10,000 (a stately sum in those days) to compete in a robotics competition that could fetch me a prize money of ₹20,000. Now, the money my father gave me was just enough to cover the booze expenses of my robotics team over a single weekend. I did not have the means to participate in the competition. However, I had to return my father's money. So, I asked my mother for ₹20,000. My mother took a loan from my father and gave me ₹20,000. I gave ₹10,000 to my father as payback and a Mont Blanc pen to make him proud. The rest was enough to get booze for another weekend.

Now, say an NBFC has lent a principal amount P to a company called D-1; D-1 is a part of the 'Defaulter' group, and other companies in the group are D-2, D-3, etc. D-1 owes the NBFC an amount of '(P + I)', where I is the interest. When D-1 defaulted, the NBFC granted a fresh loan of '(P + I)' to D-2. D-2 sent the amount to D-1 and D-1 repaid its loan. Now, the loan to D-1 was settled. After a few months, the process is repeated by giving a fresh loan to D-3, so D-2 can repay its loan.

In effect, the NBFC paid interest due to it from its own funds.

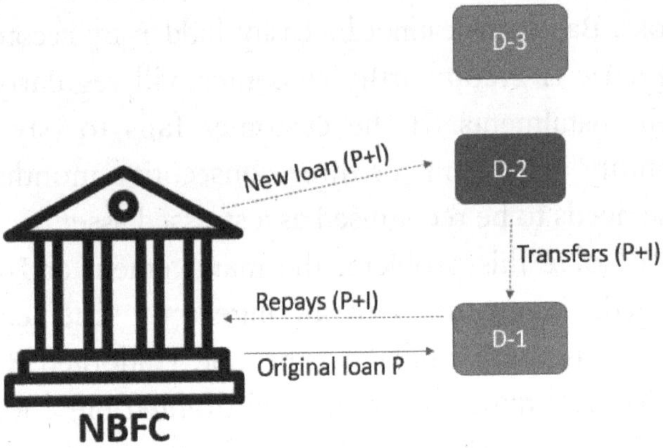

FIGURE 5: *A Type of Sham Transactions to Evergreen Loans*

Source: Author

The SFIO made the following remarks in its charge sheet against IL&FS:

> Investigation revealed that IFIN being an NBFC was in the business of lending. As part of its lending to external parties (other than Its group companies), IFIN extended loans to companies of Siva, ABG, A2Z, Pasvnath group and other corporate groups. A number of these borrowers were not servicing their debt obligation timely. The management of IFIN [] were aware of the potential problematic accounts which were getting stressed in the succeeding months of the reports generated through the Management Information System (MIS) of the IFIN. The aforesaid stressed accounts would have adversely impacted the financial statements of IFIN, therefore, the management of the IFIN [] in connivance with

> other accused adopted fraudulent practices in order not to let aforesaid loan/credit facility classified as a Non-Performing Asset (NPA) and further to avoid provisioning for such NPAs/defaulting loan facilities, which was otherwise required to be done so under the RBI Directions. In this regard, they fraudulently lent to other companies belonging to the same/aforesaid borrowers for repaying the principal and/or interest of the aforesaid defaulting borrower. This process was repeated multiple times with the earlier loan facility getting closed and a new facility being created which was again funded, on their default, through another cycle of funding through the same or another group company. Such manner of debt servicing led to ballooning up of the outstanding liabilities against a group, which were funded from the borrowings from market. Ultimately, the final loan facility was declared NPA or written off or is still outstanding in most of these cases resulting in delayed recognition of NPAs, ballooning of debt and ultimate[ly] higher loss to IFIN and its stakeholders. The above acts of the Coterie were known to the independent Directors [] and other Directors including the… CFO of the IFIN…[19]

In effect, IL&FS was burning money it raised from mutual funds, pension funds, provident funds and other sources. Profit of an NBFC is the interest it receives minus the interest it pays. Against this profit, it has to meet its business expenses, make payments to employees and give dividends to shareholders. If a company does not receive any interest, the profit it declares is actually from its own funds. This is a definite route to default.

Stated another way, IL&FS took loans from pensioners and used that to:

a. Pay interest to pensioners
b. Pay for its running expenses
c. Pay handsome salaries to its employees
d. Pay dividend to its shareholders

It, then, took new loans to pay back old loans.

Whoever did this knew that the group would eventually fall, but had no qualms in burning money as it was OPM. The SFIO held former director of IL&FS Ravi Parthasarathy and his coterie consisting of Hari Sankaran, Arun Saha, Vibhav Kapoor, K. Ramchand and Ramesh Bawa responsible for the fraud. In 2017, Parthasarathy was given a 144 per cent pay hike, which took his salary to ₹26.3 crore. Vineet Nayyar, who joined IL&FS as part of its new management team after the scam, pointed out that the erstwhile management led by Parthasarathy had no restraint on expenditure.[20] However, the SFIO went a step ahead and alleged immoral gratification by Parthasarathy and his coterie. The SFIO stated:

> Upon examination of email data of IL&FS it was found that C. Sivasankaran [Chairman of Siva group of companies] was arranging hospitality for Ravi, Vibhav Kapoor and Hari Sankaran including foreign travels, arranging private jets & helicopter ride, booking of resorts and arranging for interiors of their flats at Brussels amongst others. In-turn

> Ravi Parthsarthy, Vibhav Kapoor and Hari Sankaran were found to have facilitated/connived with Sivasankaran, by influencing the decision-making process in IFIN including the critical decisions for recovery and disbursement of loans and fees.[21]

A third problem in perpetuating a fraud of such enormity is in handling the rating agencies. Rating agencies are independent third parties that assess the ability of borrowers to repay their debt. According to the SFIO, Parthasarathi and another top manager Arun Saha met Naresh Thakkar, MD of rating agency ICRA, and convinced him to defer plans to downgrade subsidiaries of IL&FS group in 2015 as well as in 2018.

During raids conducted on IL&FS offices, the SFIO accessed company emails that indicated undue influence used by Parthasarathy's coterie to get higher credit ratings. An email sent by a subordinate to Arun Saha read as follows:

> Kotak has just informed me that some investors of IFIN will be placing call with rating agencies today so if there are any concerns on IFIN or IL&FS or overall group. Request that we handle the matter appropriately through our relationship with rating agencies.[22]

To this, Saha replied:

> Have already spoken to CARE and ICRA Ratings and they are fully briefed to handle investors' queries.

In another email, Saha wrote to Parthasarathy: 'Rating surveillance is going on and the prognosis is not good. They had taken up to their committee and came back with their plan for a downgrade with negative outlook from stable outlook at present. A meeting with you and Naresh [Thakkar] in this connection would be helpful in this regard.'[23]

To summarise, a coterie in a shadow bank wanted to avoid NPAs. So, they kept creating more NPAs until it snowballed into a big default. Finally, the shadow bank defaulted in September 2018 and set off a 'shadow bank crisis', wherein mutual funds stopped renewing their loans to other shadow banks. Shadow banks had to pull out their advances from the market to payback. This crippled the auto and real estate industries. As a result, the Indian economy experienced a general slowdown and the GDP growth rate fell to below 5 per cent in the period between April and September 2019.

Regulators Hit Back

Once a serious fraud is detected, the primary concern of bankers is to recover whatever possible from loans gone bad. Before 2016, two primary channels available with bankers to recover stressed assets were the Debt Recovery Tribunal (DRT) and Asset Reconstruction Companies (ARCs). The DRTs were set up in 1993, with the aim to help bankers recover debts. The average rate of recovery for DRTs between 2002 and 2009 was 37.25 per cent,[24] which may be considered a success of certain degree. However, 'the whole system was marred by problems like understaffing where required number of DRT benches could not be created to handle the workload. Proceedings in the DRTs also started to take a very long time to conclude and NPAs of public sector banks kept on rising. This led to severe criticism whereby DRTs were labeled as utter failure'.[25]

The ARCs, which started operating in 2002, specialise in sale, purchase and recovery of NPAs. Banks can sell their stressed assets to ARCs at a discount and avoid the lengthy process of civil suits. Between 2002 and 2009, banks have had an average rate of recovery of 39.38 per cent[26] through the ARC route, a figure close to the recovery rate of the DRTs.

The increasing NPA problems in India since 2009 convinced policymakers that a more comprehensive reform to handle the NPAs was required. Thus, the Insolvency and Bankruptcy Code (IBC) was duly introduced. The IBC achieved substantial success in faster recovery of bad loans. The average rate of recovery for banks and other financial creditors through the IBC route has been 43 per cent. The IBC has been given a deadline of 270 days to resolve corporate bankruptcy cases filed with it, which ensures quick resolution.

Deterrents Aplenty

Acts of crime need to be punished. Punishment acts as a deterrent for the delinquent, increases the faith of conformists in the system and exacts society's revenge on the fraudster. Once a fraud is detected, many agencies get involved in the investigation and recovery of funds. Multiple statutes in Indian law provide for severe punishment for fraudulent activities. Yet, statistics show that incidences of defrauding banks have actually increased over time. Why this anomaly?

The Indian Penal Code (IPC) is the primary statute governing criminal offences in India. Section 403 of the IPC states that a person who dishonestly misappropriates property is liable to be imprisoned for up to two years and has to pay up a fine. Section 406 punishes criminal breach of trust with imprisonment of up to three years and a fine. Section 477A penalises a person for falsification of accounts with imprisonment of up to seven years and a fine. Cases under the IPC are usually booked by the state police or a specialist wing of the state police called the Economic Offences Wing (EOW).

Not every case of loan default can be booked as a criminal offence. Only where a criminal intent to cheat banks exists can a case of fraud be made out under the IPC. In a case that came up for consideration of the Honourable Supreme Court (SC) in February 2019, a borrower had defaulted in loan repayment. The SC concluded from a reading of the complaint that the borrower had not dishonestly converted the loan for his personal use and 'mere inability of (the borrower) to return the loan amount cannot give rise to a criminal prosecution for cheating unless fraudulent or dishonest intention is shown right at the beginning of the transaction, as it is this (evil intent) which is the crux of the offence'.

Loan fraud activities are also hit by specific provisions in the Companies Act, Prevention of Corruption Act, Prevention of Money Laundering Act and the Income

Tax Act. Section 477 of the Companies Act gives a wide definition of fraud committed in relation to the affairs of a company or any corporate body. An offence is committed within the meaning of 'fraud' if the business of a company is carried on with the intent to defraud creditors or 'any other person', irrespective of whether or not there is any wrongful gain or wrongful loss. The Companies Act envisages punishment for furnishing false statements and for making false declarations in financial statements. It gives a wide berth to law enforcement officials to charge fraudsters and secure a conviction.

The SFIO is the agency charged with the responsibility of conducting investigations under the Companies Act. The SFIO consists of experts from banking, corporate affairs and taxation departments as well as capital market and legal experts. When a case is assigned to it, it conducts a thorough forensic audit and then submits a report to the Ministry of Corporate Affairs. Once the SFIO is assigned a fraud case, no other agency can proceed with the investigation.

The CBI gets jurisdiction over loan fraud cases under the Prevention of Corruption Act if any public servant of the central government or central public sector undertakings or central financial institutions is involved in the scam. In many fraud cases, PSB officials have been found to be complicit in the perpetuation of fraud.[27] The CBI gets a default jurisdiction to probe such fraud cases. In any other case, the CBI can investigate offences under the IPC vide the Delhi Special Police Establishment Act of 1946.

The CBI can exercise its powers under this statute in a state with prior consent of the state government.

Loan fund diversion is a criminal offence and fund diversion happens by camouflaging criminally earned money as legitimate money. This kind of activity qualifies as money laundering under the Prevention of Money Laundering Act. As a result, the Enforcement Directorate (ED) swoops in after the fraud is detected. It has the power to attach, arrest and confiscate properties having value equivalent to the value of the fraud committed.

Organised loan frauds face serious litigation risk from the Income Tax department as well. Section 68 of the Indian Income Tax Act states that any money whose source is found to be non-genuine is deemed to be income of the entity in possession of the money. Such income is taxed at a high rate of 60 per cent. A simple example is that if gold bars are found in your possession and you do not have bills to establish its source, the gold bars are deemed to be your black money. Loan frauds make liberal use of shell companies to rotate funds. Shell companies do not conduct any actual business and are often used as a protective layer for illegitimate transactions. Funds received by a fraudster or his entities from a shell company can be declared as black money under Section 68 of the Income Tax Act.

The Income Tax Act can prosecute an entity or its promoters/directors for fudging accounts and for giving false financial statement in IT returns. It can prosecute anyone, including auditors and accountants, for abetting such acts of window-dressing of accounts.

Thus, punishment for loan frauds is severe and multifarious. A swindler of loans is liable to penal action by EOW or SFIO or CBI. They get hit by a second jeopardy of prosecution and confiscation of assets by the ED. They get hit by a third jeopardy of prosecution, tax and penalty by the Income Tax department. This should act as sufficient deterrence, shouldn't it?

What Deters the Deterrents?

As mentioned earlier, the amount lost to loan frauds increased consistently between 2008 and 2019. Somewhere, severe punishment under law is not getting translated into effective deterrence. The reasons for this are societal and systemic. The systemic reasons are the easiest to pin down. A person committing a small fraud knows that they will get buried under litigation fees and bail bonds. However, a person committing a large fraud realises that the enormous amount of money he swindles can be used to fight court cases. It helps their case that criminal trials are lengthy and can drag on for years.

In the Bhushan Steel case, the SFIO filed a 70,000-page charge sheet in which it named 283 persons as accused. A counsel representing a few of the accused said: 'By arraying so many accused, the agency has ensured that the trial may not finish in the lifetime of the present lawyers and the accused persons… As they have over 200 accused, the trial cannot be held in the courtroom, they should have an alternative venue. Also, the agency has to print over two crore pages if a hard copy of the charge sheet is to be supplied to each accused which is mandated as per Section 207 of the Code of Criminal Procedure (CrPC).'[28]

Criminals committing serious frauds manage to siphon off huge chunk of funds to tax havens. When committing frauds, some feel they can escape the long arms of law and lead the rest of their life in luxury. Vijay Mallya is a fugitive of law, so are diamantaire Nirav Modi and his uncle Mehul Choksi, accused of defrauding PNB. Nitin and Chetan Sandesara, the prime accused in the ₹9,000 crore loan fraud by Sterling Biotech, are absconding. Some sources say they may be hiding in Liberia (West Africa) or Albania,[29] but no one really knows for sure. These economic fugitives end up becoming role models for aspiring criminal minds.

Social reasons for the high number of such frauds include low social stigma accorded to unethical acts and the high status of the rich in society, regardless of how they earned their wealth. Misguided norms of common society propel even some deviants to aspire for the riches by any means.

Thus, law enforcement may not be the best cure (or even a good cure) to this problem afflicting Indian economy. There is no clear evidence that punishment can deter economic crimes and, more specifically, loan frauds.

The best solution, therefore, appears to be preventive detection. Fraud cases need to be detected at early stages. For this to happen, bank employees need to maintain effective supervision over borrowers' business. Bank managers need to micromanage their employees and investors need to employ an army of auditors.

Banks will have to employ multiple valuation experts to value a single asset collateral. It increases the cost of banking (at times, making the entire banking business unsustainable) and reduces efficiency. So, in the ultimate analysis, what we have here is a problem of constraints.

For a cheap and practical solution to the problem of preventive detection, industry experts are exploring the usage of data mining and Artificial Intelligence (AI) tools. Usha Thorat, former deputy governor of the RBI, believes that there is very little that banking supervision can do to avert frauds when the management is involved. 'It is perhaps time to think of a completely new IT-based way of checking the integrity of accounts that auditors will need to do. Are there any technology solutions supervisors could use? Are there big data analytical approaches to checking out conflicts of interest and connected lending? These are questions that perhaps one needs to explore, given the reality of increasing use of technology even in perpetrating frauds,' she said.[30]

However, it is easier said than done. The key strategy of financial frauds, as we have seen, is camouflaging of nefarious transactions as genuine transactions. An IT-based system can only see one side of the transaction. It does not have the advantage of a bird's eye view of financial transactions. If, for example, funds are siphoned off through shell companies, the IT-based system will not be able to track the activities of the shell companies. Auditors in flesh and bone have the advantage of wisdom and wise suspicion, which IT-based systems lack. They are good at detecting outliers in a pattern. There is only so far an IT-based system can go.

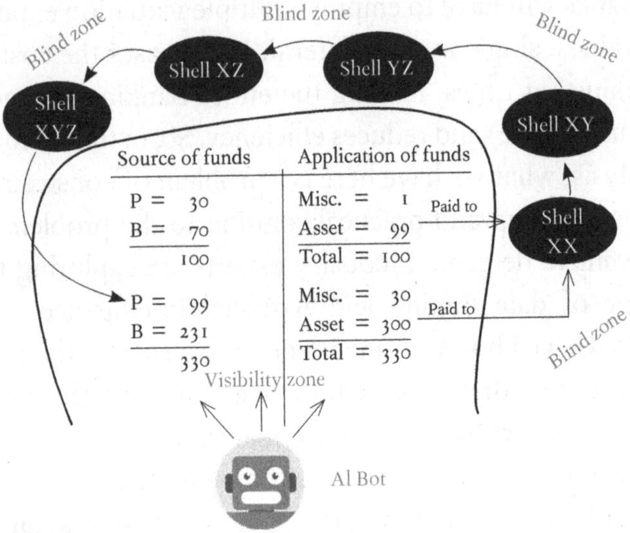

FIGURE 6: *Shortcomings of AI Algorithms in Detecting Grand Schemes Used to Defraud Banks*

Source: Author

2

Taking Stock: Securities Fraud

There were excited murmurs as Feroze Gandhi rose to speak. It was a chilly day in December of 1957, but there was a decent attendance in the Lok Sabha, the lower House of Indian Parliament. Word had gotten around that Feroze Gandhi was going to confront the treasury with an important issue in the Question Hour.

Parliamentarians eagerly look forward to bullfights on the floors of the House. This one was between Feroze Gandhi–the Congress MP from Rae Bareli–and the treasury benches represented by his own party, led by the then Prime Minister of India, Jawaharlal Nehru, and the then Finance Minister of India, T.T. Krishnamachari (TTK).

Gandhi had already earned the reputation of an anti-corruption crusader, having exposed a scam in which leading businessman and Congress supporter Ramkrishna Dalmia was diverting premiums of an insurance company under his control to fund his own business. Gandhi's revelations were taken positively by the treasury and the government had nationalised the insurance business. It merged some 250 insurance companies to form the Life Insurance Corporation (LIC).[1]

However, this very organisation had now got involved in foul play. This was the issue Gandhi was to raise in the Lok Sabha.

He started his speech thus:

> Parliament must exercise vigilance and control over the biggest and most powerful financial institution it has created, the Life Insurance Corporation of India, whose misapplication of public funds we shall scrutinise today.[2]

Gandhi then went on to allege that the LIC had invested ₹1.25 crore in the shares of dubious companies owned by industrialist Haridas Mundhra without any approval from its investment committee. Gandhi claimed that the shares of Mundhra's companies had been bought at a rate much higher than their market price to further boost their traded price. He asked how the LIC 'became a willing party to this questionable transaction with the mystery man of India's business underworld'.[3]

Exasperated, TTK claimed in the House that the allegations had little truth to them. However, the controversy soon snowballed. Public interest in the Mundhra fraud increased exponentially after Feroze Gandhi's revelations in Parliament. This public interest was fuelled more by the Nehru versus Feroze Gandhi sparring rather than the fraud itself. Feroze Gandhi's estranged wife was Nehru's daughter and that gave the controversy a soap opera-like hue.

Given the public spotlight, the government was forced to appoint a committee to examine the matter.[4] Justice M.C. Chagla, a retired judge of the Bombay High Court, was appointed as a one-man committee. The committee held quick hearings, which were attended by large crowds, and submitted its report within a month. The committee concluded that H.M. Patel, an officer of the Indian Civil Service (ICS), Finance Secretary G.R. Kamat, another ICS officer and chairman of LIC, and L.S. Vaidyanathan, managing director of LIC, may have colluded with Mundhra.

Justice Chagla said the finance minister was constitutionally responsible for the actions of his secretary. According to reports from the time, the Nehru government suffered considerable loss of face in the incident. Eventually, TTK had to resign.

Mundhra is widely acknowledged as one of the first and a leading scamster of modern India. His was the first major financial fraud of Independent India. While he is infamous for the LIC scam, there is an interesting backstory that firmly places him as a sophisticated gamer of stock markets, even superior to the likes of Harshad Mehta and Ketan Parekh, who are considered legendary scammers of the Dalal Street.

The Rise and Fall of Haridas Mundhra

Born into a trading family, Haridas Mundhra started his career as a light bulb salesman. An authorised history of the RBI states that starting 'from scratch and with virtually no education, Mundhra built a formidable industrial empire within a matter of years in the 1950s'.[5] He began with the acquisition of the Indian subsidiary of a well-known British lamp manufacturing company and followed it up with the acquisition of a controlling stake in two reputed engineering companies of Kolkata (then known as Calcutta) that were managed by the British. In 1955, he purchased a controlling stake in the British India Corporation, a well-known managing agency. This company, in turn, acquired another managing agency called Turner Morrison and Co. Ltd from a Singapore-based investment company.

Post-Independence, the new government of free India introduced stringent foreign exchange laws and high duty rates that hampered cross-border movement of goods, services and capital. Many European promoters, thus, exited their Indian businesses and a few leading industrialists of free India were on an acquisition spree.

Mundhra was no industrialist. So, where did he get the capital from to buy so many companies, one after the other?

According to a secret report sent by the then Deputy Governor of RBI, Ram Nath, to the central government in February 1956, 'Mundhra bought his controlling interest in British India Corporation by paying its former owners ₹10–12 per share. Subsequently, he drove the price of these shares up to nearly ₹14 per share. He then obtained accommodation from banks of up to ₹11 per share, thereby managing to finance the takeover almost entirely with borrowed funds'.[6]

This report deconstructed the fraudulent activity that Mundhra engaged in. He aspired to take over a company listed on the Calcutta Stock Exchange. The company's shares were trading at, say, ₹10 per share. Mundhra negotiated with the promoters of the company for a majority stake at prevailing prices in the stock market. Let's say a majority stake cost him ₹10X. He purchased these shares (by taking a short-term advance from a financier) and then engaged in circular trading.

In circular trading, multiple brokers sell shares of the same stock to one another, thus pumping up prices. For instance, Broker B purchases shares at ₹10.10 per share from Broker A. Broker B sells these shares at ₹10.20 each to Broker C. Broker C, in turn, sells the shares to Broker A at ₹10.30 per share. A steady rise in prices motivates gullible investors and speculators to purchase the shares. This further drives up the share price, culminating in a stock price of ₹14 per share.

Mundhra then applied for a bank loan by offering X number of shares of the company as collateral. Banks evaluated the value of the shares at ₹14X, based on the then prevailing stock market value. By keeping the shares as collateral, they furnished a loan of ₹10X to Mundhra (banks are usually comfortable with collateral worth 140 per cent to 150 per cent of the loan amount). Mundhra sent the loan of ₹10X to the financier. By doing this, Mundhra managed to acquire a new company without utilising any capital of his own.

This was the easy part. Problem with a stock market is that all stock prices ultimately come down (or move up) to their real market value. In a fair market situation, price discovery happens automatically in the long run. The real market value of the shares Mundhra purchased (in our recreated scene) was ₹10 per share. He had pumped up the price to ₹14 per share. If the shares were left to themselves, their value would have fallen to ₹10 per share. And if that had happened, the banks would have become cautious and asked Mundhra for more collateral. So, Mundhra had to keep buying more shares of the company to keep the price artificially high.

The manipulation, it turns out, is a vicious cycle.

This is what Mundhra actually did. By the end of 1956, 'large borrowings from banks and falling share prices were together narrowing his room for manoeuvre. Mundhra began buying his own shares back from the market to steady them',[7] but had only limited success. Brokers, who were manipulating the price of his shares, also started demanding additional margins (advance) from him. Cornered, he began raising more bank loans by offering fake share certificates as collateral.

In March and April 1957, LIC bought a substantial number of shares of Mundhra's companies in three different tranches. However, by May, the banks that had lent to Mundhra were well aware of his financial difficulties. Their only option for realising their debts was to unload the shares in the stock market. However, if any bank starts unloading shares in the market, the value of the share falls and erodes the realisable value of the rest of the shares they have. This being the nature of stocks, lending banks were in a fix.

Around this time, the general mood at the Calcutta Stock Exchange was gloomy. That year's budget had introduced a new expenditure tax, which led to a general fall in stock prices. Rumours that shares of Mundhra's companies in circulation were in excess of the shares issued by the respective companies created further panic. And thus, the bear run continued at the Calcutta Stock Exchange. This worried TTK.

Mundhra met Finance Secretary H.M. Patel on 21 June 1957, and proposed that LIC buy shares of his companies from him as well as from the market. Patel consulted Kamat and Vaidyanathan, the chairman and managing director of LIC, respectively, on this proposal. Though Patel later claimed in the Chagla Commission hearings that he had discussed the proposal with TTK as well.

A deal was finalised on 25 June, vide which LIC purchased shares of Mundhra's companies worth ₹1.25 crore. This transaction was done without consulting LIC's investment committee. It is this transaction that Feroze Gandhi questioned in Parliament in December 1957. His question was: What could be the motive behind this investment?

By the time LIC made this investment, it was already apparent to banks that Mundhra was facing severe financial difficulties. It was an open secret that Mundhra had been forging his share certificates and had hypothecated the same share certificate to multiple banks (at times, to multiple branches of the same bank). Mundhra had a bad reputation all along. Back in 1956, RBI's Deputy Governor Ram Nath had written to the central government that Mundhra possessed neither the experience nor the background to run an industrial empire. A few weeks after Ram Nath, the RBI governor wrote to Patel that he was disturbed by Mundhra's activities. Rather ironically, as Commerce and Industry Minister in 1955, TTK had written to the then Finance Minister C.D. Deshmukh, warning him about the unfair means Mundhra was adopting.

The dominant theory of commentators of the time was that Patel saw it as a bailout package for the economy.[8] The government was already worried about the negative impact of expenditure tax on the market. Mundhra had committed so many financial irregularities in his acquisition spree that, if not tempered, the stock market would have crashed if he were to go down.

When the stock market crashes, the biggest losers are retail investors. A crash paralyses the entire business ecosystem and chokes fresh capital for the industry. Policymakers view serious scams as disasters and instinctively explore avenues of averting any impending disaster.

This was a case where policymakers were aware of the impending disaster. Bailout by governments to protect markets from crashing are not uncommon. Kamat and Vaidyanathan may have felt loss aversion, which might have led them to support the measure. LIC had already made significant investments in Mundhra's firms in March and April that year.

To avoid losses on the investments in March and April, they could have been positively inclined to make further investments in June. This behavioural trait in bankers is quite common. It has been seen in many cases that even when the banker is aware of imminent default on the part of the borrower, he gives more loans with a hope that the lifeline may save the earlier loans.

The Chagla Commission, however, concluded that the objective of the transaction was to benefit Mundhra and not public interest. The Vivian Bose Inquiry Committee, which was set-up later to investigate the role of ICS officers Patel and Kamat in the matter, suggested that the only possible motive for the transaction was a quid pro quo for donations of ₹2.5 lakh given by Mundhra to Congress funds and a promise not to close down Kanpur Cotton Mills, a sick company whose closure could have thrown a large number of workers off work.

After the Chagla Commission submitted its report, TTK resigned on 18 February 1958. Patel resigned from the ICS on moral grounds. The president of Calcutta Stock Exchange also stepped down. Mundhra was arrested from a suite at the Claridges Hotel in New Delhi. Mundhra had already drained the cash reserves of the firms he had acquired, making them go bankrupt shortly thereafter. One structural engineering company, Richardson and Cruddas, was nationalised. Mundhra faced prosecution charges on account of his financial malfeasance, but was jailed only briefly,[9] from 1961 to 1963.[10]

Harsher provisions of punishment for serious frauds had not yet been introduced during Mundhra's time, since it was the first serious fraud after India's Independence. Nevertheless, tax officials chased him for a long time even after his release. He was the largest individual income tax defaulter in the 1960s.[11] All his known assets were attached by the Income Tax department to recover the huge tax demand.[12]

Interestingly, his daughter Chandrika Tapuriah got implicated in the Hasan Ali scam[13] (discussed in Chapter 6 in this book), which happened half a century after Mundhra's fraud. As on 31 March 2009, she had an outstanding tax demand of ₹20,540.83 crore. She was one of the biggest individual tax defaulters of the 2010s.[14]

In pulling off his fraud, Mundhra made deft usage of information and manipulation, the two key strategies to game the stock market. He resorted to insider information, misinformation, price manipulation and also a loan fraud. As we shall see later in this chapter, Ketan Parekh's securities fraud in 2001 was uncannily similar to Mundhra's in 1950s. Although times have changed, trading has become electronic, transparency has increased and stock markets have become even more complex than in Mundhra's time, the strategies to abuse the market remain more or less the same.

The Many Types of Securities Fraud

Any paper traded for value in anticipation of profits is a security. The paper is a contract and can be in physical or electronic form. Thus, shares, scrips, stocks, bonds, debentures, derivatives and mutual fund units are securities. Securities are an important source of capital for running business. A market for acquiring and/or trading securities increases the availability of capital for running businesses.

The Bombay Stock Exchange (located on Dalal Street in Mumbai) and the National Stock Exchange are the leading securities markets in India. Price of a security listed on these stock exchanges is automatically 'discovered' when demand for the security matches its supply. If a seller quotes a price that is higher than the fair market value, they will find no buyers. So, the seller has to bring down the price. Even now, if the price is above the fair market value, there will be no buyers. The security will have buyers only when the seller sells at the fair market value.

Fair market value depends on the information prevailing in the market. If the price of a company's shares has been discovered and there is no new information about the company, the price then is likely to remain stable. If there is any negative news or information on the company, demand for the scrip falls, and listed price on the exchange follows. Any positive information on the company signifies growth and profits in the future, thereby triggering demand for the scrip. The listed price, too, goes up as a result.

To cheat the market, one either rigs the natural process of price discovery, a strategy also known as market manipulation or controls the information flowing into the market, a strategy also known as information asymmetry. A third strategy is stealing from investors. There are three categories of market participants–issuers of stock, intermediaries and investors–and each is potently capable of defrauding the market. Only, the ways and the means vary.

Within these broad categories, the scope for committing fraud in the stock market is immense. Where information is money, a person in possession of insider information can buy or sell securities in such a manner as to make a profit when the information finally comes to public knowledge. Just like information, misinformation also affects investors' behaviour. Rumour mongering can create a hype around some scrip and drive up the price, or can create panic around a scrip and dive down the price. Advertisements too can be used to spread misinformation.

In the case of MOH Ltd,[15] it was revealed that 'a company made a false advertisement that it intended to buy shares back at a high price without intending to do so'.[16] The advertisement ran as under:

> Notice is hereby given that the Board of Directors of the Company will be meeting at registered office of the Company on 15th July, 2002 to consider possibilities of the Buy Back of equity shares up to 10% of the share capital of the company at ₹3 per share (₹1 paid-up-share).[15]

In the advertisement, the words 'buyback of shares' and 'Rs 3 per share' were in bold. The proposed buyback of shares was at a price 12 times that of the trading price of the shares at the time. This information created a perception that the shares were worth much more than the price at which they were trading. The board of directors of the company met and rejected the proposal for buyback of the shares, but did not issue any advertisement to disclose this information.

When SEBI officials analysed the balance sheet of this company, they found that the company had no free reserve or share premium. As per company law, a company can buy back its shares only by utilising its free reserve or share premium. Since this company did not have any free funds under these two heads, it anyway had no means to buy back shares. Thus, the claim in the advertisement lacked credibility.

SEBI found that '(w)hile investors were misled in such manner, the company issued shares to a related party which sold shares in this inflated market to gullible investors' at a higher trading price.[17]

Another kind of fraud involving information asymmetry is insider trading. Companies listed on the stock market are required to routinely publish their financial results and special events so that there is a regular flow of information to investors. However, when there are any news related to the company that are not in the public domain or are not published, it is only the company officials who would be privy to those. These company officials are insiders and such information are called Unpublished Price Sensitive Information (UPSI) in securities law jargon. Insiders can engage in unfair trade in the market by virtue of having access to such UPSI.

Insider trading is a fraud because 'directors of (a) company or for that matter even professionals like Chartered Accountants and Advocates advising the company on its business-related activities are privy to the performance of the company and come in possession of information which is not in public domain. Knowledge of such unpublished price sensitive information in the hands of persons connected to the company puts them in an advantageous position over the ordinary shareholders and the general public. Such information can be used to make gains by buying shares anticipating rise in the price of the scrip or it can also be used to protect themselves against losses by selling the shares before the price falls. Such trading by the insider is not based on level playing field and is detrimental to the interest of the ordinary shareholders of the company and general public.'[18] That is why insider trading is statutorily prohibited in Indian markets. Regulations on insider trading were drafted in 1992 and happen to be one of the earliest regulations of SEBI.

A fascinating, albeit tragic, tale of insider trading in Indian markets is that of Dilip Pendse. Pendse hailed from Dombivali, an urban sprawl about two hours away from Dalal Street. His father was a small-time businessman. Pendse studied in a Marathi-medium school in Dombivali and got a degree from Mulund College of Commerce in 1976. He joined Taj Hotels, a Tata group company, thereafter as a Company Secretary. It is here that Ratan Tata noticed him.

In the 1980s, Ratan Tata was embroiled in a boardroom battle to wrest control of the group from Russi Mody. Tata found an able lieutenant in Pendse, whose legal acumen and eye for detail had already been noticed by colleagues at Tata Sons. Pendse proved to be an able lieutenant in the fight against Mody. Makarand Gadgil and Murali Menon, editors at the *Mumbai Mirror*, narrate how Pendse was good at digging dirt. In one such instance, Pendse dug out muck to question Mody's integrity.[19]

In those days, steel factories had to import high-quality coal from Australia. It was alleged that Mody was pocketing a hefty commission on the import of coal. Mody would allegedly use this commission, received from suppliers in foreign currency, to purchase Mercedes cars abroad and gift them to his friends in high places. Based on a tip-off, the ED initiated an inquiry on the import of Mercedes cars and possible violations of foreign exchange laws. There was a widely held belief that the tip-off came from Pendse.[20] Pendse also regularly reported to Tata on the status of ED's investigation.

By the time Tata wrested control of the group from Mody and other satraps, Pendse was a close confidante. He was made the managing director of Tata Finance Limited in 1996. However, being a part of Tata's innermost coterie, his remit remained across Tata companies. At one point, he was a director in 18 Tata group companies.[21]

This meteoric rise in the corporate world came to a standstill when SEBI received a complaint on 12 April 2001. This complaint, signed by one Shankar Sharma, arrived just weeks before Tata Finance planned to raise ₹90 crore from the market through a rights issue. It was later found that there was no real person called Shankar Sharma and it was probably a pseudonym for an anonymous whistle-blower. However, the allegations made in the complaint were quite specific and factual.

The complainant claimed that Pendse had diverted ₹300 crore funds from Tata Finance to a subsidiary company called Nishkalp Investment and Trading as an inter-corporate loan. He had then used the diverted funds to buy stocks of certain tech companies. Value of these stocks had already tanked in the year 2000 due to the dotcom bust. As a result, the investments were not recoverable. The implication of this was that Tata Finance was in deep financial trouble, but it had not recognised the losses in its books, thus keeping investors in the dark.

SEBI swung into action. Tata Finance, which also carried the burden of maintaining the Tatas' reputation and ethical standards, started an investigation of its own. The internal investigation of Tata Finance revealed that Nishkalp had bought in shares of K-10 stocks[22] even as their prices were falling. Total investment in K-10 stocks was ₹201 crore.

SEBI's investigation, on the other hand, revealed that Pendse's relatives and friends had offloaded shares of Tata Finance weeks before the company revealed price-sensitive information to the public. The company declared on 30 April 2001, that its subsidiary Nishkalp had incurred losses of ₹79 crore in FY 2000–01. Immediately after this, the price of Tata Finance's stocks fell from about ₹90 per share to ₹30 per share (a 66 per cent haircut[23]).

However, 2.9 lakh shares of Tata Finance were sold by the following persons at ₹90 per share between 30 March 2001 and 31 March 2001:

- Anuradha Pendse (wife of Pendse);
- M/s Nalini Properties Pvt. Ltd, a company promoted by Anuradha Pendse and her father;
- Dr Anjali Beke, a close friend of Pendse; and
- M/s Anjudi Property and Investment Pvt. Ltd, a company promoted by Anjali Beke

SEBI alleged that Pendse was aware of the financial results that were released on 30 April 2001, when his relatives and friends offloaded their shares. Thus, these results were UPSI in his possession and he passed them on to his friends and relatives in March 2001. This helped his friends and relatives avoid losses of ₹1.74 crore. SEBI imposed a penalty on Pendse, and his friends and relatives he had allegedly tipped off.

Pendse appealed to the Securities Appellate Tribunal (SAT) against SEBI's actions. He claimed that his friends and relatives had sold the shares way back in September 2000 and what happened in March 2001 was merely the reporting of the sale to the exchange.

Such physical sale of stocks is called 'off-market' sale. Whenever an off-market sale happens, the broker is required to report it to the exchange within 14 days. Pendse claimed that the broker delayed it and reported only in March 2001. It appears that neither SEBI nor SAT bought this argument. Off-market transactions can be doctored and back-dated. The rule to report all off-market transactions within 14 days was brought to counter this kind of manipulation.

The Tribunal observed that the UPSI 'was available with Shri Pendse by virtue of his being the MD of (Tata Finance) and a Director and member of (the) investment committee of Nishkalp... (He) was specifically aware of the estimated financial results of (Tata Finance) for the quarter ending March 2001 which were discussed with him by the Finance Department of (Tata Finance) in the second week of March 2001. Apart from this information, admittedly he was aware of the estimated erosion in value of the investment portfolio of Niskalp and its subsidiaries. He was also getting (a) copy of the NAV (Net Asset Value) statement of Niskalp which was prepared daily and circulated to him.'[24]

Anuradha Pendse was his wife, so SAT did not bother much to prove that Pendse had tipped her off about the impending news. During the investigation, Dr Anjali Beke confessed that Pendse had done the trading of Tata Finance's shares in her name. She and her company Anjudi Property were merely name lenders (*benami*). The tribunal observed that Anjudi Property 'was maintaining two accounts with Canara Bank, BS Marg Branch and Citibank and that Shri Pendse had introduced them to the banks'. Anjudi Property did not have any capital of its own and Pendse had arranged for all its funds for trading. Further, Mona Ludhwani was the accountant of both Nalini Properties (Anuradha Pendse's company) and Anjudi Property and she worked in Pendse's office at Churchgate in South Mumbai.[25]

These circumstantial evidences and Dr Beke's confession were enough for SAT to conclude that Dr Beke was Pendse's *benami* and Anjudi Property was his front for trading in the stock market.

Penalties were imposed. Prosecution proceedings were launched. Dilip Pendse and his associates were restrained from accessing the securities market for a period of five years.

Parallelly, Tata Finance filed a First Information Report (FIR) with EOW against Pendse for misappropriating ₹400 crore through Nishkalp. EOW later handed over its investigation to the CBI.

A disgrace of such magnitude destroys careers, howsoever bright. Pendse's was no different. After leaving the Tata group, he opened an office on the ground floor of the building complex in Dadar East in which he resided and spent a large part of his time in the office studying the many legal cases that were booked against him.

Early in the morning of 5 July 2017, Pendse had his breakfast at his first-floor apartment and went down to his office. He locked his office from inside and put his mobile phone on airplane mode. At lunchtime, his wife tried calling but could not reach him. Anxious, she went down with her house help and found Pendse's office locked from inside. A carpenter was called and a hole was cut into the office door. Pendse's body was found hanging.

Then 61 years old, Pendse left a suicide note in which he mentioned that he was frustrated due to the protracted legal cases going on against him and decided to end his life. Three weeks later, on 28 July 2017, SEBI disposed of proceedings against him in the insider trading cases, saying that penalty had already been imposed in earlier orders.[26]

Pendse was meant to reach heights. Had he stayed on course, his career graph would have risen to great heights and he would have reached a position similar to N. Chandrasekaran, who rose through the ranks to become the CEO of TCS and the chairman of Tata Motors, Tata Global Beverages and ultimately Tata Sons. However, that was not meant to be. Many commentators believe it was foolish of him to have squandered a promising career. Although Tata Finance lost about ₹400 crore because of his improper actions, not much of the loss resulted in personal gain for him.

Of course, he avoided losses in crore of rupees by resorting to insider trading. It is human nature to avoid losses. When he realised that the stock price of Tata Finance was bound to fall on publication of the financial results, probably he could not resist the temptation to avoid the loss.

Some commentators, however, are unequivocal in chastising him. Sundeep Khanna, who runs *The Corporate Outsider* column for the *Livemint* said his 'is the story of a con-man who may have got his comeuppance but not before he had plunged his company and his group into chaos. His personal misdemeanours were manycheating, forgery, criminal conspiracy and misappropriation of funds were the stated charges along with criminal breach of trust, falsification of accounts but it was the misuse of his position to dupe small investors and the impact that such actions had in the loss of faith in NBFCs that was his biggest crime.'[27]

This then is the first lesson from the tragic tale of Pendse. A promising career and life can end up in depression and misery if one follows the path of deviance. This is not always true for petty theft, but this is true for white-collar crimes. Only a financial genius can pull-off serious frauds. If one is a financial genius, s/he does not need to pull-off a fraud for fame and fortune. A little bit of honest work is enough to achieve their goals.

A second lesson from the insider trading case against Dilip Pendse is the position of law on tip-offs. When dealing with Dr Anjali Beke, the SAT ruled that a person receiving unpublished price-sensitive information on a company becomes an insider even if they are not part of the company's management. This exposes well-meaning *benamidars* to the risk of legal action.

This also exposes many innocent traders and brokers to the risk of insider trading. How does that happen? In November 2017, it was reported that financial results of reputed companies were leaked on private WhatsApp groups much before they were released to the public. SEBI initiated a preliminary enquiry and conducted search operations on various members of the said WhatsApp groups. It seized many mobile phones and extracted the WhatsApp chats. On the basis of the seized records, it initiated penal proceedings against two individuals, Neeraj Agarwal and Shruti Vora. In her defence, Vora submitted that the information she got on WhatsApp chat groups was Heard on Street (HOS) grapevine and not UPSI, as she did not get the information from any insider. She said: 'It is a well-known fact that nobody gives undue weightage to HOS while making investment decisions as it is pure speculation/gossip from unverified sources. However, a lot of traders and investors rely upon HOS to get a pulse of market and make their decisions on the basis of several factors, one of which is HOS. HOS functions like a grapevine whereby the said is shared by news agencies (like CNBC/Reuters), analysts with broking houses, traders, active investors etc. News agencies typically are a part of such groups for sourcing their news and also share news on such groups. It is common knowledge that HOS cannot be a sole factor for making a trade decision. However, traders consider awareness about the same as important to understand market sentiment.'[28]

However, SEBI concluded in an order passed in April 2020 that they had indulged in insider trading, and imposed a penalty of ₹15 Lakhs on each of them. Leak of a company's UPSI on a WhatsApp group technically makes members of the group guilty of insider trading. A WhatsApp group member who has missed the post but has traded in the company's shares is also at the risk of lengthy litigation.

A third lesson is that an insider may be under the perception that his gain is not anyone's loss, but it is not true. When, say, an insider buys certain shares of a scrip, they not only hurt their sellers, but also impact the market at large. Investors rely not only on the available information, but also on price movements when trading in the stock market. When an insider trades at a certain price, the price movement affects the decision of innocent traders.

Hypothetically, consider a stock that trades at ₹90 per share. An insider knows that the company has incurred sudden losses and the fair value will be somewhere around ₹30 per share. He does a short-sell of significant volume. This increases the availability of the stock in the market and its price goes down to, say, ₹80 per share. A genuine investor will make his assessment and conclude that the stock is trading at a price below the fair value (for him, fair value is still ₹90, as he does not have the inside information). So, he will invest in the stock. Thus, insider trading frauds affect not just the party the insider traded with, but the entire market.

Commenting on this phenomenon, the US Congress had said:

> No investor, no speculator, can safely buy and sell securities upon the exchanges without having an intelligent basis for forming his judgment as to the value of the securities he buys or sells. The idea of a free and open public market is built upon the theory that competing judgments of buyers and sellers as to the fair price of a security brings about a situation where the market price reflects as nearly as possible a just price. Just as artificial manipulation tends to upset the true function of an open market, so the hiding and secreting of important information obstructs the operation of the markets as indices of real value.[29]

The Magic of Manipulation

Information asymmetry is an important strategy to game the market. Only the company or its insiders are in a position to use this strategy. Brokers, investors and launderers use a different strategy to defraud the market: manipulation.[30]

Manipulation is the illegal practice of raising or lowering a security's price by creating the appearance of active trading.[31] There are two broad types of manipulation: price manipulation and volume manipulation. Both the forms are meant to instigate the basic human nature of herd mentality.

While manipulations can take many forms, 'pump and dump' is the basic price manipulation technique and 'wash sales' is the basic volume manipulation technique. The pump and dump scam happens when a small group of persons keep purchasing shares of a specific company over an extended period of time. The available shares of a scrip in the market are called 'float'. As the float in the market decreases, the price goes up. Genuine investors see a rising trend in the scrip's price and purchase shares at a higher price. The manipulators then purchase additional shares, thus pushing the price further up. The price rise is a reinforcement for genuine investors and they are inclined to invest more in the scrip. The manipulators then sell all their shares at the peak price and exit with a windfall. Now the supply of shares in the market is high. So, price sinks to the real market price of the scrip.

To better understand how this happens, let's analyse Sai Baba Investment and Commercial Enterprises, a live penny stock whose prices might have been manipulated in recent times (according to an allegation by the market news portal *MoneyLife*[32]). Stocks that have low market capitalisation and trade at a low price are called penny stocks. So, when the price of this penny stock zoomed, *MoneyLife* observed its price was obviously manipulated.

Sai Baba Investment and Commercial Enterprises claims that it is into real estate and in the business of buying, selling, distributing and marketing of goods and all kinds of commodities. It claims to provide loans and advances, financing industrial companies and offers management and financial consultancy. It did not have any revenue in FY 2010–11 and 2011–12, while its revenue in FY 2012–13 and 2013–14 was less than ₹0.5 crore. In FY 2016–17, its total sales were ₹1.56 crore and net profit stood at ₹0.74 crore. Its revenue remained in the same range in FY 2017–18 and 2018–19. Although it claims involvement in so many business activities, its meagre revenue comes only in the form of interest, indicating it is not active in any real business.

Its share price movement, since it started trading on the stock market, is represented in the figure below:

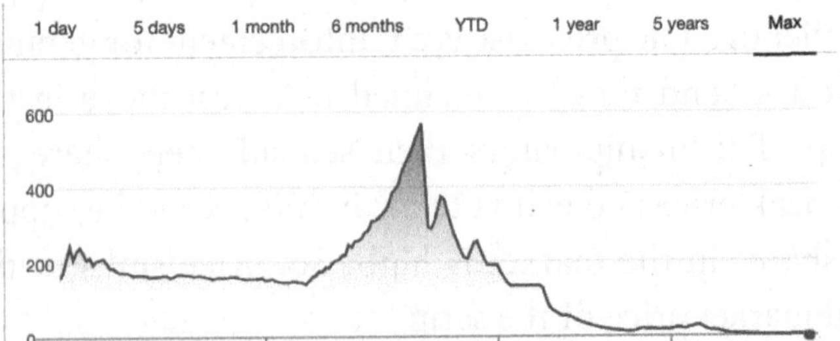

FIGURE 1: *Sai Baba Investment and Commercial Enterprises*

Source: Author

Shares on BSE (in INR)

MoneyLife observed in a news report on 9 August 2017, that even with no real business, 'the company's shares rose by 244 per cent, from ₹139 on 21 November 2016 to ₹478 on 23 June 2017... Why?' It claimed that the scrip price was 'obviously manipulated'. True to the prognosis, the price fell to ₹100-ish in April 2018, and then to ₹12 in October 2018. In December 2019, the scrip was trading at a price less than ₹2 per share.

The finances of Sai Baba Investment and Commercial Enterprises were never impressive. Nothing has changed until now. It never did any active business. It still does not do any active business. It did not have any future in the past, it still does not have any future. However, it traded at a 400-plus price before falling to a price below ₹2. This does not make sense. In an ideal market, price closely follows the value of the stock. It is a penny stock, with a value less than ₹2. If the author is allowed to speculate, those who pumped the price to 400-plus might have pumped the stock price further, if not for *MoneyLife's* divulgence. After the article was published, they sold their shares and made an exit. When they dumped, the stock's float in the market increased manifold. As a result, its price tanked.

The pump and dump scam is a zero-sum game. Manipulators gain, innocent investors lose.

The wash sale scheme, on the other hand, boosts the volume of transactions of a scrip. If shares of a company are illiquid, investors feel that it is not sought after. So, what do you do to show the scrip is hotly traded? You open up many front companies and trade the scrip between these front companies. A sells a share to B, B sells that to C. Again, C sells it to A. And the process repeats itself. This scheme helps maintain the price of a stock at a certain level. If genuine investors in the stock see no activity, they may try to offload their shares. If they offload, the price goes down. To assure genuine investors that their investment is secure, the manipulator indulges in wash sales. This is a way to keep investors assured by showing them the stock is being traded regularly and the prices are stable.

Big Bull

The Harshad Mehta scam of 1992 was so shocking that the name Harshad Mehta has become emblematic of fraudsters gaming Dalal Street. The scam 'shook the very foundations of the financial industry in India and continues to hold a place in the imagination of many'.[33] It was a simple case of pump and dump and the author was tempted not to include the story of Harshad Mehta in this work. However, ignoring Harshad Mehta in a narrative on securities fraud is like disregarding an appropriate eulogy to Dracula in a review of vampire fiction.

Mehta was a Gujarati Jain from a middle-class business family. His association with the stock market started in 1980, when he joined a brokerage firm as a clerical staff. By 1990, he had established himself as a prominent investor and broker in the securities markets. At this time, he was fondly referred to as the 'Big Bull'.

The fraud he perpetrated on the stock market was a plain vanilla pump and dump scheme. He purchased shares of older companies listed on Dalal Street, thus reducing their float in the market. This increased the price of these stocks. He kept purchasing the stock as its price went higher and higher. Retail investors, who are mired by a herd mentality, also jumped in and purchased shares of these stocks. By doing this, Mehta pumped up the price of ACC's stock from ₹200 per share in early 1990 to ₹9,000 within three months. This translated into a 4,500 per cent returns on investment in a matter of three months! He dumped the shares of ACC at this peak price and netted neat profits. The natural process of demand-supply worked and the price of ACC shares dropped to the fair value. It was a windfall for Mehta and a huge loss for the herds of gullible investors.

There are two key problems in this scheme. First, you need huge funds to do this. To pump the prices of a stock with large capitalisation to such high figures in a short time, you need to put in a large amount of money to acquire the stock. Mehta managed to get the funds from a mysterious source.

The second problem is that of building credibility. Agreed, retail investors have a herd mentality. When the Big Bull charges ahead, they are most likely to follow. However, your retractors can speculate or spread rumours. Bear cartels may try to influence the herd. So, you need a narrative to keep the herd from meandering. Mehta built this narrative by projecting wealth and success. He stayed in a 15,000-square feet sea-facing penthouse at Worli in Mumbai, that had a mini golf course of its own and a luxurious swimming pool. He maintained a fleet of imported luxury vehicles. He wore expensive suits and wined and dined in the most expensive hotels of Mumbai (then Bombay). Such opulence was unheard of in the India of 1992, which had just opened up its economy to usher in globalisation. Mehta was covered by a number of business publications. It is not known if he had any conscious PR strategy, but the ode by the media added to the halo of his success and his invincibility.

To counter cynics, he put forth a theory called the replacement cost theory. This theory stated that older companies were trading at a price much lower than their actual value. The real worth of older companies was the cost one has to incur to replace the company. That is, build the company from scratch. He reasoned that cement maker ACC had been in the market for a long time and thus its real worth was not its potential to earn in the future, but the money that would be incurred in building its business legacy from scratch. His was a get-rich-quick narrative, which he supported with a theory and a role model (himself).

Pump and dump was not a new scheme at the time. It was used in stock markets at least a century before that. Pump and dump was used much after the scam as well, as we saw in the case of Sai Baba Investment and Commercial Enterprises. The frauds rigging share price of Sai Baba Investment hoodwinked some people (targeted investors) at some times. However, Mehta's was a mega pump and dump scheme. One needs huge funds to run it and Mehta had managed to garner those funds. His scheme turned so big that he ended up deceiving all the people time and again.

As Abraham Lincoln's saying goes: You can fool some people all of the time and you can fool all the people some of the time, but you cannot fool all the people all the time. Some people began wondering from where Mehta was getting all the liquidity to put in his chosen stocks. A journalist by the name of Sucheta Dalal investigated and found that Mehta was diverting bank funds to the stock market to execute his mega pump-and-dump fraud. She exposed the modus operandi in *The Times of India* on 23 April 1992.

So, what was Mehta's modus operandi? Banks took short-term loans from other banks by hypothecating government securities. These deals were facilitated by brokers. These interbank loans were directly transferred by the lender bank to the borrower bank and the borrower bank issued a receipt to the lender bank. The broker only facilitated the process. Mehta convinced lender banks to transfer loans to him under an understanding that he would transfer the amount to borrower banks and get a receipt from the borrower banks. He diverted these funds to the stock market. Armed with bank funds, he thus played pump and dump on Dalal Street to earn huge profits in the short term. Then, he returned the funds back to the lender bank.

For the short-term period that he was using the interbank loan to speculate on the stock market, he had to deposit a receipt with the lender bank. Mehta convinced the Bank of Karad and Metropolitan Cooperative Bank to issue fake bank receipts for a fee.

Upon reconciliation of accounts in April 1992, SBI realised that it had advanced interbank loan of ₹500 crore through Mehta to some bank for a period longer than 15 days (the usual period of these short-term loans). It demanded immediate repayment of ₹500 crore from Mehta. Mehta did not have ready cash to pay back SBI as his money was invested in his favourite stocks. He managed to get a fresh loan from National Housing Bank (NHB) to repay a major part of SBI's loan. However, Sucheta Dalal got a whiff of this before he could repay SBI. *The Times of India* released the exposé on 23 April 1992, upon which people realised that Mehta's stocks were overpriced. They started selling these stocks and the value of shares Mehta held tanked.

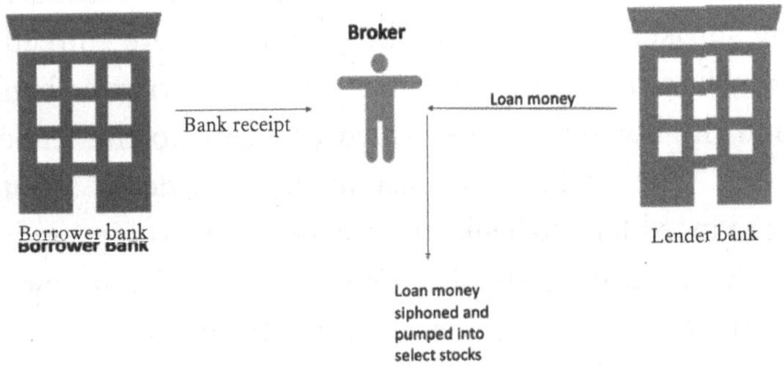

FIGURE 2: *Harshad Mehta Scam Modus Operandi*

Source: Author

There was an absolute mayhem in South Mumbai after the exposé. The Bombay Stock Exchange crashed. Many people who had been swayed by Mehta's get-rich-quick dreams and had invested their life's savings in the stock market were in for a rude shock. Chairman of Vijaya Bank, which had transferred an interbank loan to Mehta, committed suicide on the same day. His was the first sacrifice at the altar of the Big Bull. Many other suicides were attributed to the Mehta scam. M.J. Pherwani was then the Chairman of NHB, which was a subsidiary of RBI. Pherwani, seen as Mehta's mentor, made NHB advance a loan to Mehta that he could not return after the crash. Pherwani resigned as chairman of NHB in May 1992, and was found dead at his residence 12 days later. The death was ascribed vaguely to heart attack, but many believed that he committed suicide.[34]

Seventy-six criminal cases and 600-odd civil suits were filed against Mehta and his family members after the scam became public. Thanks to his financial might, Mehta afforded the best lawyers of the time. Ram Jethmalani was the lead lawyer in the criminal cases. Many lawyers from Mumbai were paid upwards of ₹1 Lakh per appearance, which was much more than the usual fees of lawyers at the time. However, as the cases against him and his family dragged on, the situation became so dire for his family that his brother Ashwin Mehta acquired a law degree in his 50s just so he could represent the family in the dispute.[35]

While the cases continue until this day, Mehta died of a heart attack while still in jail on 31 December 2001.

The scam had some unintended beneficiaries as well. Mehta had invested ₹453 crore in various stocks through *benami* bank accounts.[36] When the scam came to light in 1992 and Mehta's fall was imminent, the *benamidars* turned opportunistic. They sold the shares held in their names and pocketed the proceeds.

Another beneficiary was the Income Tax department. Academic leader Douglas Horton had famously said: 'When all is lost, ask the IRS (Income Tax department of the USA), they'll find something.' When financial frauds happen, accommodative entries are made in account books to hide actual transactions. Income tax law considers many of these accommodation entries as 'unexplained cash credits' and deems them as income. In the aftermath of the scam, the Income Tax department conducted detailed scrutiny and found many instances of accounting manipulation. It went on to raise a demand of ₹3,200 crore.

As on 15 March 2011, the custodian appointed by the courts to control assets of Mehta and family had paid claimants ₹4,000 crore. Of this, ₹800 crore was paid to SBI and ₹3,200 crore (total tax demand) to the Income Tax department. On receiving the tax payment, Nilima Mansukhani, the then Mumbai Chief Commissioner of Income Tax, said: 'Our priority demand has been settled. This extremely large demand was pending since long. But we will pursue our other claims towards interest and fines.' The tax demand was fully paid by March 2011, but Mehta and family still owed the Income Tax department. Apparently, the interest and penalty as per tax laws summed up to ₹11,174 crore, according to a report released by the custodian on 8 January 2016.

The biggest beneficiary of the fraud was the system. Markets were, till then, operating without any watchdog. SEBI was set up as a non-statutory body in 1988, but it got real powers only with the enactment of the SEBI Act after the Mehta scam. The scam came in the wake of India's decision of Liberalisation, Privatisation and Globalisation (LPG). The new era of private capital demanded cheap capital to run the economy. Cheap equity capital could be raised from the average investor by assuring them that their money would yield better returns if invested in equity rather than if parked in gold or land.

However, market abuse by the high and mighty erodes investors' confidence. Thus, there is a need for a market regulator, who can protect the interest of small investors. A second argument is that fraud should not go unpunished. The securities market needs a watchdog and a body to take scamsters to task. Justice Arijit Pasayat, while upholding the conviction of Mehta, had thus said:

> The entire community is aggrieved if economic offenders who ruin the economy of the state are not brought to book. A murder may be committed in the heat of the moment upon passions being aroused. An economic offence is committed with cool calculation and deliberate design with an eye on personal profit regardless of the consequences to the community. A disregard for the interest of the community can be manifested only at the cost of forfeiting the trust and faith of the community in the system to administer justice in an even-handed manner without fear of criticism from the quarters which view white-collar crimes with a permissive eye, unmindful of the damage done to the National Economy and National Interest.[37]

SEBI's role in the national economy has to be seen in this context. The SEBI Act was enacted in reaction to the Mehta scam. It was not the first time though that a pump and dump scam was detected. Such scams had been detected many a time in the past. Neither was it the only fraud severe enough to bring down a stock exchange. Consider the crisis in the Calcutta Stock Exchange in

1937. A report on this crisis by the economic advisor to the finance minister in 1948 read as under:

> The crisis in the Calcutta stock market in 1937 (followed) the tremendous boom in the Indian Iron & Steel Co's shares. The price of these shares, standing below par (₹9.2) in June 1936, shot up to ₹30 by January 1937 and further up to (₹79) on 6th April 1937. No dividend, let it be noted, had been till then paid by the company. About that time, □ boom conditions prevailed also in New York and London; but the position at Calcutta went far beyond anything known before in the annals of that market. 'For the first time in its history, the stock market became the playground for all comers. Seized with an insatiable lust for money-making, uninitiated in the technique of stock speculation, ill-informed as to the relative position of and the value of the various speculative shares, the man-in-the-street was wildly dragged into the maelstrom of stock market boom.' After reaching the above record price on 6th April, Indian Irons fell abruptly to (₹43) by the end of the month, causing immense loss to numerous persons and benefiting only a few clever manipulators who had taken full advantage of the pitiable *laissez faire* policy then pursued by Government.[38]

While the language appears dated, it clearly conveys how a pump and dump scheme in shares of Indian Iron & Steel Co. in 1937 created a crisis in the Calcutta Stock Exchange. When the price of Indian Iron & Steel Co. shares shot up, it was evident to many that the price rise was artificial. No such boom in iron and steel stocks were seen in New York or London. Had there been a regulator at the time, it would have intervened pre-emptively and prevented the crisis.

Many other instances of fraud have plagued the stock markets over the years. They were dealt with under penal provisions in the IPC and the Companies Act. Then why was there a need to empower a watchdog after the Mehta scam?

The answer lies in LPG. Earlier, stock markets were perceived as platforms for speculation and gambling.[39] Major industries in pre-LPG India were under State control, and private enterprises were tolerated in only a limited number of activities that the State did not deem fit to monopolise. The government did not give any serious thought towards sources for raising capital for private enterprises.

With LPG, the role of the State changed to a facilitator. It was supposed to take a back seat and allow private enterprises to run business. An alignment was achieved in goals of private enterprises (profit) and the State (economic welfare). As a result, it was now in the State's interest to promote private economic activity. A key measure of fostering private business is to make available cheap capital. Hence, running fair capital markets is the State's responsibility.

Fairness in the system instils confidence in investors. Confident investors put their money in capital markets (by purchasing shares and mutual funds) rather than in passive assets like gold and land. This lowers the cost of raising capital for companies. Thus, ensuring fairness in capital markets is a matter of national importance. This is the responsibility reposed with SEBI.

Commenting on the role of SEBI in tackling securities frauds, the Supreme Court said: 'SEBI, the market regulator, has to deal sternly with companies and their directors indulging in manipulative and deceptive devices, insider trading etc, or else they will be failing in their duty to promote orderly and healthy growth of the Securities market.'[40] The Supreme Court went on to observe that SEBI should ensure that fraud, deceit and artificiality 'have no place in the securities market of (India) and market security is our motto. People with power and money and in (the) management of the companies, unfortunately often command more respect in our society than the subscribers and investors in these companies. Companies are thriving with investors' contributions but they are a divided lot. SEBI has, therefore, a duty to protect investors, individual and collective, against opportunistic behaviour of Directors and Insiders of the listed companies so as to safeguard market's integrity.'[41]

Over the years, SEBI has reinforced the faith of retail investors on the markets. It's true that SEBI has not managed to detect every disaster before it happened: no regulator can detect all financial frauds even with the boon of foresight. A majority of market analysts believe that SEBI has been quick in plugging loopholes and reducing the scope of abuse.

And yet, SEBI could not foresee the Ketan Parekh scam.

Big Bull Volume 2

Ketan Parekh was an employee at Harshad Mehta's firm Growmore Investments when Mehta's fraud was exposed. In fact, he was one of the accused in some of the cases filed against Growmore Investments, but was never convicted. He went on to commit a major fraud between late 1998 and 2001. The 2001 stock market crash is credited to this financial virtuoso. This book, however, refuses to pay any homage to Parekh. His scheme is uncannily similar to the scheme perpetuated by Haridas Mundhra in mid-1950s. We do not know if Parekh was inspired by Mundhra or he just reinvented the wheel, but the only credit that is due to Parekh is that he executed the scheme under SEBI's watch. There was no market regulator at the time of Mundhra's fraud.

Parekh's strategy was to pump the prices of select scrips and then engage in wash sales to stabilise the prices at artificially high levels. Then he used the artificially priced shares as collateral to take loans from banks and siphon off loan money. To do this, he identified companies with a low float.[42]

He started off by identifying a stock with low float. He purchased some shares of this stock and held on to it. This reduced the supply of the stock in the market and prices increased. Say the stock's price was ₹100 per share. He purchased some shares and held on, whereby the stock's price increased to ₹120 per share. Then he maintained the stock at this price by doing circular trading at the same price. That is, he made his front companies sell and purchase shares under his ownership. This created a perception among investors that the stock was trading actively at ₹120 per share. It enhanced their confidence in the stocks and resulted in more demand for it. Consequently, the price of this stock rose to ₹150 per share.

Then Parekh approached banks and asked for loan against X shares under his ownership. He had purchased the shares at ₹100 apiece, but now they were trading at ₹150 apiece. Banks accepted the shares as collateral and provided a loan of ₹100X. They were happy because they had advanced a loan of ₹100X, while they had security worth ₹150X as collateral.

Parekh then pumped the loan of ₹100X to purchase more shares of the stock. This started off a second round of price rise. Illustratively, the price of the stock rose from ₹150 per share to ₹175 per share when he purchased more shares. This boosted investors' confidence and increased the demand for the stock. Thus, the share price further increased to ₹200 per share.

Parekh again went to the bank and offered Y shares of the same stock worth ₹200 apiece. Against a collateral of ₹200Y, banks advanced him loan of ₹130Y. This time, he pumped the loan into shares of a new stock. And the process continued.

Parekh had identified 10 stocks that he manipulated this way. These stocks began to be called the K-10 stocks. As a broker, he drove the narrative that technology and entertainment companies were underpriced and that they had a strong future due to revolution in communication and other technologies. As a manipulator, he had to ensure that the price of K-10 stocks did not go down. If prices were to go down, banks would have panicked and invoked the shares pledged by him. Once banks were to start selling the pledged shares, the stock would be more in circulation and prices would have further fallen, triggering a downward spiral.

To stabilise prices at the artificial high levels he had driven the stocks to, he resorted to wash sales, that is, his companies traded in stocks among themselves at his desired price level. The challenge here was in escaping the prying eyes of SEBI. SEBI officials spent a great deal of time analysing transaction patterns. If they understood his scheme, they would have taken action against him for engaging in fraudulent and unfair trade practices.

In its simplest form, circular trading involves two firms trading among themselves. That is, A sells a stock to B and B sells it back to A (A -> B -> A). Economically, the transactions are meaningless, but create a perception of huge trading volumes. However, this is also the easiest pattern to red flag. Circular transactions involving three parties are easy for an attentive investigator to red flag. A sells to B, B sells to C and C sells it back to A (A -> B -> C -> A). A longer pattern can be detected by data mining software running on a good algorithm.

Parekh deceived SEBI by using a complex network of companies that traded among themselves. These companies avoided forming a pattern by trading at random with one another. Consider this pattern: A -> B -> C -> D -> E -> C -> F -> G -> D -> H -> B. There is actually no pattern, as no chain gets repeated. It becomes more complex if the trading pattern is like a tree. Consider a case where A sells four shares to B. B sells two shares to C and two shares to L. C sells two shares to D, while L sells two shares to M. D sells its two shares to A and L also sells its two shares to A. And the pattern is not repeated a second time for the same scrip.

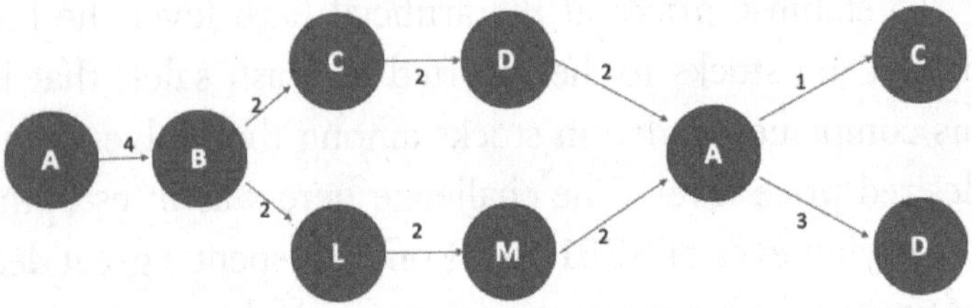

FIGURE 3: *Circular Trading without a Pattern*

Source: Author

Being a qualified Chartered Accountant, Parekh knew the benefits of using shell companies as fronts to create the smokescreen of trading activity in the market. Parekh controlled these companies through a complex corporate structure.

Mayur Joshi, founder of Indiaforensic Centre of Studies,[43] hints that Parekh used unethical means to influence institutional investors to invest in K-10 shares. 'UTI's mutual fund division, allegedly under Parekh's influence, invested heavily in the stocks he favoured. Other mutual fund investors followed suit, believing that the market activity indicated that these companies had a good future', Joshi said.[44] UTI was a public sector enterprise and contributed to the speculation around the K-10 stocks.

Parekh apparently pulled the promoters of some of the K-10 companies into his scheme. The promoters would allegedly give funds to him to trade in shares of their companies. This is because when Parekh manipulated prices on the stock market, the price of promoter-held shares also rose. This allowed promoters to offload their shares at high prices and pocket huge profits.

The scheme worked fine for a long time. The only risk to the scheme was a fall in the prices of K-10 scrips, which Parekh ensured did not happen by doing wash sales. Parekh had not, however, accounted for sudden market shocks when he developed his scheme. An economic bubble called the dotcom bubble burst in the United States in 2000, which shook the confidence of Indian investors and they began selling their shares.

To understand how a burst in America led to a crash in India, we need to understand what the dotcom bubble was.

The release of Mosaic web browser in 1993 was a historic event. As important, if not more, as the invention of the printing press in 1440. This enabled masses to use the World Wide Web and, thus, brought internet access to the common man. The usage of computers and information technology increased meteorically.

This coincided with low interest rates in America. Low interest rates meant easy availability of capital. So, there was cheap capital waiting to be invested and a sector growing by leaps and bounds. This fuelled investment in internet-enabled companies, so much so that it turned into an economic bubble.

This bubble, the dotcom bubble (named so because internet sites generally use the suffix .com), continued from 1994 to 2000. However, most of these internet companies were consistently incurring operating losses. Many of these companies spent heavily on advertising and market promotion expenses, aiming to get big fast rather than turn profitable. Around the turn of the millennium, some investors realised that their investee companies may never make profits. On top of this, interest rates increased steadily from February 2000 onwards, as part of a conscious policy of the Federal Reserve of the US. A series of bad news for internet companies led to a crash of internet stocks in March 2000.

Incidentally, the K-10 stocks consisted mostly of companies that rode on the information and telecommunications revolution. Crash in stock prices of this industry in the US led to a crash in India. This was partly because the Indian companies had American companies as clients and partly because of anxiety among investors about the future of information technology stocks.

The prices of these stocks fell quite suddenly, faster than Parekh could contemplate a Plan B. When prices fell, panic hit the banks that had advanced handsome loans to Parekh against the shares of K-10 companies. Fearing further slump in prices, they invoked pledged shares and sold them in the market. This further reduced the prices of these stocks. On observing the trend, mutual funds also started selling their shares to minimise their losses. This too accelerated the price fall. Parekh did some crisis management and tried to control prices. For this, he took more loans against shares, chiefly from a cooperative bank called Madhavpura Mercantile Cooperative Bank.

In March 2001, a bear cartel in Mumbai, opposed to Parekh, tried to dump shares of Parekh's stocks. He panicked and sold off his entire ownership of K-10 shares in a single evening after regular trading hours. Overnight, the prices of these stocks tanked. The shares he had hypothecated to various banks were now worth a small fraction of the price at which they were hypothecated. Madhavpura Mercantile Cooperative Bank suffered a loss of ₹888 crore and was forced to shut down. Other banks and mutual funds faced heavy losses. The asset value of UTI, which had a significant exposure to the K-10 stocks, got depleted and the government had to step in to bail it out.

In 2001, SEBI banned Parekh from trading in the stock market for 16 years. A special CBI court convicted him in 2014 on charges of cheating and sentenced him to two years of rigorous imprisonment. SEBI also initiated prosecution proceedings against him for indulging in unfair trade practices.

Loan Against Shares (LAS) is an age-old instrument used by entrepreneurs to raise loans for business. Haridas Mundhra, the original scamster, misused LAS by taking loans against artificially-priced shares. He used the loan to artificially jack up prices so that he could get more LAS. Ketan Parekh's scam was quite similar. We know about these scams because they were huge and had affected the entire market. Market insiders swear that there have been many smaller schemes using similar modus operandi from the time of Mundhra until Parekh and even later.

This brings us to the recurring theme of this book: Why do fraudulent activities recur? Once a fraud is revealed, why can't regulators devise sufficient control to prevent the same kind of fraud in the future?

TABLE 1: *Parallels in Mundhra and Parekh Scams*

Features of the scam	*Mundhra (1956)*	*Parekh (2000)*
Modus Operandi	Took loan against shares of own companies. Used the loan to purchase more shares of own companies. Then, took new loan against new shares.	Took loan against shares of K-10 companies. Used the loan to purchase more shares of K-10 companies. Then, took new loan against new shares.
Stock Price Trends	Used loan funds to pump up prices of stocks under his control. Then, used wash sales to maintain high prices.	Used loan funds to pump up prices of K-10 stocks. Then, used wash sales to maintain high prices.
Defrauding Government	Managed to make LIC invest in artificially priced shares of his companies.	Managed to make UTI Mutual Fund invest in artificially priced shares of K-10 companies.
Trigger for Crash	Government policies advocating import substitution and high tax rates.	Dotcom bubble bursting in the US.
Fraud Expose	Rumours and exposé by Feroze Gandhi in Parliament.	Article by journalist Sucheta Dalal on the scam.

Source: Author

To understand why, I made a field trip to, quite literally, Dalal Street. I followed the price trends of Gitanjali Gems. Its price tanked in 2013, leading to a reduction in value of its shares. It was reported at the time that the promoter group had pledged significant number of shares with NBFCs like Macquarie Finance for loans. I tapped the alumni network of IIT Kharagpur, from where I graduated, and connected with Vivek Mishra, who was working in Macquarie at the time it forwarded loans to Gitanjali's promoters.

Vivek, who has worked across banks in the role of a foreign exchange and derivatives trader, lived in Mumbai. I went to Mumbai to meet him. We could have met just about at any place–Juhu, Andheri or Hiranandani–but zeroed in on Pizza by the Bay on Marine Drive. Incidentally, it is just a kilometre away from Dalal Street.

Vivek came over to the café directly from his office. Dressed in a casual tee and jeans, he did not look like one of the 'suits' of the world of high finance. Although a person of unassuming demeanour, Vivek is highly respected among his peers for his understanding of risk and volatility. He ordered a thin-crust pizza with extra olives, while I went for the waiter's recommendation–a lasagne-type dish that I later regretted trying.

I found in Vivek a man bursting with ideas and experiences. He was frank in admitting failures. He narrated a most troubling episode of his career where he could not read an artifice of Mehul Choksi, promoter of Gitanjali Gems, who is now an economic fugitive after the PNB scam of 2018. Vivek took me to a time much before the PNB scam.

'Choksi had committed a sleight with the stock market and with Macquarie Finance much before the famous PNB fraud of 2018,' explained Vivek. 'Well, I have to use the word allegedly… Choksi had allegedly defrauded both the stock market and Macquarie

Finance back in 2013. Macquarie also incurred a loss, just like PNB. But unlike PNB, Macquarie suffered its losses and moved on. SEBI continues to investigate the alleged fraud and has drawn some adverse conclusions on Choksi.'

The Macquarie group is an Australian MNC providing investment banking and other financial services. Vivek worked with Macquarie's India office way back in 2012. Choksi approached Macquarie office for a loan against shares of Gitanjali Gems. Choksi was promoter of Gitanjali Group, which was one of the top branded retailers in India at the time. It owned popular jewellery brands such as Nakshatra, Gili, Asmi, D'damas, Maya and Giantti. Gitanjali Gems was the flagship company of the group and was listed on both the Bombay Stock Exchange and the National Stock Exchange.

The risk team at Macquarie did its due diligence. This was a time when gold and jewellery stocks were doing well. The sector was consistently showing good results. Price of the Gitanjali Gems scrip was hovering around ₹300 per share. They found Gitanjali a good customer to do business with. Choksi hypothecated promoter-owned shares, numbering some 3 lakh or so and received a loan from Macquarie that roughly amounted to ₹150 per share. However, within months, the price of Gitanjali Gems scrips shot up and stabilised at around ₹600 per share. A collateral worth ₹600 for a loan worth ₹150 is always a comfortable position for a finance company. Vivek made a smug face when the good news was brought up in a team meeting. Team members congratulated each other on taking a good call on the Choksi deal.

Choksi was soon back at Macquarie's office, requesting for more LAS. The promoter-owned shares he was offering as collateral were now worth ₹600 apiece. Macquarie eagerly negotiated and finalised a deal in which Choksi hypothecated another about 3 lakh shares against a loan from Macquarie that roughly amounted to ₹300 per share.

The risk team at Macquarie categorised the loan to Choksi and his group as prime assets. They never expected this LAS to go bad. Gitanjali Gems was steadily trading around ₹600 figure as late as June 2013. Then suddenly in just two months, the price plunged, with the shares trading at just ₹63 in August 2013. An erosion of 90 per cent value in a matter of two months meant only one thing: the company's stock price had not reflected its actual value.

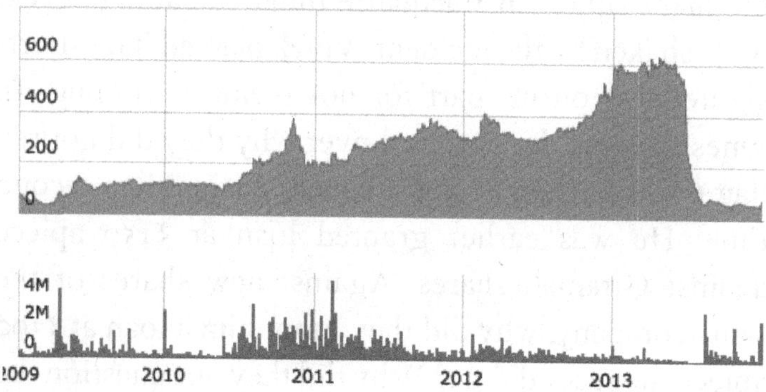

FIGURE 4: *Gitanjali Gems Trading Price on BSE between 2009 and 2014*

Source: BSE

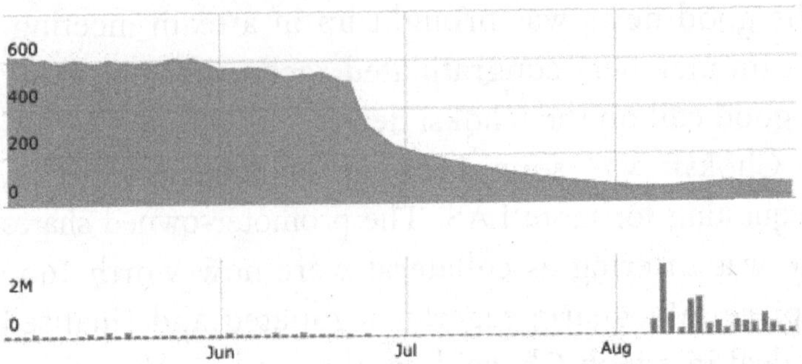

FIGURE 5: *Gitanjali Gems Share Price in 2013*

Source: BSE

The risk assessment team at Macquarie was continuously monitoring the stock price movement. On detecting a high value erosion in a matter of days in June 2013, they invoked the pledged shares in two tranches on 28 June and 1 July 2013. Finally, on 22 August 2013, Macquarie sold 5.63 lakh shares of Gitanjali Gems at just ₹4.56 crore, which is ₹81 per share.

That haircuts are a part of the game in the business of financing kept some of Vivek's colleagues going, but many others in Macquarie India, including Vivek, were shaken by the incident. Vivek blamed it on short-sightedness on his part for not seeing it coming. In times to come, he obsessed over why they did not red flag Choksi when he approached Macquarie a second time. He was earlier granted loan at ₹150 apiece against Gitanjali shares. Against new shares of the same company, why did they grant him a loan at ₹300 apiece the second time? Why did they not question the meteoric rise of the share price in a matter of months? Sometimes, you start asking basic questions only in hindsight.

In hindsight, Vivek felt that the share price of Gitanjali Gems was rigged. This prompted him to inquire further and his findings, although inconclusive, provided shocking revelations on unfair practices in the stock market.

The immediate reason that market experts cited for the fall in Gitanjali Gems' share price in June 2013 was a change in government policy. Earlier, jewellery manufacturers would purchase their raw materials (i.e., gold bullion) using bank finance. Banks termed it as gold loan facility. RBI scrapped gold loan facilities of most banks on 4 June 2013, which seemingly led to the crash in prices of Gitanjali Gems.

'But how exactly did this change in government policy affect jewellers?' Vivek asked me rhetorically. He then went on to explain that gold loan facilities were basically short-term loans, given to complement the working capital. Removing the facilities restricts access to cheap working capital. Jewellers can still raise working capital from the market, albeit at a higher interest rate. The change in government policy does not fundamentally affect the jewellery business. Can this be reason enough for Gitanjali Gems to lose 90 per cent of its market capitalisation in a matter of weeks?

Vivek clearly did not think so. Gitanjali Gems was grossly overpriced. Policy change at RBI served as a nudge for bears in the market to offload shares of Gitanjali Gems. As bears offloaded shares, the prices went down. Since most serious investors did not have real confidence in Gitanjali Gems, the price fall induced them to offload their shares. This further reduced prices.

Once it was clear that Gitanjali Gems was grossly overpriced, the next logical question was to see how it got overpriced. Journalist Pavan C. Lall made an observation in a book he wrote about Choksi's nephew Nirav Modi (the prime accused in the PNB scam) that helped us construct the modus operandi. Lall said: 'Choksi had... been pledging his shares with lenders on the premise that his business model was insulated and that his stock would only go one way, up. The idea was to use borrowed money to increase his stake in Gitanjali by 20 per cent to a controlling majority of 60 per cent. But when the price of his shares plummeted (in June 2013), he was saddled with another problem. He had to take on further liability to plug the leaks and ended up with an amount close to ₹200 crore in personal debt.'

Vivek tapped on traders' grapevine and gossip of Gujarati jewellers' community to construct a modus operandi. As per the grapevine, Choksi pledged shares of Gitanjali and got loan from the likes of Goldman Sachs and Macquarie. He used the loan to purchase and hold more shares of Gitanjali. This reduced the supply of Gitanjali shares in the market and increased their prices. He then allegedly hypothecated newly-acquired shares and took more loans. This time, it is rumoured, he invested the loan funds in Dubai real estate.

However, if he really diverted loan funds to Dubai, the money trail would clearly demonstrate remittances to Dubai. Market intelligence that Vivek gathered (at this point he warned me that he was building a theory based on market chatter) on the money trail did not clearly demonstrate any siphoning of loan funds overseas by Choksi. Choksi purchased cheap gems and stones from Dubai at high prices and made payments to a supplier company that he owned in Dubai. The excess amount paid by him to his Dubai company was then siphoned off and invested in properties in Dubai.

An earlier incident in Macquarie office adds credence to this theory, Vivek said. When the prices of Gitanjali shares fell, Macquarie had asked Choksi to give additional collateral, as per loan terms. Choksi explained that he had no liquidity to pledge, but offered high value gems and stones as collateral. But determining the value of gems is no easy task. So, Macquarie insisted that it would get the gems valued by an external valuer, before accepting the gems as collateral. Choksi backed out at this point, and never got his gems valued by an external valuer. A third-party valuer could easily identify cheap gems being braided around as high value gems.

After being hounded by the Indian government in the PNB scam, Choksi escaped to Antigua and got citizenship there. He has managed to thwart diplomatic efforts by India to deport him up until now. All this requires funds. How did he manage the funds when all his assets in India had been attached by enforcement agencies? Vivek used this to buttress the argument that the loans taken by Choksi were siphoned out of the country.

On its part, SEBI initiated investigation on possible manipulation of Gitanjali Gems' shares. In an order passed in March 2017, Wholetime Member of SEBI S. Raman analysed the trades in shares of Gitanjali Gems in a short period and found that nearly 100 per cent of trades of 15 traders was only in shares of Gitanjali Gems. This period–July 2011 to January 2012–was one of the occasions when there was a steady rise in the price of Gitanjali Gems' shares. Genuine traders would trade in scrips of multiple companies. The very fact that these 15 traders were trading almost exclusively in shares of Gitanjali Gems indicated that they were indulging in manipulative trading to affect the price and trading volume of Gitanjali Gems.

Raman observed that these companies were 'acting as front for the Promoters of Gitanjali Gems and while acting as such, the Promoters remained invisible to the public in so far as their trades were concerned'.[45] To discourage company promoters from manipulating share prices, SEBI bars promoters from acquiring shares in excess of 5 per cent of traded shares through exchanges. If a promoter group desires to acquire more than 5 per cent of the company's shares in the stock market, it has to make a public announcement well in advance.

By using these 15 traders as front, the promoters were actually engaging in acquiring Gitanjali shares in excess of the 5 per cent limit in 2011–12. Raman, therefore, instituted an investigation into the conduct of Mehul Choksi. His modus operandi was similar to Ketan Parekh's. Parekh had used a web of shell companies as fronts to trade in the K-10 shares and manipulate their prices. In 2011–12, Choksi ran a similar racket.

A modus operandi that was used in the 1950s by Mundhra was repeated by Parekh towards the end of the millennium and again rerun in the 2010s by

Choksi. Can't we devise an algorithm or a control system to detect early warning signs of such frauds? Vivek said SEBI had devised many internal monitoring mechanisms to detect early warning signs. On detecting signs of a fraud, it immediately moved to ban the guilty from trading in stocks. The problem is, fraudsters also improvise. They manage to stay a step ahead of law enforcement agencies. If algorithms mine trading data to find patterns, the scamsters find ways to ensure their trading activities do not reveal any clear pattern.

Another problem is that of the corporate structure. Corporate structures allow brokers to hide behind a corporate veil or a web of companies that do circular trading and colour unfair trading activities as genuine trades. Hiding behind corporate veil also protects these schemers from fraud detection algorithms.

As for the misuse of LAS and other financing instruments to commit securities-cum-loan frauds, Vivek believes that this can never be fully curbed. Whether or not to advance a loan to a customer is ultimately a subjective call. However, the risk officials in banks and NBFCs often have to toe the line of the marketing and operations managers. Managers have business targets and they are supposed to meet these targets. They perceive risk officials as obstacles and try to recruit risk officials who adhere to their diktats. In some cases, risk officials are members of the team and are expected to be a part of any consensus. Keeping risk officials away from managers' supervision is a good way of maintaining their independence.

One way of doing this, according to Vivek, is to make a rule that the chief risk officer (CRO) of banks of certain size cannot be fired without RBI approval. RBI should get involved in selection of CROs of large banks, be they privately owned or publicly held.

In the ultimate analysis, deterrence is the best solution to any act of fraud. When a person with an evil mind endeavours to commit a fraud, he will weigh the risks and rewards. The rewards of committing a fraud in the stock market are remarkable and immediate. A trader with insider information can make crores in a single day's trade. Risks include the risk of being banned from trading in the future, the punishment (penalty and prosecution) and a tarnished reputation. Being banned from trading in the future is but a weak deterrence. It is easy to find a dummy trader in whose name a banned trader can speculate in the stock market. In fact, many have alleged that Parekh was an active player in the stock market through proxies even after SEBI banned him from the stock market.

Penalty pinches a fraudulent trader, but there are many ways of dodging a SEBI penalty demand. Once the trader makes a windfall by manipulating the stock market, all he needs to do is to transfer the gains overseas or to a relative. By the time SEBI detects the unfair trades and follows the due process, the trader could have very well parked the fraudulent gains in a tax haven. We will revisit this in the chapter on the art of siphoning funds (Fraud Ecosystem).

Prosecution is serious business, but the due process in criminal law is more stringent than civil law. Penalty is imposed under the procedures established under civil law, but to prosecute an individual, SEBI has to follow the procedures of criminal law.

Criminal law demands higher standards of proof. It is difficult to prove beyond reasonable doubt that, for instance, the girlfriend (or boyfriend) of a company's accounts manager has used insider information to trade in the company's shares. To take another example, two companies engaging in circular trades of a scrip are not committing any crime. Thus, a person engaging in fraudulent activities can theoretically be prosecuted, but the number of prosecution cases remain lower than the number of unfair trade practices that SEBI detects.

Thus, the rewards of committing fraud in stock markets are disproportionately higher than the risks involved. This is not true for all kinds of financial frauds, but this appears to be the case for securities frauds.

Reputation loss is, by far, the most potent punishment for committing securities fraud. Individuals who can commit serious frauds in stock markets are often persons of some stature in society. Society looks up to them as achievers and that's a perk they don't want to forgo. Take the case of Sanjay Valvani, a New York-based hedge fund manager, to understand how loss of face affects the psyche of traders in the stock market. Industry experts credited Valvani for driving up profits of Visium Asset Management, a hedge fund that essentially invested in healthcare and pharmaceutical stocks.

His success drew the attention of all those who follow market trends, including the Federal Bureau of Investigation (FBI). The FBI alleged that Gordon Johnston, a senior official at the US Food and Drug

Administration (FDA), had supplied confidential information to Valvani and another of his colleague.

FDA is the regulatory body in the US that approves release of drugs in the US markets. Pharmaceutical companies have to apply to the FDA for approval for selling any new drug in the US, the biggest market for pharma companies. So, FDA's decision has a direct bearing on future profits of any pharmaceutical company based in the US.

The FBI alleged that Johnston leaked out some confidential information on the FDA's assessment of generic versions of a blood thinner.[46] Sanofi held a patent on this particular blood thinner and, thus, had a monopoly over sales in the US market. Momenta Pharmaceuticals had applied to FDA for approving a generic version of the blood thinner. Were Momenta Pharmaceutical to get the approval, it could have sold the generic version at a low price in the US markets. This would snatch significant market share from Sanofi, leading to more profits for Momenta and less profits for Sanofi.

Valvani bought shares of generic drug maker Momenta Pharmaceuticals and bet against shares of Sanofi. FBI alleged that Valvani had insider information through Johnston's leaks and used it to make dishonest gains to the extent of $25 million in the stock market. In June 2016, federal prosecutors brought an indictment against Valvani, claiming that he deserved 85 years in prison for committing fraud in the stock market. 'As alleged, Valvani, Johnston and Plaford conspired to extract highly confidential and tightly guarded information about pending applications for generic drug approvals from the FDA, and traded on such information, reaping millions of dollars in illegal profit,' said Preet Bharara, US Attorney for the Southern District of New York.[47]

Valvani, who was just 44 years old at the time, committed suicide the same month, on 21 June 2016. In the suicide note, he said he was innocent. Since the accused himself is dead, we may never know if he really committed the fraud that he was accused of. So then, what drove a rich and successful professional to commit suicide? He had only been accused, not convicted. Getting a conviction in insider trading cases is anyway difficult. So, why commit suicide within days of an indictment? A quick look at his background helps understand Valvani better.

Born to immigrant parents from a modest background, Valvani graduated from the University of North Carolina and worked as a healthcare consultant for four years following his graduation. Then he received an MBA degree from the Fuqua School of Business at Duke University and soon became the best healthcare investor on Wall Street.[48] He was driven by achievement motives rather than greed and would often donate generously to local causes. He funded two scholarship funds in Fuqua School of Business by committing $250,000 to it.

Naturally, the indictment hit him hard. Sociologist Emile Durkheim explained in his seminal work *Suicide* in 1897, how community perceptions affect individual behaviours. He had demonstrated from empirical results that perceptions of friends, family and peer groups drive a person to commit suicide. This is what probably happened with Valvani. It has been reported that Valvani was 'professionally isolated' after FBI investigations became public.[49] He was also worried that his indictment would affect his hedge fund and its employees as well. In short, he could not cope with the massive reputation loss that came with the indictment.

Reputation loss does not equally affect all people tried for fraudulent acts. A complex society like ours is a conglomerate of numerous sub-cultures. Some sub-cultures equate money with success and subliminally believe that money has no colour. For them, the rewards from fraudulent activities are still much more than the reputation loss from getting exposed. A fraudster hailing from such a sub-culture would not feel the severity of reputation loss when the fraud stands exposed. Hence, it is a necessity to correlate the severity of the penal action with the crime.

3

Hustlers of High Seas: EXIM Fraud

The Telegraph, a British national newspaper, released an exclusive video in March 2019, shocking the people of India. In a feature headlined *India's most wanted man Nirav Modi–accused of £1.5 bn fraud–living openly in London*, the video on *The Telegraph*'s online edition showed Nirav Modi, a short fellow with jovial countenance, having a good time on the streets of London. The video went viral and evoked angry reactions from the Twitterati in India. Apparently, they were appalled that Modi was roaming the streets of London in a jacket worth ₹9 lakh. The jacket he wore was made of Ostrich skin, which comes third in the pecking order of pricey leathers after crocodile and alligator leather.

Just 14 months before Nirav Modi's sighting in Ostrich-skin jacket, in the first week of 2018, he and his uncle Mehul Choksi had escaped India after allegedly committing a fraud of legendary proportions on PNB. Subsequently, on 29 January 2018, PNB filed a police complaint accusing Modi, Choksi and their other accomplices for a major fraud. It was later found that he defrauded the bank of a whopping ₹11,356 crore.

When the PNB scam was revealed to the public, it hogged headlines for months. The media fervently reported on what experts were saying about the scam, reactions of business and political leaders, activities of law enforcement agencies and speculation on where the uncle-nephew duo were hiding. Yet, it took this author a lot of time to understand what the scam exactly was. I reached out to auditors and lawyers to better understand the scam, just to realise that they too did not understand it.

The dominant narrative in the media was that two employees in PNB were issuing Letters of Undertaking (LoU), kind of a bank guarantee, to foreign banks vouching for Modi's firms. Modi's firms took short-term loans from foreign banks against the bank guarantees. This happened over a period of time. One employee retired sometime in 2017 and was replaced by a new employee. This new employee found that PNB was issuing the bank guarantees without taking any collateral and refused to issue fresh bank guarantees. As a result, Modi's firms defaulted on their old loans and the foreign firms invoked the guarantees, asking PNB to pay up.

Well, if PNB was issuing bank guarantees without taking any collateral, it's the bank's fault. Modi defaulted, but defaulting on loans is not a crime. There are ups and downs in a business. An entrepreneur is consistently exposed to all kinds of business risks. What was the fraud that Modi committed?

The picture was not clear for quite a while after the scam came to light. The modus operandi remained as elusive as Modi himself. This was because the fraud was being presented as a loan fraud, while it was actually an export-import fraud. Every fraud preys on OPM and, in this case, it was PNB's money. This fraud was basically a trade-based money laundering. It was evident from the facts marshalled by both the CBI and the ED in their charge sheets.[1] This was also evident from the findings of John Carney, the examiner appointed by US Bankruptcy Court to examine the involvement of US-based companies of the Nirav Modi group in the fraud. Most experts who attempted to understand the fraud looked at it as a loan default and so their understanding of the most-talked-about fraud of the decade remained hazy.

Diamantaires of the Caribbean

Diamonds have always been a source of concern in cross-border trades. They are tiny, so easy to carry, but cost a tidy lot. An exhaustive report of the Financial Action Task Force (FATF) in 2013, titled 'Money Laundering and Terrorist Financing through Trade in Diamonds'[2] explains how brazenly diamonds were used to transfer value from one country to another by people who had their reasons not to go through the formal forex banking channels. For long, Hawala dealers have used diamonds, but instances of terror financiers using this channel have increased.

Another vulnerability of the international diamond trade is that the valuation of diamonds is quite subjective. There are rough, cut and polished diamonds. The value of a diamond is determined on the basis of four Cs: cut (shape of the crystal), carat, colour and clarity. Measures like cut and clarity are themselves subjective and cannot be precisely determined. Different professional evaluators may arrive at different prices for the same diamond. Valuations are even fuzzier around rough diamonds. As a result, diamonds are ideal products for under-invoicing and over-invoicing manipulations.

Under invoicing refers to a condition in which a product imported into a country (or exported out of the country) is done at a price below the fair market price. The difference is paid to the seller through some other means. In over invoicing, a product is imported into a country (or exported out of the country) at a price above the fair market price. Both these manipulations have serious consequences. Some simple consequences are evasion of income tax, customs duty and capital flight. Complex money laundering can also be committed using under invoicing or over invoicing. We will keep revisiting these two concepts in this chapter. For now, it suffices to understand that diamonds are ideal goods for committing trade misinvoicing as they can be valued way above or below the fair market price.

With this information in hand, let us design a simple export import (EXIM) fraud. An import transaction involves two parties: The importer (also the buyer) and the supplier (the seller). Customs and trade authorities impose taxes on imports and grant incentives on exports. So, they become a third party in the import process. Shippers, transporters and couriers facilitate the supply of goods across borders and seas. Call them the fourth party.

Since the importer and the supplier do not know each other well and may not trust each other, the supplier prefers to get money as soon as it sends the goods. The importer, however, needs time to make the payment. It does not have money in the foreign currency that the supplier wants to be paid in. Imported goods take a long time to sell to domestic customers, thus increasing pressure on the importer's working capital. To solve this problem, an overseas bank chips in. The overseas bank pays the supplier on behalf of the importer as soon as the supplier dispatches goods. Within a short period (six months to a year), the importer sells the goods in the domestic market and receives proceeds. It pays back the principal amount to the overseas bank along with an interest. So, why does it choose an overseas bank? This is because the interest rate on dollar loans is much lower than interest rate on rupee loans. The overseas bank, which provides trading finance for smooth operation of EXIM businesses, is the fifth party involved in a typical EXIM activity.

Why will the overseas bank extend this facility to the importer? The supplier does not trust the importer. They are based out of different countries, following different legal systems. Then why would an overseas bank trust the importer? The importer could theoretically give collateral to the overseas bank, but it makes the process more cumbersome. So, the importer applies to a domestic bank for a Letter of Credit (LC) or a bank guarantee. The importer is a regular customer of the domestic bank and the domestic bank knows this customer well. It is aware of the creditworthiness of the customer. So, it extends a bank guarantee to the importer in return for a fee that varies from 0.25 per cent to 2 per cent of the principal amount. The importer presents this guarantee to the overseas bank and gets a loan to pay the supplier. The overseas bank no longer needs to trust the importer. If the importer defaults, the guarantor bank will pay. So, this guarantor bank is the sixth party.

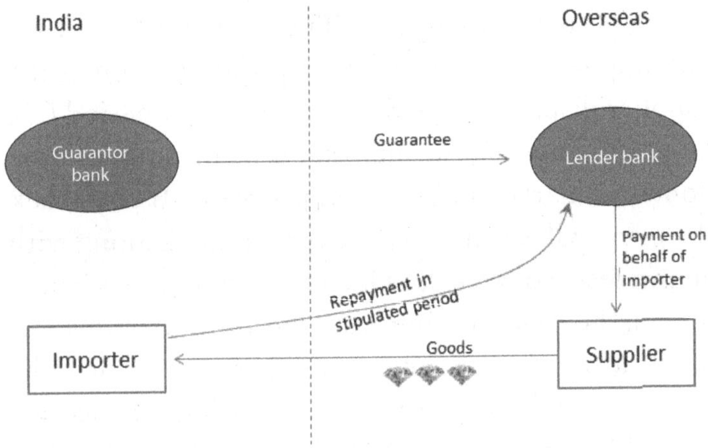

FIGURE 1*: How Are Imports Financed*

Source: Author

An importer commits a fraud when it swindles other people. These other people can be the supplier, the customs and trade authorities, the transporter or the guarantor bank. The overseas bank is secured as it has been guaranteed by the domestic bank. Here, we shall design an EXIM fraud committed by the importer on the guarantor bank.

Our importer trades in marbles. It incorporates a shell company in Dubai and purchases Italian marbles from this shell company for ₹1,000 per square feet (sq. ft).

The real value of these marbles is ₹100 per sq. ft. The steps involved in the over-invoiced import are:

1. The shell company dispatches Italian marbles at ₹1,000 per sq. ft.
2. The importer maintains its bank accounts with, say, PNB, Brady House branch. This bank gives a bank guarantee.
3. The importer presents the bank guarantee to Overseas Bank No. 1. Overseas Bank No. 1 pays ₹1,000 to the supplier, the shell company.
4. The shell company layers the funds and parks them in a Swiss bank account of the importer.
5. Now, the importer is supposed to sell the marbles in Indian market and pay the customer, but it won't make much on selling the marbles (since the fair market price is ₹100).

If the importer does not pay back the advance given by the overseas bank, it will be blacklisted. The overseas bank would invoke its guarantee and take ₹1,000 from PNB's Brady House branch. The importer wants to fleece more money from the bank (after all, it's a bank. Why loot such a small amount!). So, the importer goes for a second round. In this round, it exports the very same marble it had imported. The marble worth ₹100 per unit is imported at ₹1,000 per unit and is lying in the importer's godown. The importer incorporates a shell company in Hong Kong under the directorship of its employees. It exports the marbles at an under-invoiced price of ₹10 per unit to the shell company in Hong Kong (apparently, they are from cheap quality mines of Rajasthan, not Italy).

The shell company in Hong Kong sells the marble to the shell company in Dubai at the same price. The shell company in Dubai supplies the marble (now they are rebranded as Italian marble) to the importer at ₹2,000 per unit. The importer gets a bank guarantee from Brady House branch of PNB and deposits it with Overseas Bank No. 2. The steps followed now are:

1. Overseas Bank No. 2 pays ₹2,000 per unit to the supplier.
2. The supplier delivers the 'Italian marbles' to the importer.
3. The supplier gives ₹1,020 to the importer through a backchannel. The importer uses this to pay back Overseas Bank No. 1. Remember from the earlier round that principal amount was ₹1,000. The importer adds interest of ₹20 and pays back Overseas Bank No. 1. Since the loan stands fulfilled, the importer's creditworthiness gets some brownie points.
4. The supplier still has ₹980 left (₹2,000 less ₹1,020). This is sent to the importer's Swiss account.
5. The importer is a successful imposter.

The modus operandi in this fraud is similar to a ponzi scheme. The fraudster uses a new financier's money to pay back the old financier and pockets the balance. The scheme goes on and on till one day it finds no financier. The scheme gets exposed only then, but by then the importer might have siphoned off a significant amount.

The fraud works because of the sham trading in marbles. Same marble is round-tripped again and again so as to get more money and fleece banks of more and more money.

A problem with this fraud we designed is that it involves painstaking transportation of heavy goods like marbles. Not only are they just rocks, their cost is also not high. The amount that a fraudster acting on our design can siphon off is not high. After round-tripping shipments multiple times, the marbles may be invoiced at ₹1 lakh per unit, which is absurdly high for marbles. Customs authorities would intercept the shipment and bust the fraud.

The most appropriate good for misinvoicing, as we discussed earlier, is diamond. Although both diamond and marble are stones, a handful of diamonds cost more than a shipload of marbles. And diamond value is so subjective that no law enforcement agent can nail you for under invoicing and over invoicing. It is the ideal good for a round-tripping operation. So, we replace marble with diamonds in our fraud design to arrive at a common EXIM fraud scheme.

This is precisely the fraud Nirav Modi is alleged to have committed. It is alleged that his firms executed the scheme from 2011 to 2017. In each round of round-tripping, the value of imports increased. Thus, the loan taken kept increasing. New loans were used to pay off old loans and balance was siphoned off. Bank guarantees in the form of LoUs were provided by the Brady House branch of PNB. Only when a new employee at PNB refused to grant further bank guarantees, his firms could not (allegedly) take any new loan to pay back old loans and the firms defaulted on a colossal loan quantum.

The ED charge sheet alleged that Modi and his associates 'created and managed a global network of related shell companies that posed as independent third parties in sham transactions to import gemstones and other jewellery related goods valued at billions of dollars in order to obtain bank financing in the form of LoUs'.[3] It claimed that Modi's entities 'shipped stones back and forth among themselves and other Modi-controlled entities around the world, generating shipping invoices that were provided to PNB to secure the LoUs'.

On critically assessing the role of PNB in this fraud, some see a failure of control and due diligence. Post-mortem investigation revealed that the SWIFT network (through which PNB sent confirmation of its guarantee to overseas banks) was not linked to the internal banking system. As a result, the bank guarantees given by local employees in Brady House between 2011 and 2017, escaped the attention of senior officials and auditors. It was also revealed that bank employees had not taken any collateral against the bank guarantee given.

However, it must be kept in mind that bankers need either creditworthiness or collateral to extend bank guarantees. Modi's firms had taken bank guarantee multiple times between 2011 and 2017, and had not defaulted on the guarantees even once. These firms had an exemplary track record. Thanks to the import of over invoiced diamonds multiple times in a year, the entities also had heavy transactions in their balance sheet. These facts are positive pointers of creditworthiness for any banker.

Modi's firms paid bank guarantee fees to PNB at the rate of 0.25 per cent to 2 per cent per annum, depending on the percentage set by the PNB corporate office. In the fiscal year 2016-17, the fees that PNB's Brady House branch received from Modi's firms would be in the range of ₹100 crore to ₹150 crore. Banks set internal revenue targets for managers of all bank branches. So, it can be safely presumed that the bank guarantee fees from the Modi group was important to meet revenue target and that the Modi group was an important customer. Revenue of this quantum from a single financial instrument (LoUs) should have come to the attention of the branch's internal and statutory auditors as well.

Bank employees directly involved in facilitating the bank guarantee to Modi's entities were accused of being co-conspirators in the fraud. However, the mere fact that the guarantee fees from Modi's entities made up a significant portion of the branch's revenue explains to an extent why they might have got involved in the fraud. This also explains why the key bank employee who signed off on the bank guarantees, Gokulnath Shetty, took a measly bribe (according to allegations of law enforcement authorities) for facilitating a fraud of such magnitude.

When journalist Pavan Lall interviewed ED officials, they revealed that the bribe taken by Shetty from time to time amounted to under ₹2 crore.[4] The CBI has filed a disproportionate assets case against Shetty and his wife, alleging that they have amassed disproportionate assets to the tune of ₹2.63 crore.[5] Possibly, Shetty was not aware of the fraud he was facilitating. He might have gone out of the way and jumped some rules of the rulebook to please a big customer and meet his branch's revenue targets.

Large frauds are successful when they manage to camouflage their scheme as a genuine business. Frequent round-tripping of funds boost the balance sheets of entities involved in such a fraud. Any auditor would look at the balance sheet of such an entity and conclude that it is engaged in significant economic activity. Import and export transactions are with shell companies based in tax havens that shroud the shell companies in a veil of secrecy and protect them from any probe.

Carney's investigation revealed that the shadow entities under Modi's control were officially declared as third parties (anyone will find a trader importing from related parties as well as exporting to related parties suspicious), but were internally treated as related parties. The employees of Modi's firms were made directors and signatories of these shell companies. For instance, Ashish Bagaria, a data entry operator at Firestar India (a Nirav Modi group company), was made the manager of Eternal Diamonds Corporations Ltd, a shell company incorporated in Hong Kong. Nilesh Khetani, a data entry operator at another group firm, was made the director of Fancy Creations Company Ltd in Hong Kong.[6]

Jinesh Shah, an employee of Firestar India, was the sole shareholder and director of UAE-based Pacific Diamonds FZE, which supplied diamonds to Modi's group companies in India. On investigation, it was found that Pacific Diamonds PZE is registered at

Office 608, Desk A, Building Number B1, Ajman Free Zone, Ajman, UAE. During a physical verification, it was found that Room Number 608 was a small room and had eight desks and each desk was registered in the name of a company![7] Carney's team went for physical verification of the so-called 'diamond merchants' based in Dubai and Hong Kong who had traded with Modi's companies and found that none of them had any real business operation.

Carney's examination also revealed that Modi's firms in India and Belgium regularly sent fancy, loose diamonds to his American firms in bulk along with 'email instructions to export them immediately upon receipt to either the Modi firms in India or certain Shadow Entities at prices and quantities that Firestar India defined'.[8] Following interviews with the employees of Modi's firms in America, it was found that the diamond department in these firms received emails from an office in India containing instructions, shipping documents and invoices for a shipment of loose diamonds. The instructions revealed the originating entity that sent the diamonds and explained how the diamonds should be allocated for subsequent shipment outside the US. The diamonds were then sent from the US to either an overseas entity of the Modi group or a shell company under his control.[9]

The PNB fraud has had a definitive impact on the Indian economy. It led to a general sense of pessimism about the banking industry in India. PNB is one of the larger public sector banks and a fraud of this magnitude left doubts about the health of other public sector banks. On the positive side, the RBI forced banks to conduct rigorous performance audits and housekeeping exercises to trace unmonitored areas that could be misused by the next big fraud.

The fraud increased the cost of doing business for genuine importers and exporters. The RBI banned the use of LoU as a financial instrument.

We have used LoUs, bank guarantees and LCs interchangeably earlier in this chapter because they are conceptually similar instruments. However, they differ significantly in their contractual terms. The advantage of LoU as a financial instrument is that once it is produced in an overseas bank, the entire onus of creditworthiness shifts from the importer to the domestic bank issuing the LoU. In case of LC and bank guarantees, importers have to prove their creditworthiness to the overseas bank even if they have LC or bank guarantee from a domestic bank. Exposure of domestic banks to the LC is limited. Hence, LoU was a convenient and cheaper option to raise trading finance. Now, importers have to fulfil additional documentation formalities in overseas banks to pay suppliers.

This fraud jolted the diamond industry. So much so, that tremors are felt to this day. Banks immediately reduced their exposure to diamond merchants and were reluctant in taking diamonds as collateral when forwarding new loans. This led to a contraction in diamond traders' working capital.

While the fraud had a long-lasting impact on the Indian economy, it is pertinent to mention that there was nothing original about it. A similar modus operandi was allegedly used by Jatin Mehta of Winsome Diamonds, whom law enforcement agencies had accused way back in 2012 of having defrauded banks of ₹6,500 crore. Mehta is also a fugitive economic offender from India and is cooling his heels somewhere in the Caribbean Islands. Interviews with diamond traders revealed that this is, in fact, a common and rampantly used modus operandi for committing financial fraud.[10]

In conversation with a news channel, a Mumbai-based diamond merchant explained 'how quite a few companies operate in cartels to move the same shipments over and over again in order to obtain bank credits in the name of working capital'.[11] The channel came across other merchants who disclosed this as a common fraud in their business. What differentiates the PNB fraud from other similar frauds before and after this case is the magnitude to which it had ballooned.

Frauds are ultimately control problems. It is impossible to maintain control and supervision over all the elements of a complex system. In any given system, fraudsters exploit the weak areas where control does not exist. That is the reason frauds of similar types keep recurring. It is not that the system does not learn from past mistakes. The system patches one loophole, only to find that there is another. Every time the system increases control, the cost of supervision also increases.

The problem of control is especially acute in the case of EXIM frauds. Export-import supply chains involve multiple parties and multiple systems. No actor in the supply chain can supervise the entire supply chain. The supply chain spans multiple sovereign jurisdictions and multiple businesses.

When an item is imported, Indian customs authorities do not know what happened at the supplier's end. The exporting country does not know where the goods ultimately end up. Banks that provide trading finance can see only their transactions. Transporters and logistics companies are responsible for verifying each and every cargo they carry but verification is an additional cost burden on their operations. Trade valuers furnish certifications without knowing if the goods they certify are loaded onto ships or are exchanged by stevedores. That's why EXIM activities are mired by all kinds of frauds: smuggling of contraband, laundering, transfer mispricing, narcotics trade, tax evasion, customs frauds, GST frauds, etc. In fact, some types of EXIM frauds defraud sovereign states and jeopardise their economic security. Most serious of such frauds is 'origin fraud'.

'Made in China'

The management team at Indian Stainless Steel Development Association (ISSDA) huddled in their Gurgaon office with India's steel import data sometime in early 2019 to solve a puzzle: Where was the cheap Chinese stainless steel coming from? Official import data did not show any spike in Chinese stainless steel in Indian market, but ISSDA members kept complaining of unfair competition from underpriced Chinese steel. K.K. Pahuja, President of ISSDA, had spent 36 years in Steel Authority of India Limited (SAIL) making steel and he knew that the grouse was true. Import data that India's Customs released, however, did not show that Chinese steel was flooding Indian markets.

The US–China trade war had started a year before, in March 2018, with the US imposition of 25 per cent tariff on imports of steel products. Although these were non-country-specific tariffs, they were meant to hurt Chinese steel exports. China is the largest steel producer in the world, with a total share of 13.5 per cent of world exports in 2018. It produces over 50 per cent of the world output of steel. While steel production elsewhere has stagnated, it continues to grow in China.[12] When the US tariffs were announced, other countries got jittery that China may dump its steel exports in their country.

Such concerns did not initially dawn upon Indian steel manufacturers, since India does not have a free trade agreement (FTA) with China. India imposed a countervailing duty of 18.9 per cent on the import of stainless steel from China, over and above the standard customs duty. This was considered enough safeguard for the Indian stainless steel industry.

Despite this, ISSDA kept getting complaints from its members about price undercutting as China was dumping cheap stainless steel in the market. It was affecting Indian steel manufacturers. 'The domestic stainless steel industry is witnessing under-priced imports and is operating at a mere 60–70 per cent of its total installed capacity,' Pahuja had said at the time.[13]

Team ISSDA's analysis of import data, however, revealed something shocking. The import of stainless steel from Indonesia into India had grown from about 8,000 tonnes in FY 2017–18 to 67,000 tonnes in 2018–19. It implied an import growth of more than seven times in a single year. Stainless steel is a high value-added alloy. A country does not suddenly develop the capacity to manufacture stainless steel. Setting of manufacturing plants requires capital, machinery and skilled labour. There is no way the installed capacity in Indonesia could have grown in leaps in just a year.

ISSDA concluded that these imports were of Chinese origin, but routed through Indonesia because China has an FTA with the Association of Southeast Asian Nations (ASEAN), of which Indonesia is a member and ASEAN has an FTA with India. By the virtue of its FTA with ASEAN, Chinese exporters could export to Indonesia without incurring any duty. These exports were then re-exported to India duty free because of the FTA between ASEAN and India.

The ISSDA believed 'cold rolled material from China is exported to Indonesia for minor value additions like slitting into smaller widths, after which, the same consignment is exported to India'. In some cases, 'Indonesia imports hot rolled stainless steel coils from China and then converts the same consignment into cold rolled stainless steel coils. These cold rolled materials are then exported to India' at preferential duty rate of zero per cent.[14]

The FTA between India and ASEAN stipulates that preferential duty rate could be claimed by an exporter to India only if the country of origin is in ASEAN. FTA benefits can be denied by India if the value addition in ASEAN region is less than 35 per cent. Chinese exports should have 'certificate of origin' from China. The ISSDA alleged that Chinese exporters routed their goods through Indonesia with cosmetic value addition in Indonesia, but managed to get origin certificates from

Indonesia, thus hoodwinking Indian customs officials. This is called origin fraud or country of origin (COO) fraud.

Origin fraud is one of the few economic offences that are not financial frauds and yet they have colossal impact on a country's economy. Origin fraud instances have destroyed industries, decimated economic security of sovereign states and driven farmers to suicide. Perpetrators of origin fraud may be the exporters, authorities of third country who issue fraudulent certificate of origin or the exporting country itself. A country of origin may collude with a conduit country to dump goods into a market. Possibilities are numerous, but origin fraud investigation generally does not throw up conclusive evidence. This is because one sovereign country cannot investigate another sovereign country or its customs agents without cooperation from the other country.

Thus, when a country detects such circumvention of duty rules by routing shipments through a third country, it imposes anti-circumvention duties on the conduit country. Some economists believe that origin fraud is good for the economy as it gives consumers access to cheaper goods. When the local industry competes with cheap imports, they also become more competitive. This argument flows from the free trade theory, which states that eradicating customs duties leads to increased efficiency. However, I feel it is a flawed theory.

Take the example of stainless steel. Indian manufacturers have to invest in land, machinery and skills to manufacture stainless steel. It takes time to develop supply chain routes and ancillary industries to support the manufacture. There can be cost efficiency when Indian manufacturers take advantage of economies of scale. Scale manufacturing is possible with the formation of industrial clusters in an area. Thus, cheap manufacturing does not happen in a day's or a year's time. Manufacturing infrastructure and ecosystem evolve over a period of time.

Theoretical economists love to draw supply-demand curves (or partial equilibrium curves), in which they draw a straight line to show how supply varies with price. This is erroneous and reductionist. Supply is not as elastic as it appears in the graphs. Theory states that supply automatically increases when price increases in a competitive market, thus bringing down the price to the fair market value. However, it is not so. Supply depends on the ability to produce, which, in turn, depends on the manufacturing infrastructure and ecosystem in a country. If such an ecosystem does not exist or has fallen into disuse, the country cannot promptly increase its production. In such a scenario, the country will be purely dependent on imports and prices determined in exporting countries.

Manufacturing in China is much different from manufacturing in India. China subsidises raw materials and other inputs. Its labour laws and environmental protection norms are more liberal than India's. So, its stainless steel costs are lower than India's. China also has a fixed exchange rate viz-a-viz the dollar. It has a huge manufacturing capacity and cannot afford the losses arising from capacity underutilisation. In 2016, about six million people were employed by China's steel industry. International trends, such as the trade war, force Chinese manufacturers to export their goods at prices that are artificially lower than the price at which these goods sell even in the Chinese market.

So, when Chinese exporters dump goods at cheap prices in India, they drive the domestic industry out of business. A domestic industry that grows organically over years can get destroyed in just a few years, but once the local industry is decimated, local markets have only one source to purchase stainless steel from: China. At that time, Chinese exporters could resort to surge pricing and make a tidy profit.

While business associations in India have complained about unfair trade practices by Chinese exporters, Rajya Sabha's Parliamentary Standing Committee on Commerce went a step further and hinted that China engages in unfair trade practices that harm domestic industries in other countries. In a report presented to the Rajya Sabha in July 2018, the standing committee observed: 'China is not recognised by WTO as a market economy mainly because of the lack of transparency in its trade policy. A large number of companies which are dominant players in exports are government-controlled enterprises. While China has long been accused of manipulating its currency to maintain export competitiveness, it has also been found guilty of unfair trade practices like export subsidies that are in contravention to WTO regulations. China accounts for the maximum number of Anti-Dumping Duty/ Countervailing Duty investigations around the world. China being unmindful of the WTO is acknowledged as a matter of concern by the European Union and the

United States. The Committee was given to understand that Chinese Government gives export rebate to the tune of 17% to their exporters. Effectively, this makes Chinese goods being imported cheaper by 5%–6% than the Indian counterpart. Further, regional provinces in China extend incentives and rebates on the tax structure and are competing with each other to attract industries in their region and also promoting exports big time by extending sizeable incentives (even on software downloads and logistics compensation for long distance freight) which makes Chinese products cost effective.'[15]

The report noted that the Chinese government ensured cheap supply of raw materials and this automatically lowered the price of finished goods. These low prices are essentially artificial because they do not result from efficient production or fair market rules. The committee said: 'Apart from WTO non-compliant trade measures, Chinese competitiveness is also led by an enabling policy environment wherein the government has made considerable interventions in ensuring that all the factors of production i.e. land, labour, capital are available at the cheapest cost to its manufacturers. The lending rates in China are very industry-friendly while in India, the banks offer one of the highest lending rates to the industry. Our industry is borrowing anywhere between 11 and 14% while the Chinese are getting loans at 6%. Also, logistics costs in China are one of the lowest in Asia and much lower than India. The Chinese cost of logistics is 1% of their business. In India, it calculates to 3%. Similarly, the effective cost of electricity in India is anywhere between 12 and 14 rupees, which is higher in comparison to China. India suffers cost competitiveness by almost 9% to their competition with China on account of energy, finance and logistics.'[16]

Lending rates are cheap in China because public sector banks advance cheap loans to exporters. Electricity is subsidised by the government. Basically, the government has an export-driven strategy, which includes subsidy on all factors of production, on input costs, tax incentives by both central and provincial governments and artificially low foreign exchange rates. Thus, the price of Chinese goods remains artificially low.

A country with economic might can monopolise Indian market by resorting to predatory pricing strategies. It would sell its goods at dirt-cheap prices in India, thus destroying local industry and local industrial ecosystems. Once local supply is unavailable, it would have monopoly over Indian market and could sell at high prices. China is not the only country which poses such risks to India. But China is India's top source of imports and follows certain opaque and maverick trade policies that increase vulnerability of Indian markets.

For instance, India imported about 65 per cent to 70 per cent of its bulk drugs and intermediaries from China in both FY 2016–17 and 2017–18. India is hopelessly dependent on China for Active Pharmaceutical Ingredients (APIs), which forms the key raw material for the pharma industry of India. If, someday. China uses this as a leverage, Indian pharma industry will be rendered helpless. In early 2015, Dr Y.K. Hamied, Chairman of the Indian pharma and biotech behemoth Cipla, said in a conference organised by the Delhi-based Research and Information System for Developing

Countries (RIS): 'If China decided one bright day to stop export to India, we would be finished. The pharma industry is zero, both domestic and export, and we are looking at that danger objectively.'[17] The Parliamentary Standing Committee on Commerce also voiced similar sentiments in 2018:

> India is called the "pharmacy of the world", but a substantial part of the bulk drugs that are used to manufacture the Finished Dosage Formulation (FDF) that India is famous for, come from China. China is the main supplier of raw materials for Active Pharmaceutical Ingredients (APIs) and Key Standing Materials (KSMs). It is a matter of concern that India's pharma sector has critical dependence on Chinese bulk drugs import for its drugs manufacturing. It is noted that in some cases, including in the life-saving drugs category, the dependence on Chinese imports is as much as 90%. (Report No. 145 of the Rajya Sabha, *supra.*)

The committee also noted that about 75 per cent of the APIs used in the formulations of National List of Essential Medicines (NLEM) are sourced from China. Our API-manufacturing capability, based on fermentation technology, is quite negligible. Owing to its dominance in APIs/KSMs and intermediates, including those belonging to antibiotic class cephalosporin and vitamins, the Chinese bulk pharmaceuticals products have competitive edge in our domestic sector/market.[18]

There is also a strategic angle to this issue. When the Indian market is over-reliant on foreign supply, the supplying country can withhold supply to harm India. This is the idea behind economic warfare. India, or for that matter any independent country, needs to protect its domestic industry as an economic defence measure. Economist Michael Taillard explains how subsidies and dumping can be used in economic warfare in his book *Economics and Modern Warfare: The Invisible Fist of the Market*. Taillard observed:

> During the course of economic warfare, one reason that subsidies are used is to increase the volume of a specified product… that the consumers of the targeted nation are purchasing from the businesses of the issuing nation. The other purpose is to make the goods produced within one's own nation cheaper to decrease the volume of exports purchased by people domestically. The intended goal of both these methods is to redirect profits and production away from the businesses of the target nation and turn them to benefit one's own businesses.[19]

Taillard explained that dumping was possible through the use of government subsidies or deep discounting by individual companies attempting to use predatory pricing strategies.

Trade defence refers to measures taken by a host country to protect itself from such tactics. Trade defence measures generally include anti-dumping and countervailing duties on import of goods and withholding taxes on import of services. Anti-dumping duties and countervailing duties are imposed in India by the Directorate General of Trade Remedies (DGTR) under the Department of Commerce.

Before 2018, India did not have a coordinated strategy for defending its economic borders from predatory exporters. Anti-dumping duties were imposed by the Directorate General of Anti-dumping and Allied Duties (DGAD) under the Ministry of Commerce. The Directorate of Safeguards (DoS), in the Department of Revenue under the Ministry of Finance, took safeguard measures. The Directorate General of Foreign Trade (DGFT) imposed Quantitative Restrictions (QRs).

Since the defence measures were vested with different bodies under different ministries, coordination took substantial time. As a result, the trade defence mechanism in India lacked optimality and took more than a year to complete proceedings in cases pertaining to unfair trade practices. Delay of a year or more in acting upon concerns of domestic industry can be fatal for the domestic economy. Hence, proposals were made since 1997 to institute an integrated 'national authority' for trade defence measures.[20] Finally, the DGTR was constituted on 7 May 2018. All powers of imposing anti-dumping duties, safeguards and QRs now vest with this single authority.

India's Customs department is the first line of defence against unfair trade practices by exporters. The second line of defence is an enforcement body under the Department of Revenue called the Directorate of Revenue Intelligence (DRI). However, industry bodies and domestic businesses can petition the DGTR, highlighting unfair trade practices by export-import businesses of other countries. The time taken to initiate anti-dumping investigations was a matter of concern until recently. However, the average number of days taken to initiate investigations came down from 259 days in 2016 to 110 days in 2017 to just 32 days in 2019.[21]

Origin fraud works as a cheat code to circumvent the defences laid out by the DGTR. There are broadly two types of origin fraud through which circumvention of trade defences happens: transhipment and assembly operations. Under transhipment, goods from the country of origin are sent to the destination country, but certificates of origin are obtained from a conduit country. Under assembly operations, parts are sent from country of origin to conduit country; they are then assembled in the conduit country and shipped to the destination country. Assembling involves scant value addition, yet the assembled products carry certificate of origin of the conduit country.

India introduced the anti-circumvention law in 2011 through a new sub-section, 1A in Section 9A of Customs Tariff Act, 1975, to impose duties on conduit countries as retaliation of origin fraud. It states that a conduit country can claim to be the country of origin of any product if value addition in that country is more than 35 per cent of the value of the product.

Juhi Dion Sud, an advocate in the field of international trade defence laws, claims that India's anti-circumvention rules have been sparingly used since their promulgation. No circumvention investigation was initiated by India from 2011 to 2015.[22] Notwithstanding this slow start, anti-circumvention investigations have picked up and have revealed the fraudulent practices followed by exporters.

In one such instance, the domestic industry complained that after India had imposed anti-dumping duty on imports of a certain type of glass fibres called chopped strand mats (CSM) from China, Chinese exporters were routing their goods through a Thai company called Asia Composite Materials (Thailand) Co. (ACM Thailand).

On investigating, it was found that ACM Thailand was importing a different variant of glass fibre from China and was converting it into CSM glass fibre before shipping them to India as Thai-origin goods.

Investigations also revealed that ACM Thailand was a subsidiary of a Chinese company Sichuan Weibo New Material Group. Investigators concluded that ACM Thailand was a part of Sichuan Weibo's production line and the value addition it did in Thailand was insubstantial. In fact, ACM Thailand's website unabashedly mentioned that it could provide 'good (export) service to customers world-over, particularly in areas where anti-dumping duty was imposed on CSM made in China'. This shows a malafide intent of circumvention. When confronted with this statement on its website, ACM Thailand did not furnish any rebuttal.[23]

Zero Deterrence

Origin fraud is often viewed as an arbitrage rather than a trickery, primarily because of lack of punishment on the fraudulent exporters. This is because a country defending its markets has no jurisdiction or control over exporters from another country. In short, the only deterrence against an erring exporter is detection and imposition of new duties. Conduit countries, through which imports are routed to circumvent trade barriers, are also apathetic towards concerns of the importing country because they don't lose anything in the process. Conduit countries make nominal economic gains in the form of increased assembling activities, logistics business, shipping business, etc.

This condition encourages serial offenders to find new routes to circumvent trade defences. Take, for example, the trade defences imposed by European Union (EU) against Chinese bicycles. Back in 1993, the EU imposed anti-dumping duty on imports of cheap Chinese bicycles into EU markets. Japan and the US did not place any trade barriers. Consequently, Japan and the US are today flooded with Chinese bicycles and do not have any indigenous bicycle industry left.

Although the domestic industry of bicycle manufacturers survived in the EU, they complained that Chinese bicycles still managed to sneak into EU markets by committing origin fraud. The European Commission initiated investigations against bicycle imports coming from Indonesia, Malaysia, Tunisia and Sri Lanka on receiving complaints from domestic industry associations. The Commission found that Indonesia and Sri Lanka were used as transhipment points through which Chinese bicycles were shipped to the EU. In Indonesia or Sri Lanka, there was no value addition. Traders in these two countries managed to get certificates of origin so as to ship into the EU without additional duty. There were still some assembly operations in Malaysia and Tunisia, but the value addition was much lower than the 25 per cent minimum prescribed by the EU.

The Commission extended the bicycle anti-dumping duties on China to Indonesia, Malaysia, Tunisia and Sri Lanka in May 2013. To its chagrin, domestic industry associations came back with a new complaint in 2014. Chinese bicycles were now being routed through Pakistan, Cambodia and The Philippines. The Commission initiated an investigation in September 2014, with officials from the Commission undertaking a physical verification of the manufacturing plants in Pakistan, Cambodia and The Philippines. They found that the so-called manufacturers in these three countries were importing parts from China and merely assembling in these countries. The local value addition was insubstantial. Thus, anti-dumping duties on China were extended to Pakistan, Cambodia and The Philippines in May 2015.

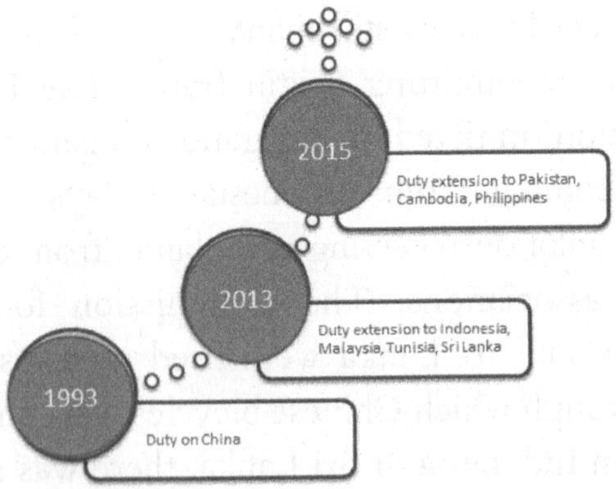

FIGURE 2*: Timeline of Action by European Commission against Chinese Bicycles*

Source: Author

God knows what route Chinese bicycles are currently taking to reach the European Union! Their expedition into India is a matter of concern for the domestic industry in India as well. The Parliamentary Standing Committee on Commerce believes that there is rampant under invoicing of Chinese bicycles coming into India. As per the Committee's estimates, about 85 per cent of Chinese bicycles imported into India are under invoiced.[24] India has kept a high rate of duty on imports of bicycles from China. Nevertheless, 'under-valued bicycles of Chinese origin are being imported from non-existent and fake or shell conduit companies of Hong Kong etc., mainly at Ludhiana ICD and JNPT Port'.[25]

Origin fraud is here to stay. Even a hegemonic power like the US finds it difficult to contain origin fraud. The trade war that US President Donald Trump unleashed on China in early 2018 by imposing stiff tariffs on Chinese goods faced a challenge from rampant origin fraud. US officials claimed that soon after high tariffs were imposed on Chinese imports, Chinese goods were being sent to the US through countries like Vietnam, Cambodia and Hong Kong. Certain EXIM traders were replacing 'Made in China' labels with 'Made in Vietnam' labels and transhipping Chinese goods to the US through Vietnam.

In June 2019, US customs authorities found that Chinese goods were being re-routed through a Special Economic Zone (SEZ) in Cambodia to escape the tariffs imposed on Chinese goods. This SEZ–Sihanoukville Special Economic Zone–is jointly owned by the government of China and the government of Cambodia, and was started as part of the Belt and Road Initiative (BRI) of China.[26] China controls border and shipping infrastructure in many other countries that have joined the belt-and-road initiative. How feasible is it to verify the origin of shipments from each of these countries?

BRI is seen by foreign policy mandarins as a strategic encirclement of India by China, but the author has always believed that BRI is an economic encirclement of India. The infrastructure and industrial clusters developed by China in countries along the BRI remain under Chinese control. It will be extremely difficult for Indian authorities to determine whether goods shipped from these locations were made in that country or made in China.

Owing to its economic might, the US government could influence Vietnam to act against origin fraud. Following that, Vietnam led a massive crackdown on fraudulent transhipping of Chinese goods in November 2019.[27] However, other countries through which Chinese goods moved to the US were not as willing as Vietnam to use their enforcement resources to clamp down on activities that affect another country. Patrick Conway, a professor of economics at the University of North Carolina at Chapel Hill, pointed out that many Chinese products were transhipped through Hong Kong in the period. The US Customs Service tried to detect and crack down on this , but the job proved to be too daunting. He believed that origin fraud violated international law, but the efforts to contain them were hard and costly.[28]

The best that a country could do to counter such unfair trade practices was to take up investigations promptly upon receiving complaints from the domestic industry or customs authorities. The malady is widespread and the cure takes time as a country governed by the rule of law has to follow due process. Intergovernmental cooperation can effectively counter such unfair practices. Sharing of intelligence among customs officials of different nations can also help in dealing with such unfair practices.

Political will of countries not to be used as a conduit for origin frauds can bring about positive changes. It is important for the 'victim countries' to enter into agreements with countries that have high vulnerability to being used as a conduit for mutual cooperation and conduct capacity building of customs and trade officials of such countries. FTAs are especially prone to abuse by origin frauds. Hence, FTAs should incorporate mechanisms for joint inspection and audit of goods traded among member countries.

Fake Exports

The Ahmedabad office of the newly-formed Directorate General of GST Intelligence (DGGI) received a peculiar intel from a source in Gandhidham in September 2019. That, a syndicate from the National Capital Region (NCR) was making fake exports of tobacco products through the Kandla SEZ in Gandhidham.

DGGI Ahmedabad quickly formed three teams and mounted raids on three units in the SEZ. The teams found that the Delhi-based syndicates actually exported tobacco, but the tobacco that they exported was of low grade, such as scented *jarda*, *kimam* (a tobacco extract) and filter *khaini*. These tobacco products were not of export grade. These products could be procured in local markets at ₹150–₹350 per kg but were being exported at the rate of ₹5,000–₹9,000 per kg.[29] Why would any foreign trader in their right mind purchase low-grade tobacco at such a high price?

Apparently, it was done to defraud the exchequer and happens to be a common modus operandi to defraud the government. The Goods and Services Tax (GST) was rolled out in India only in July 2017, and many incidences of fake exports have been detected by the DGGI in quick succession after the GST rollout.

As a fraudulent activity, fake export scam is much older than the GST itself. Most countries offer incentives and subsidies to promote exports. One such scheme is the duty drawback scheme, whereby exporters of some items get points depending on the value of exports. These points can be redeemed against customs duty on the import of other items. In India, these points are granted in the form of Duty Entitlement Pass Book (DEPB) scrip since April 1997. An exporter can sell the scrips in open market to an importer. The importer can redeem the points against customs duty it has to pay on its imports.

Illustratively speaking, exporter Ram gets 10,000 points on his exports, which he can redeem against customs duty, but Ram only exports. So, he sells the scrips to Hari at a 10 per cent discount. That is, he sells the scrips to Hari at ₹9,000. Hari, an importer, has to pay customs duty of ₹15,000 on his imports. He shows the scrips to customs authorities and pays only

₹5,000 (₹15,000 – ₹10,000). Both Ram and Hari benefit because scrips are transferable. Ram gets an incentive of ₹9,000. Hari saves ₹1000 (₹10,000 – ₹9,000).

Export scams earlier concentrated on gaming this scheme. Fraudsters exported cheap and condemned goods as high-value products and claimed DEPB scrips. The dummy exports were then dumped mid-sea! Organised syndicates would export cheap goods at a high price, then import the same goods at a cheap price and then again export the goods at a high price, thus round-tripping the same goods to claim DEPB scrips.

So as not to get caught, EXIM syndicates float multiple shell companies. When one shell company makes high-value exports, it is expected to get payment in foreign exchange. Since the exports are fake and there is no real buyer, no payment actually comes. RBI and customs authorities then start asking questions. By the time authorities get alerted, the syndicate sells the shell company's DEPB scrips to genuine traders and abandons the shell company. Shell companies usually have dummy directors (discussed in detail in a separate chapter). So, investigators face a stonewall and cannot recover the loss.

EXIM syndicates rank the highest in the value pyramid of fraudsters because they directly defraud the treasury of a country. They are audacious enough to steal from the revenue collected by the government.

The amount that such syndicates can fleece can be staggering, thus giving them the tag of serious frauds. For instance, in March 2016, DRI sleuths conducted a raid at the Tughlaqabad container depot and found a few businessmen exporting rags as ready-made garments in order to claim DEPB scrips.[30] They went on to allege that businessman Ramesh Wadhera fraudulently made ₹700 crore by getting DEPB benefits on fake exports in just two years before their action.[31]

Wadhera had allegedly used a network of 488 agents to conduct a circular trading in which he exported rags to Dubai at a high value and imported back the same rags at a low value. He got duty drawbacks every time he exported.

Another businessman operating from the Tughlaqabad container depot, Vikas Sharma, had allegedly made ₹300 crore in the same period by using the same modus operandi. The DRI had estimated in 2016 that out of the ₹28,000 crore that the government gives as incentive under the duty drawback scheme every year, as much as ₹7,000 crore is taken by conmen alone![32]

It is not possible for customs officials to conduct physical check of all export containers. Physical checks are time consuming and reduce the efficiency of port logistics. Thus, customs officials check consignments randomly or on the basis of specific intelligence, a constraint that is exploited by syndicates making fake exports.

GST and Fake Exports

The problem of fake exports has become even more acute with the advent of the GST. The GST is a tax on value addition done by a party when supplying any good or service. Tax is calculated at every point of supply. For example, supply happens when a firm purchases a good. Supply also happens when it sells the goods. The firm has to deposit the difference of the GST on sale and the GST on purchase with the government. The firm computes the GST on sales and collects it from the party it sells to. We call it the output GST. The firm also pays GST to its suppliers. This amount, called GST input tax credit (ITC), is deductible from the output GST. Net amount has to be paid to the government.

Confused? The logic of GST is confusing indeed, so much so that advocates sweat when explaining to courts how VAT and GST frauds happen. We have no choice though. We cannot appreciate the arbitrage of EXIM conmen without understanding the nuances of this tax.

The GST is an indirect tax, in the sense that the burden of this tax falls ultimately on the end consumer. Revenue officials, however, do not know who the end consumer of a good or service is. A good, say iron ore, may be traded by multiple persons and ultimately lands up in a steel plant. Is the steel plant the ultimate consumer? It converts iron ore into steel and sells steel to the automotive industry. Is the maker of auto parts the ultimate consumer? Supply chains are complex and, thus, every party in a supply chain deposits GST on the value addition it is attributable to. The GST liability of each party in a typical supply chain is calculated in the following way:

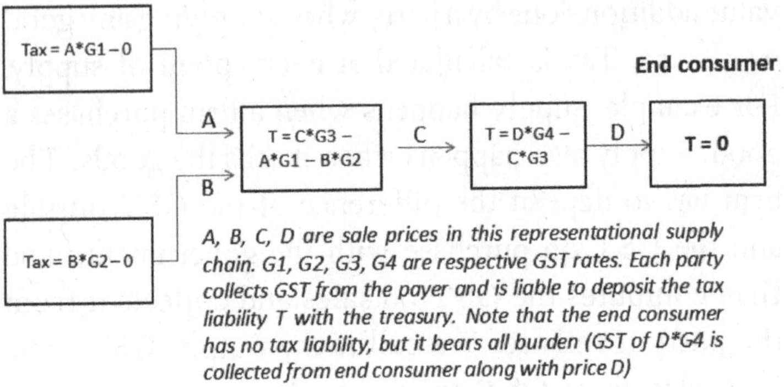

FIGURE 3: *How GST Works*

Source: Author

If the output GST liability for any firm is higher than the input GST credit (ITC), the firm has to pay the difference to the government. However, if the output GST liability is lower than the ITC, the government has to refund the difference amount to the firm. Ideally, no refund should arise in the above scheme of affairs, but refunds do arise whenever there is an inverted duty structure. That is, when the GST rate on sales is lower than the GST rate on purchases.

For instance, the GST on non-woven fabric is 12 per cent, but the GST on fabric bags is 5 per cent. A boutique purchases non-woven fabric at ₹100, weaves it into a bag and sells the bag at ₹200. Its output GST liability is 5 per cent of ₹200, which works out to ₹10. Its ITC is 12 per cent of ₹100, which works out to ₹12. Since GST credit is more than GST liability, the boutique can claim the difference (₹12 – ₹10) as a refund from the government.

This is where an arbitrage opens up for scammers. The scammers incorporate a shell company, draw a fake invoice for purchasing fabric raw materials from a *benami* supplier and a fake invoice for selling fabric bags to a *benami* shopkeeper. And then they can claim a refund from the government.

Revenue officials have booked 6,641 cases of GST fraud, involving 7,164 entities up until November 2019.[33] A mind-boggling number of GST frauds have been reported in the two years following its introduction in India, which, I grudgingly admit, points to the ingenuity of Indian fraudsters. Tax evasion comes naturally to people, but tax frauds do not. Tax evasion is a practice by which a person hides their tax liability from the government, but tax fraud is all about fleecing from the government. Rampant fraud behaviour that we see immediately after the introduction of the GST points to two key traits of Indian fraudsters. One, their propensity for innovation and *jugaad* (a quick fix to a problem, using limited and innovative methods). Two, a low moral barrier to justify stealing from the government.

Although GST refund fraud can happen wherever there is an inverted duty structure, large refund frauds happen in connection with the export of goods. As stated earlier, the GST is ultimately borne by the end consumer, it being an indirect tax. Whenever goods or services are exported, the end consumer is located outside the country. The country does not have the right to tax an end consumer living outside its borders. Hence, no output GST is levied on exports. Export of goods and services is 'zero-rated supply', to use the jargon used in indirect tax practice. Thus, exporters can claim refunds on the entire ITC accruing to them.

In the case of Delhi-based syndicates exporting tobacco through Kandla SEZ, it was found that although low quality tobacco was purchased in cash from local markets at ₹150–₹350 per kg, fake purchase invoice was drawn at ₹5,000–₹9,000 per kg. The DGGI found that fake invoices were issued by 25 different suppliers in Assam, Bihar, Delhi, Haryana, MP and UP.

Sin goods attract GST at a rate of 93 per cent. By drawing fake purchase invoices, the exporters got input tax credit of 93 per cent of the purchase price. After making fake exports, they claimed the entire ITC as a refund from the government. The mathematics behind it is represented by the illustration below:

Entities in the supply chain	ITC (A)	Sale price (B)	GST on sales (C = 93% of B)	Tax liability (D = C− A)
Manufacturer	0	150.00	139.50	139.50
Trade 1	139.50	180.00	167.40	27.90
Trade 2	167.40	250	232.50	65.10
Trade 3	232.50	2000	1860	1627.50
Exporter	1627.50	*Export price*	0	**- 1627.50**

Never pays tax to government as it is a fictitious entity

Negative figure means refund

GST rate on exports in zero

FIGURE 4: *Method of Generating Fake Refunds (Amounts in INR for 1 Kg of Tobacco)*

Source: Author

By the time DGGI acted against the syndicate, it had claimed refund of ₹400 crore on fake invoices worth ₹1,000 crore.[34]

In an unrelated case, the Gurgaon unit of DGGI found that Deepak Mittal and Ankur Garg, both Delhi-based traders, had issued sale invoices for cigarettes to various dummy and fictitious entities. These fictitious entities, in turn, posed as traders and issued sale invoices to certain export firms. The export firms claimed refund of ITC on the pretext that the cigarettes were exported, whereas there were no actual exports of cigarettes. This way, these two men availed of ITC of ₹141 crore.[35] DGGI later arrested these two individuals.

Tobacco, cigarettes and other sin goods are the preferred items of export for this scam. They attract high GST rates. So, refund generated from fake exports is also high. And, it is difficult for customs officials to ascertain their value without expert assistance. Other goods preferred for fake exports are readymade garments and carpets.

The fraud runs deep and rampant. The Central Board of Indirect Taxes and Customs (CBIC) revealed in January 2020 that a data audit had led them to as many as 1,200 exporters who are untraceable![36] These 1,200 exporters had together claimed GST refunds of ₹350 crore. It is possible that multiple export firms are run by a single fraudster and that the actual number of export frauds that the CBIC detected is lower than 1,200. The CBIC has stated that these frauds involved fictitious entities with no physical presence. These entities were incorporated by fraudsters using stolen identity and morphed documents.

While the situation may appear dire, most of these frauds will soon be contained and controlled. The DGGI is a new body formed after the introduction of a new tax regime. Any new system that is introduced to tackle the kind of complexity that GST entails is bound to have multiple control failures in initial days. However, if the enforcement arm quickly learns and punishes frauds, the deterrence forces behavioural change in scam entrepreneurs. Also, the GST architecture is woven around GST Network, an e-governance portal. The technology portal collects information on a real-time basis and throws interesting clues to detect fraudsters. Data analytics on GST Network has enabled CBIC officials to block many fraudulent refund claims.[37] Data mining on GST Network helps identify high-risk traders that may be fraudsters. GST officials can then use this lead to determine if a claim of refund is genuine or fraudulent.

4

Chefs Who Cook Books: Accounting Fraud

On 6 December 2008, the Hyderabad chapter of the CEO Clubs India held an interactive session with tech magnate Ramalinga Raju on the topic *Secrets of Success: Lessons Learnt from Life*. As the founder and promoter of Satyam Computer Services, Raju had catapulted the company to being one of the top global software firms in just about two decades. Aspiring entrepreneurs were thus keen to pick his brains and get insights into his success story. Stumping his interviewers in the course of the interaction, Raju said: 'Why should somebody share his secret of success with anybody else!'

Although Raju came across as selfish, he did reveal his secrets exactly a month later: in a confession letter, to market regulator SEBI. In the letter dated 7 January 2009, he admitted that he had been cooking the books of Satyam for the past several years. It had started by inflating profits marginally in the audited accounts but as the company grew by leaps and bounds, the fictitious profits also grew. That is, till they reached unmanageable levels.

Raju revealed the company had a fictitious bank balance of ₹5,040 crore, accrued interest of ₹376 crore that did not exist (fictitious bank balances yield fictitious interest) and other bogus receivables. In total, there was a hole of ₹7,136 crore in the balance sheet of Satyam, which was then one of the four largest IT companies of India. Subsequent investigation by the CBI and the SFIO revealed that the extent of fudging was much higher.

The investigations also shed light on how easy it was for Satyam to fudge its accounts. It generated fictitious revenue by billing fake customers for fictitious software services provided. The company created fake customer identities, fake invoices and some 6,000 fake salary accounts to justify the fake services that it provided.[1] This happened over eight years. The window dressing went undetected despite the company having been listed on three international exchanges: NYSE, Dow Jones and EURONEXT.

For the quarter ending September 2008, the company overstated its revenue by 75 per cent and its profits by 97 per cent. Its balance sheet for the quarter showed ₹1,700 crore parked in current accounts. Current accounts do not yield any interest, so no one in their right mind parks such huge funds in current accounts. Some market analysts had asked the rationale behind the decision. The hole in the balance sheet had become so big, almost like a crater, that it was glaring. When Raju realised that the crater could no longer be hidden behind fictitious figures, he confessed. Probably that is why he expressed in the confession letter that his situation was like that of 'riding a tiger and not knowing how to get off without being eaten'.

Riding the Tiger

Raju had started Satyam with a cousin in Secunderabad in June 1987. It got its major break when it acquired a large US-based customer, John Deere, a Chicago-based farm equipment maker. John Deere engaged Satyam to develop software for its business operations. The general practice in those days was to develop the software on the client's premises so that the client could be taken through each phase of the development process. Satyam proposed an alternative to this onshore model, suggesting its engineers would code their software offshore from India. Satyam said only a small team will be there at the client location to integrate the software. Such a model, Satyam reasoned, would lead to considerable cost savings. Engineers in India would have to be paid much less than engineers working onshore.

However, John Deere's management was not convinced about this. To give them a proof of concept, Satyam divided its development team into two. One team was stationed at the John Deere plant, while another team of 35 engineers was based out of an independent office elsewhere in Chicago. The second team would develop software and upload it at night onto John Deere's mainframe computers using a satellite link.

The experiment was successful and John Deere's management allowed Satyam to develop software for its Chicago-based business operations from India itself. And, thus, started a movement for offshoring software operations to India. Satyam was the pioneer of the software outsourcing industry in India.

Satyam's role in the genesis of software development clusters of India places it at a high pedestal in the minds of the Indian business community. This is also a reason the revelation of the fraud came as an utter shock to all. Many compare it with the Enron scandal of 2001, which involved massive accounting manipulations and eventual bankruptcy of the company.

Raju started cooking the books of Satyam in April 1999. One reason for manipulating the books was that Satyam never had the kind of profitability that other companies of similar size–Infosys, Wipro and Tata Consultancy Services–had. Raju wanted Satyam to be at par with these competitors. A second reason might have been personal gains by portraying that the company was doing well.

According to the CBI, the Rajus made a windfall by divesting shares of Satyam. A gain of ₹707 crore from the sale of 1.09 crore shares. This was tainted money as shares were then trading at artificial prices due to the company's fake profits. The SFIO investigation threw up a much higher figure. It showed a gain of ₹3,029 crore from the sale of 3.91 crore shares.[2]

Journalist Kingshuk Nag alluded to a more devious reason behind the fraud. He alleged that Raju's principal focus was on his real estate business and he saw Satyam as a milch cow.[3] In Nag's narrative, Raju was building two companies for his sons, Maytas Infra and Maytas Properties (Maytas is Satyam spelt backwards). Between 2000 and 2007, he acquired large tracts of land in and around Hyderabad at prices much higher than their fair value. To fund the huge land banks, he pledged his shares in Satyam to banks and borrowed money. By declaring false profits, he ensured that the share price of Satyam remained artificially high in the stock market. Since the shares were trading at a high value, banks gave large loans against these shares. Raju pumped the borrowed money into real estate. He sold some shares held in the name of relatives and used the proceeds to buy more land. He also allegedly siphoned funds from Satyam to finance his appetite for real estate.[4]

Such schemes are like a house of cards. They work well as long as the economy is robust, but fall the moment a storm starts. Raju's scheme worked quite well until the subprime mortgage crisis happened in the US in 2008 and the American economy went into a recession. Since India's software companies exported software primarily to US-based clients, share traders forecast a fall in revenues of Indian software companies. This resulted in a fall in prices of most software scrips.

Such fluctuation in share prices does not bother genuine investors for they know that economic conditions are cyclic. In Raju's case though, he had pledged his shares to banks and financial institutions at a time when the share price was much higher. If the share price falls below the price at which it was pledged, banks expect the borrower to pledge more shares or return the loan. This is because banks use the collateral to cover their exposure in the loan given. However, Raju had already pledged all his shares.

Raju also did not have any cash. He had utilised the entire loan amount in buying up land and real estate for Maytas. To make matters worse, real estate prices had begun crashing as the subprime mortgage crisis led to an economic slowdown in India as well. In Hyderabad, land prices fell the most in areas such as Medchal, Nizampet, Miyapur and Bachupally, where Maytas held large land banks.

One option for Raju was to sell land at a loss and get the much-needed cash. Prospective buyers were not eager to make a quick deal as they were expecting the prices to fall further. As a result, Raju could not muster enough cash to pay the banks.[5] Satyam began facing financial distress. The company had managed to sail through with outrageous figures of non-existent bank balance up until now because Raju and his coterie had fudged documents. They had prepared fake bank account statements as documentation and furnished the same to their auditors, PricewaterhouseCoopers (PwC). They did not verify the genuineness of the bank documents.

In fact, no one questioned Satyam's profits and large cash balances when the economy was doing good. When market sentiments turned negative, analysts started questioning why Satyam was not utilising the ₹1,700 crore it had parked in non-interest-bearing current accounts. Who keeps cash in current accounts in bad times! In reality, this cash did not exist and it seemed imminent that the scam would be found out.

To salvage the situation, Raju proposed a merger of Satyam and Maytas. While the cash assets of Satyam were all fictitious, Maytas had real assets at its disposal. In the proposed merger, Satyam would use its fictitious bank balance and other assets amounting to ₹7,000 crore to purchase Maytas. This way, it would get real assets and the company could tide over the economic storm.

The merger proposal was presented to Satyam's board of directors on 16 December 2008. While some members had apprehensions about the merger of two companies working in completely different verticals, they eventually approved the amalgamation. However, the institutional investors who held majority shares of Satyam did not take the move kindly. They thought Raju was trying to save his family's real estate business by merging it with Satyam. The merger decision was, thus, reversed just eight hours after the board of directors had passed it. A statement was given to the press that said: 'We have decided not to move ahead with the acquisition of Maytas in deference to investor community views.'

The real story was completely different. The family business was being used to save Satyam and hide the fraud, but the institutional investors did not know about this. The merger attempt had, in fact, put the spotlight on Satyam. Investors realised that everything was not alright with the company.

The failed merger attempt was quickly followed by an anonymous letter to Krishna Palepu, a member of the board of directors, that the account books of Satyam were fudged. One director, Mangalam Srinivasan, resigned from the company's board on 25 December 2008. Two more directors, Vinod Dham and Palepu, resigned two days later. This unnerved the investors.

Under pressure from all sides, Raju agreed to appoint DSP Merrill Lynch as a consultant to recommend steps to strengthen the board of directors. The firm was hired on 27 December 2008, and was given just 10 days to submit its report. However, it took only about a week to conclude that Satyam's accounts were fudged. It wrote a letter to Raju stating that it had found 'material accounting irregularities' in the company's books. It marked copies of the letter to SEBI and the Bombay Stock Exchange (BSE) as well. Raju had been cornered and he knew that SEBI and the BSE would make the Merrill Lynch report public. So, he wrote the letter confessing the fraud on 7 January 2009.

In hindsight, the Satyam scandal presents three key lessons. First, it was a massive audit failure. All the cases of accounting manipulations result from some form of audit failure, but this one was glaring. Accounts were fudged on a regular basis for eight long years and the auditors did not make any qualification. On the other hand, Merrill Lynch found 'material accounting irregularities' in less than 10 days.

After the Enron scandal, one of the Big 5 audit firms had to close shop. What remained after the scandal was the Big 4, and one of these Big 4 firms was the auditor of Satyam.

An FIR was filed against the individual auditors of the firm and they were charged with criminal conspiracy. In January 2018, SEBI banned PwC from auditing firms listed in the stock market, and there was penal action on the auditors. However, the ban was quashed by the SAT.

More importantly, the Satyam scandal prompted lawmakers to relook at audit norms and introduce better control and supervision, a process that culminated in a complete overhaul of the corporate laws of India in

2013. Accounting frauds are criminal offences under the new Companies Act of 2013. The new Act has bestowed enforcement powers to the SFIO. It has also proposed setting up an independent regulator for auditors, called the National Financial Reporting Authority (NFRA). The NFRA became fully functional towards the fag end of 2018, and now exercises regulatory and penal powers over errant auditors.

Many audit professionals believe that auditors and company managers are over regulated now because the new laws are reactive.[6] They reason that since the regulations came in response to the Satyam fraud, they are not balanced. There are now six different authorities regulating the function of auditors:

1. Ministry of Corporate Affairs (MCA) regulates auditors of all companies
2. The SFIO undertakes criminal proceedings against errant auditors
3. The NFRA imposes penal action for audit lapses
4. The ICAI undertakes disciplinary proceedings against auditors
5. SEBI regulates auditors of listed companies
6. The RBI regulates auditors of banks and NBFCs

However, multiple authorities regulating audit behaviour does not necessarily mean over regulation. Neither do they act in a pre-emptive manner. These authorities jump into action only when irregularities in auditing are revealed. Multiple regulatory bodies create a greater deterrence among auditors. All that the auditors need to do to keep these regulators at bay is to perform their job cautiously and make appropriate comments in their audit reports. True, these institutions are still new and only time will tell how effective they are in creating a sense of deterrence against audit lapses.

A second lesson is that the past behaviour of decision makers gives adequate hints about fraud risk. A 360-degree profiling should be a part of large institutional investors' due diligence. In Satyam's case, exhaustive profiling might have informed investors about the serious allegations of siphoning off funds by the promoter family.

Other than personal gain from the sale of Satyam shares at high prices, the Raju family benefited from Satyam in other ways too, as alleged by the investigating agencies. The ED found that funds from Satyam were used by the family to acquire 287 properties in major Indian cities. The CBI found that Raju had listed Satyam on the New York Stock Exchange (NYSE) in 2001, by issuing American Depository Shares (ADS). By doing this, he raised ₹760 crore, but remitted only ₹397 crores to India. Rest of it was transferred to unknown accounts in the US, which the CBI believes are *benami* accounts of Raju.[7]

While these acts had gone unnoticed at the time, other acts of similar nature had come to the notice of outsiders. For instance, the Income Tax department had found much before the fraud came to light that Raju had transferred approximately ₹19.5 crore from Satyam to the bank accounts of his mother, father and other elderly relatives of his extended family. This he did apparently because income tax laws exempt banks from levying TDS on senior citizens. The investigating officer in this case was S. Padmaja, an Indian Revenue

Service officer of 1992 batch. When she went to the Satyam office to check documents, she was locked in a room for a few hours. Later, the Rajus allegedly used pressure and got her transferred.[8]

Whatever be the truth, such allegations demonstrate poor conduct by the promoters. A 360-degree profiling of the promoter group could have informed institutional investors about these serious allegations. Once past behaviour raises red flags about promoters and founders, the investors should insist on multiple internal audits by different auditors. A certain degree of investor activism is always good for the transparent functioning of a company.

In Satyam's case, Raju and his family held less than 10 per cent of the company's shares. Institutional investors held more than 50 per cent shares. Raju managed to fudge accounts for eight long years because he kept the finance team insulated from other divisions. Institutional investors should have insisted on access of their audit teams to finance records. They failed in performing the basic supervision functions of majority shareholders.

A third lesson from this fraud is that accounting frauds are the easiest to commit and most difficult to catch. Raju could keep up the facade for so long because the devil is in the numbers. Accounting manipulation is rampant, but rarely comes to notice. The higher the volume of transactions in a company, the greater the difficulty in tracing manipulation.

Creative accounting generally happens with one of two motives: Either to show a rosy picture or to avoid taxes. The two classes of manipulations are mirror images. To show a rosy picture, the fraud artificially increases revenues and profits. To avoid taxes, the fraud suppresses revenues and profits. I had ventured to discuss various manipulations to reduce tax liability in my book *Loophole Games* and ended up with more than a hundred different modus operandi. I still cannot claim that the list in that book was exhaustive.

In this book, we discuss accounting frauds that demonstrate a rosier picture of their business. These frauds may be promoters trying to increase their company's valuation before a stake sale or founders window dressing books to attract investors. Or top managers trying to meet a target for bonus and employee stock options. And accounting fraud is quite common. In a survey conducted by the Economist Intelligence Unit in 2014, 80 per cent respondents from India said they had come across frauds in their firm. Globally, around 75 per cent respondents said they had encountered a fraud in their firm.[9]

Accounting frauds do not get detected most of the time. In most cases, they get noticed when there is a change in management. For instance, Vijay Mallya sold his stake in United Breweries to Diageo in 2014. After getting control of the company, Diageo realised that funds had been diverted by Mallya to other companies under his control. Diageo appointed EY to conduct a detailed forensic audit of the company's accounts. The forensic audit revealed a clear diversion of funds in the form of loans and advances to other companies under Mallya's control. Diageo's due diligence team could not detect these irregularities before the transfer of stake.[10]

Detection is difficult in big companies because of the complexity of transactions. Peculiarly, detection of accounting fraud is equally difficult in small companies because no one is looking. Small companies are often family controlled and all you need to fudge accounts is a pliable auditor ready to abet the act. It is relatively easier to influence small audit firms than the large ones. One data analysis reveals that there are only 15 audit firms that audit 10 or more listed companies. Whereas, as many as 654 audit firms have just one listed company as their client.[11] Such audit firms value their clients more than the big audit firms. They have a greater need to retain the client and so try to keep the client in good humour. Thus, it is easier for companies to control smaller auditors. Small companies contracting small audit firms are best placed to commit an accounting manipulation. An investigation in recent years that best exemplifies this is the case of Celestial Biolabs, an India-based biopharmaceutical company.

Master of Profit Management

Celestial Biolabs was a small enterprise providing clinical research and bio-IT services. Its turnover was ₹25.32 crore in FY 2010–11 and ₹21 crore in FY 2011–12. It clocked decent profits in both the years, but there was nothing particularly impressive. That is, until you find out that the company had provided services to marquee pharmaceutical companies such as Pfizer Limited, Glenmark Pharmaceuticals Limited, Merck Limited, Zandu Pharmaceuticals, Claris Lifesciences Limited and Themis Medicare Limited. These are top pharma companies. The pharmaceutical industry itself is a research-intensive industry and none of these companies would hire technical services from a small firm unless it had a unique technical knowhow or expertise. If all these companies hired technical services from a single firm, it definitely had valuable intellectual property.

Celestial's client list had drawn attention of many investors in the BSE and the NSE, the two stock exchanges where the company was listed. Unfortunately, as it often happens with success, Celestial drew the attention of tax collectors. Sleuths from the service tax office found Celestial had not paid any service tax for the services it provided to the top pharma companies of India.

In the course of their investigation, the tax sleuths found while Celestial had been booking the sale of service to the top pharma companies, the purported recipients had not received any service. They were not even aware of Celestial and their account books did not have any transaction listed with it.

If no service was provided, how could taxmen impose service tax! Piqued, the tax officials informed SEBI about this in May 2015. SEBI swung into action and started its own investigation. It asked the purported service recipients–Pfizer, Piramal Healthcare, Serum Institute of India, Themis Medicare, Wockhardt, Zandu Realty, Narayana Institute for Advanced Research and many other entities–to confirm if they had received any services mentioned in the audited accounts of Celestial in FY 2010–11 and 2011–12. These companies verified their books of accounts and confirmed they had not availed of any service from Celestial Biolabs Limited.

SEBI served a show-cause notice to the directors of Celestial. The Celestial MD responded saying since the clinical trials' business was new in India, its clients wanted complete confidentiality. Government regulations were not clear and there was confusion over whether or not a service tax was applicable on Celestial's business. That's why the clients apparently refused to issue written contracts and preferred to engage services on the basis of verbal contracts.

The MD stated that the matter was discussed internally at Celestial and the company decided to raise an invoice for the time spent by its team members on work allotted by these clients. The company raised invoices against these clients and booked sales in its profit and loss sheet. The MD claimed that the amounts mentioned in the invoices were discussed with the clients and was mutually agreed upon. The clients did not pay but the company did not declare the receivables as bad debt, even years after the 'services' were provided.

SEBI did not buy this argument. The market regulator held that it was 'highly improbable that not one but all the pharma companies wanted to carry out such sensitive/confidential work without entering into a formal agreement' and did not communicate with Celestial via emails or letters even once. 'All the nuances and nitty gritty of the project were discussed without leaving a paper trail. This practice of not maintaining any kind of records for an ongoing project was followed not with one pharma company but uniformly with all the pharma companies. Further, even all the pharma companies used to communicate their requirements' orally only to Celestial.[12] These were big, multinational pharma companies and maintained detailed documentation of all their work, except the work that Celestial apparently did for them.

SEBI called for timesheets, which are generally approved by clients. They were not produced. SEBI called for proof that the invoices raised by Celestial were sent to clients via post or email. Celestial's directors could not produce that either. Following this, SEBI concluded that the services provided by Celestial were non-existent. It alleged that artificial sales were booked by the company to show retail investors it had a robust business and this was done to boost the company's valuation. Promoters sold part of their stake to gullible investors at artificially high valuation.

SEBI barred Celestial and its promoters from the capital market for a period of 10 years for fabricating sales and giving false disclosures. It initiated penal action against the company's promoters and auditor.

The modus operandi of the alleged fraud at Celestial is quite elementary. Most companies are constrained from committing such elementary fraud by multiple checks and balances. Most auditors adhere to professional codes of conduct. Even those who are inclined to overlook fudging cannot afford to ignore such blatant acts, thanks to the multiple regulators overseeing their conduct. Then there are internal auditors, tax auditors, independent directors, audit committee and ethics committees.

Luckily for them, accrual accounting allows them many other techniques of fudging, which are comparably less conspicuous than fake sales. Profits for a year are determined by a very elemental equation:

Profit in year Y = Sales in year Y - Costs in year Y

Now, a company's managers have significant control over the timing to recognise a cost or a sale. To increase profit in year Y, they need to either increase sales or decrease costs. They may recognise advertising and research and development (R&D) costs in a future year, even if the costs were incurred in the same year. Alternatively, they may advance the revenue recognition of future years by booking credit sales. This is exactly what happened at Ricoh India, where the senior management of the company was accused of committing an accounting fraud.

Ricoh India, now Minosha Digital Solutions, is the Indian arm of Japanese multinational corporation Ricoh Global, a leading supplier of office automation equipment and IT peripherals such as scanners and printers. Ricoh Global owned about 74 per cent shares of Ricoh India. Other shares were traded in India's stock markets. The company had an impressive performance between FY 2013 and FY 2015 as its sales shot up from ₹633 crore to ₹1,638 crore. As a result, its share price on Dalal Street shot up from less than ₹100 in November 2013 to more than ₹1,000 in June 2015. This was a jump of over 900 per cent in just 18 months.

Something unforeseen, however, happened around the time the company was reaching such heights of success. The Companies Act of 2013, came into force following the Satyam scam. The Act requires a company to rotate its statutory auditor every 10 years. Ricoh India's auditor for the last 15 years was Sahni Natarajan & Bahl, an Indian firm. The company was forced to hire a new auditor. The company's board decided to appoint BSR & Co., a KPMG affiliate, as its auditor. BSR & Co. refused to sign off on the company's quarterly financial results for third quarter of 2016, citing 'financial irregularities' and recommended a forensic audit of the company.

The company appointed PwC to do the forensic audit. PwC found that the company was booking revenue from IT services much before the projects were completed. They also found circular transactions in which Ricoh India sold services to a party and then purchased the same service. Such circular transactions end up showing higher sales even though they do not result in any profit. About 71 per cent of Ricoh's sales in IT services comprised such circular transactions.

The company's core business was the sale of scanners and printers of the Ricoh brand. In this segment too, the company's managers booked sales even before the delivery of the product to vendors. More stock was pushed to vendors than they could sell. Vendors do not mind taking stock if it is on credit. The company booked sales upon pushing stocks to vendors. It was a win-win for both.

Managers have discretion in deciding the time of booking a revenue, but they have no control over the receipt of payment. Customers pay only when they make the purchase. If revenue is booked before that, then payment receivables from customers also increases. High receivables from customers raised alarm for KPMG's auditors and they insisted on a forensic audit.

Ricoh India's earnings were manipulated to such an extent that the company was forced to book losses of ₹1,118 crore in FY 2016. The company admitted in a public release on 19 July 2016, that its accounts appeared to have been falsified.

Equity-to-Profit Models

Why do some frauds get caught while others don't? Success stories in this profession are rarely found in the public domain for the simple reason that successful fraudsters never get caught. We can, however, tell with reasonable certainty that frauds that create a self-sustaining cycle seldom get caught. Accounting manipulations are superior techniques to generate self-sustaining cycles. The myriad figures in books of accounts are overwhelming even for professionally qualified accountants. They successfully hide grand schemes that defraud investors.

One typical model that creates a stable fraud cycle is the equity-to-profit scheme. In this scheme, a company fraudulently shows high profits, indicating that the company is doing well. This pushes up the company's valuation. The company then lures investors to buy its equity at a high valuation. Investors pump capital into the company. The company then converts the same capital into profits. Genuine profits arise from regular business activities, but artificial profits can be generated by showing the capital as profits.

The company can further increase its valuation on getting more profits. Then it lures other investors at a higher valuation and the process continues. The promoters benefit because they sell part of their original stake in each round of investment. The company valuation goes up with each round. Sometimes, the valuation jumps in leaps from one round to the other, thus luring more bullish investment banks.

The key steps in each equity-to-profit cycle are:

1. Show high profits
2. Get high entity valuation
3. Sell equity at valuation determined in Step 2
4. Capital received upon selling equity gets converted into profits
5. With new profits, go back to Step 1

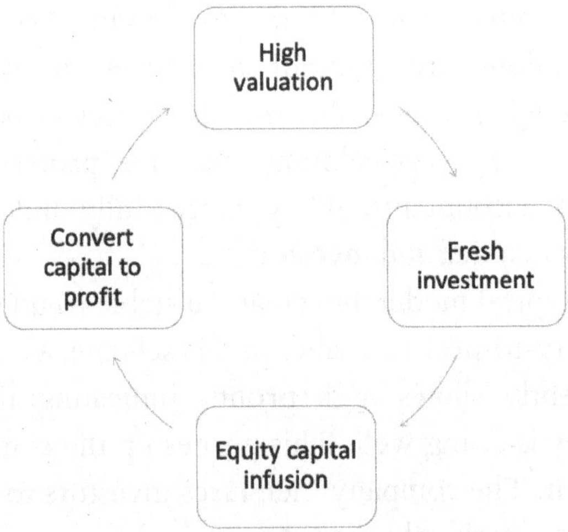

FIGURE 1: *A Self-sustaining Fraud Cycle*
Source: Author

Fraudsters face two major problems in implementing this scheme. First is the issue of converting capital into profits. Capital received from investors is recorded in the balance sheet. Profits are generated when sales are made to outsiders. How can capital already recorded in accounts be shown as sales in the same accounts? To resolve this problem, creative accountants have advanced an ingenuous solution. The capital in this company's accounts is further invested in 'related parties', entities over which the company's promoters have control. They can be influenced to abet the promoters' nefarious schemes.

Now, the capital has moved to related parties, who will use this capital to pay the company for goods or services. This way, the capital comes back to the company's books as revenue. In many cases, related parties receive capital from the company and pay rents to it in the form of property rent, IP royalty or brand royalty. The company can then claim that it is in possession of valuable property or IP rights, which helps further boost the company's valuation.

Related party transactions (RPT) are an important innovation in the history of accounting frauds. Most related party transactions are benign and rather help genuine businesses prosper. When related parties cooperate in conduct of their businesses, group synergies and economies of scale result. This, in turn, leads to higher efficiency. Some MNCs have grown in the last few decades largely because they have managed to tap the hidden synergy benefits that come from cooperation between related parties.

On the flip side, related party interaction gives more room to managers to manage and manipulate profits. That is why corporate laws and accounting standards prescribe strict reporting norms for related parties. Yet, related parties used for accounting manipulations are often not disclosed. These entities are registered by top executives as *benami*. That is, directors and partners in such entities are relatives, drivers, cooks and company employees but the control over the entities and their bank accounts rest with the executives committing fraud.

The *Economic Survey of India 2020* presented results of a study of companies that had taken bank loans and defaulted. The *Survey* found that a low percentage of wilful defaulters had disclosed related party transactions in comparison to non-defaulters. It also revealed that the percentage of distress defaulters disclosing related party transactions was higher than that of wilful defaulters. Wilful defaulters are those borrowers whom banks have accused of siphoning off loans and committing fraud.

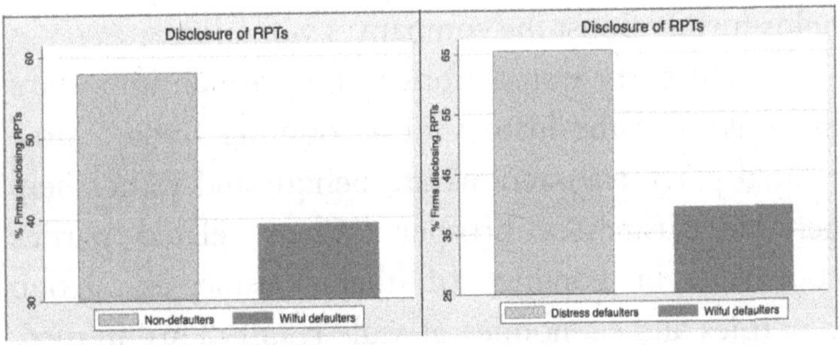

FIGURE 2: *Disclosure of RPTs by wilful and distress defaulters in comparison to non-defaulters*

Source: Economic Survey of India 2020

All major fraud investigations by the SFIO and other agencies in the last decade, including that of Satyam

Computer Services, IL&FS, Vijay Mallya group, and Bhushan Steel group, have revealed questionable related party transactions.

Related parties are important to equity-to-profit schemes because they facilitate conversion of capital into profits in the books of a company.

The second major problem in running an equity-to-profit scheme is that of taxation. Taxes are predatory costs on profits and can be as high as 25 per cent of the declared profit. While profits in these cases are not genuine, the tax outgo is genuine. In essence, the company has to pay 25 per cent to the government every time it rotates its funds between its capital account and profit account. Taxes end up disrupting the entire model.

To solve this problem, creative accountants resort to exemption shopping. They study direct tax laws to find out sectors for which the government offers tax incentives. Such incentives can be as high as 100 per cent relief from taxes. India's Income Tax Act gives attractive tax benefits to software exporters, SEZ-based businesses, power and infrastructure companies. Exemptions are also available to companies operating from certain underdeveloped and hilly areas. Since revenue of such companies is anyways fictitious, it can be given any colour. Related parties can be made to pay the company for software development or development of power plants or SEZ construction. It is relatively easier for a fraudulent business than a genuine business to claim an exemption it is originally not eligible for, as it can tailor its front business to match the conditions laid out by direct tax law.

A variant of the equity-to-profit model is the loan-to-profit model, in which fraudsters run the fraud cycle using borrowed funds instead of equity capital. Saurabh Mukherjea, former CEO of brokerage firm Ambit Capital, found that many power and infrastructure companies based out of Hyderabad in the 2000s were using creative accounting to boost their stock valuations. The schemes that he found these companies using were quite similar to equity-to-profit schemes. Mukherjea observed:

> The listed company (let's call it ListCo.) was lending money to various shell companies. Those shell companies then took equity stakes in the power plants that ListCo. had won tenders for. Each of these power plants was being managed through a SPV, which then gave the 'construction' order to ListCo. Thus, the loans advanced by ListCo were also being accounted for in its profit and loss (P&L) account as revenues and hence profits. Put simply, ListCo. was borrowing money from the bank, lending to itself and then showing it as profit!
>
> These profits that ListCo. showed on its P&L obviously boosted its shareholders' equity. That in turn allowed ListCo. to borrow more money from the banks, which in turn allowed it to finance more power plants (for which the construction order would of course come to ListCo.). Thus, the insane spiral...[13]

The companies Mukherjea analysed were part of the power and infrastructure cluster of Hyderabad. They used related parties to convert loans into profits. Major expense in this process is the tax cost on the profits, but then Section 80IA and 80IB of the Income Tax Act provide tax exemptions for power and infrastructure companies. The companies that Mukherjea analysed had gamed investors and lenders by using accounting tricks. Their promoters might have made neat, legitimate profits by selling their stake when valuations were high.

However, as with all kinds of financial frauds, these schemes are difficult to sustain in times of economic crisis. Companies without sound fundamentals are the first to tumble down in the times of crisis. Mukherjea explained that the share price of these companies plummeted from a peak in 2008 and lost significant market capitalisation. The coincidence of the fall with the 2008 subprime mortgage crisis is not lost on us. Ultimately, banks and retail investors lost money. The promoters purportedly made money by selling their stake at high valuations, while some promoters went a step ahead and siphoned off loan funds.

Death of Accounting

The last two decades have seen a tectonic shift in the way businesses are valued. This is where the next generation of accounting frauds–let's call them 2G accounting frauds–are happening. Traditionally, an unlisted company's value is calculated on the basis of profits it makes by exploiting its assets. Profit trend of past years is extrapolated onto future years and cash flows of future years are determined. These cash flows are discounted to find their present value. This is called the discounted cash flow method of valuation. There is always room for error in any valuation process, primarily because valuers make certain assumptions. That's why expert valuers give a range of fair values rather than a single fair value.

What has happened in the last two decades is that accounts, as we know, has failed to be a true description of business.[14] Accounts record the assets in possession of a firm and how these assets can be exploited to earn profits, but accountants record only the cost of assets in their books. The value in a business has shifted from tangible assets to intangible assets in the past two decades. Intangible assets derive immense value on the basis of their uniqueness and replicability. A machine has an installed capacity beyond which it cannot produce. When valuers calculate the productivity of the asset, they have an upper limit in sight.

Intangible assets have no upper limit of utilisation though. They can be replicated, licensed to millions of people and exploited any number of times. Data, the new gold, works in even funnier ways. While data can be sold and exploited by itself, it derives even more value from network effects. The asset value recorded in books does not reflect the real value of such intangible assets. The variance between book value and actual value is so high that books of account have become misleading.

On the flip side, much of the intangible assets in possession of companies are duds. According to one study, fewer than 5 per cent and as few as 2 per cent of a high-tech company's patents have discernible value to a company. About 50 per cent or more are unnecessary.[15] Unique IP rights are invaluable, but IP that one takes years to develop can turn redundant if an alternative is discovered anywhere else in the world or if someone else develops a similar IP and releases an open source version. For such IPs, the book value may be high, but the real value is zero.

This is why there is no connect between valuation theory and prices that new tech companies command. Start-ups without any assets in their books manage to make astronomical valuations, using the argument that their ideas will fetch cash flows in the future. Cash flows from exploitation of ideas is the most ludicrous thing I have ever heard and I still cannot get a hang of the idea. Venture capitalists and private equities, on the other hand, are buying stakes in these companies.

The books of these tech start-ups resemble books of shell companies in their early years. No asset, no business activity and no revenue. What they have is an idea, which they claim can change your life, and a couple of geeky founders in polo t-shirts. Some angel investors understand the value that professional valuers have missed and pump money into it. And then, their books still show no assets, but a lot of business activity. The geeks are so bad at business that they keep making losses, but curiously, the more losses they make, the more they are valued.

Many of my classmates at IIT Kharagpur have founded start-ups and become rich (many more have burnt their fingers, but this is not their story). They usually benchmark their start-up's performance by the amount of money they have burnt. 'Burn' is an actual jargon of the start-up world and the money a start-up burns is an actual measure of its success. These classmates have been my source of inspiration: I, too, aspire to burn money for a living. Sometimes, I look back and rue the stress and strain of a career in public service, when I could have burnt money and lived an affluent life.

The concentration of intangible assets in modern business has effectively killed the utility of accounts. Accounts no longer give you a true picture of a business. Value has become a subjective construct. Beauty is in the eyes of the beholder and value is in the perception of the venture fund manager. Start-ups still play by the rule. They prepare discounted cash flows to value their company, but you can neither agree nor disagree with them. Their projections are ad hoc and are subject to the idea clicking. Projections change in a matter of months. Many start-ups have doubled their valuation from one round of investment to another in a year's time.

When a start-up has managed to make heavy losses for years and cannot possibly claim to make profits anytime in the future, it junks the discounted cash flows approach and uses sales as a measure of value. Sales-to-value ratio of listed companies are calculated and applied to the start-up to get its value. Then they plough with messianic zeal to generate sales. E-commerce start-ups even use gross merchandise volume to determine their value.

The scenario today has created a fertile ground for frauds. Develop an idea and convince others to invest in the idea. This is what swindlers do for a living! There is a thin line separating good swindlers from good founders. You do not know if the teens pitching their idea to you are sheep or wolves.

One must not forget the contribution that genuine start-ups make to the economy and society. They innovate and create value for consumers. Their innovation incubates more entrepreneurs, and drives a virtuous cycle of tech-driven growth. But that won't stop a criticism of start-ups peddling dreams to investors. After valuations of Silicon Valley start-up WeWork tanked in September 2019, the Guardian ran a tirade against start-ups:

> big business, until around the 21st century, was at least bound by a few basic laws of monetary gravity. You were successful when you produced more revenue than the cost of running the business. You expanded when your profit margins increased... In the startup world, the logic is inverted, the math alchemic. You are worth the appeal of your idea to a bunch of rich people and companies who will keep giving you money in the hope that one day a fiction will be made real. You can keep losing money at spectacular rates as long as you, like a junkie after the next quick fix, keep expanding, at whatever maniacal clip the market justifies. [16]

Some business analysts in America have speculated that investors lost confidence in WeWork because it came in the run up of the Theranos fraud and the realisation that many start-ups will never make profit. Theranos was a health tech start-up in the US that claimed to have devised rapid blood tests. Its CEO

Elizabeth Holmes and COO Ramesh Balwani were charged by the US SEC in September 2018 of 'massive fraud'.

Commenting on the effect of Theranos on WeWork's valuation debacle, one commentator had railed that 'two things had changed in the nine years since Neumann began constructing the myth of WeWork with the help of starry-eyed tech journalists and hungry investors: Theranos and Uber. In the fall of Theranos, the investing public saw how a multi-million-dollar alleged fraud could be spun up from Silicon valley bromides and the image of an idiosyncratic, enigmatic founder who inspired cult-like devotion. In Uber, they saw how machismo, hubris, and accounting tricks could obscure fundamental business challenges.'[17]

What is true about Silicon Valley is true about Bangalore too.

The structural shift in what is valuable has brought new challenges for both law enforcement and corporate governance. If a start-up fails, there is no way of knowing whether it was never valuable or was a genuine one that did not click. It is due to this that it is difficult to do a post-mortem analysis of the start-ups.

In a post-mortem analysis, the forensic auditor tries to determine if a company has failed due to genuine reasons or due to fraud. Founders usually make money by selling their stake when investors pump money into the start-up. A fraudulent founder does not need to siphon off money from the start-up. S/he can simply pay herself/himself a hefty salary from the funds received from investors. If the start-up tanks, there is no way of finding out if the founders conned investors or failed in their venture.

The mystery of Israeli firm, Panaya, is an apt illustration to explain the dilemma forensic auditors face with relation to start-ups. Let us discuss a hypothetical situation before delving into Panaya. Tech companies have to constantly innovate to stay in the game. To do this, they continuously acquire new companies with specialised knowhow. Professionally appointed CEO of one such tech company zeroes in on a start-up that has developed expertise in 'impact analyses of code change, applied in code comparison of enterprise resource planning (ERP) systems to help reduce the application life cycle cost' (whatever that means). His team feels that acquiring this start-up can help the company automate much of its coding activities.

The CEO negotiates with the venture fund owning majority stake in the start-up and arrives at an acquisition price of $200 million. The price is 6X (revenue multiplier: another start-up jargon), that is, six times the start-up's revenues. An independent valuer hired by the company affirms that the start-up's fair value hovers around this figure. The board of directors and the investment committee give their go ahead and the acquisition happens.

A year later, the company writes off $90 million off this price. Not happy with the way the company is functioning, a promoter alleges that the CEO has committed a fraud. His allegation is that the CEO owned the start-up through legal entities. He made the company purchase the start-up at a gross overvaluation. The company immediately appoints a forensic auditor to investigate the matter. Can the forensic auditor come to any conclusion?

The forensic auditor, I bet, can neither prove nor disprove any fraud. The start-up was loss making. An independent valuer certified a 6X fair value for the start-up, but received her fees from the company. A really 'independent' valuer may value the start-up at any figure from NIL to 10X of revenues. Discounted cash flows (DCF) methodology will give it a low value. Book value of the start-up is nil because it has consistently made losses. If the valuer appreciates the disruptive technology the start-up has developed, she may give a 10X value, but how can a valuer (usually a merchant banker or chartered accountant) really appreciate disruptive technologies?

When the value of an apple varies from ₹1 to ₹1,000, why can't it be sold for ₹600? A forensic auditor can never prove that the apple, sold at ₹600, is overvalued. In fact, the wide variance in values makes valuation itself a joke. In our case as well, the forensic auditor can never prove that the start-up was acquired at a price higher than the fair value. Neither can she ever prove that the start-up was acquired at the right price. If the CEO's action was bona fide, he suffered due to the complaint and protracted investigation by forensic auditors. Such an act would discourage the CEO from making aggressive acquisition of new technology start-ups and hurt the business. But if the CEO's action was mala fide, he escapes punishment as the fraud cannot be proven.

Coming to Panaya, it's an Israeli start-up that develops disruptive technologies to automate software development. Backed by venture funds, it applied for patents in 2008, 2009 and 2013. The company though was in the red and experienced a severe liquidity crunch in 2013. It laid off 25 per cent of its staff in 2013 and 2014. It remained in a state of crisis in 2014, and was on the verge of shuttering in the year. Indian IT major Infosys acquired Panaya in February 2015 at 6X its latest yearly revenues, which added up to $200 million. Of this, $90 million was written off by the company after a short period.

Meanwhile, a whistle-blower alleged to SEBI that Panaya was purchased at a much higher price than its real value.[18] Crux of the insinuation was that Infosys' CEO Vishal Sikka had a vested interest in the purchase. So he purchased bad apples at a much higher price. The whistle-blower also claimed that the company's CFO was not comfortable about the deal. So Sikka got him an attractive severance package of ₹23 crore in exchange for leaving the company and agreeing not to disclose anything about his tenure in Infosys to anyone.

Infosys cofounder and shareholder Narayana Murthy jumped in and demanded an independent probe. Two independent firms were hired by the company to investigate the matter. They gave a clean chit and claimed that they could not find any financial impropriety. Murthy shot off a letter stating that he did not believe the reports by lawyers who had been hired by the accused (Vishal Sikka and other senior employees).

Following a public spat between Murthy and the board, led by Sikka, Sikka stepped down from his position in Infosys in August 2017. Cofounder Nandan Nilekani took over the reins. Subsequently, in October 2017, the Infosys board gave Sikka a clean chit. The new board unequivocally stated that there was no merit to the allegations of wrongdoing.

The Panaya case will remain a mystery. The circumstances in which the CFO's services were terminated appeared suspicious to Narayana Murthy. The CFO was awarded a severance package of ₹23 crore even though he was not entitled to such a pay, as per his employment terms. He signed a non-disclosure agreement (NDA) with the company. Could the high severance pay be a payment for the non-disclosure commitment? At the same time, there is nothing wrong with a 6X valuation. Enterprise value of start-ups vary from 5X to 30X of revenues, so a 6X deal is not a bad deal. There is no way an investigator can conclusively prove or disprove the allegations of fraud in the Panaya deal.

This brings us to the question of whether or not revenue multipliers are reliable metrics of an enterprise's value? Theory says that the value of a company is its ability to produce profits in the future. That's why standard valuation calculates future profits and adds present value of all future profits to get enterprise value. However, since some start-ups do not make any profit for many years, they are valued at a multiple of their sales revenue. In this elementary formula, valuation is directly proportional to revenue. So, the message start-ups receive is: increase revenue. To increase revenue, they forgo profits. At times, they give deep discounts and sell at a price below the cost. By doing this, they end up burning investor money.

In the tech sector, it is not clear where entrepreneurship ends and fraud starts. There is a thin dividing line, if at all.

5

Merchants of Delusive Dreams: Pyramid and Ponzi Schemes

Once upon a time, there was a king crazy about the game of *chaturanga* (chess). His advisors informed him one day that a sage, who was a champion in the game of chess, was travelling through his kingdom. He invited the sage to his palace to play a game of chess with him. The king then magnanimously offered the sage any reward should he manage to beat him in the game.

The sage asked for grains of rice as his reward. He wanted the grains to be calculated using a simple rule: one grain of rice in the first square of the chess board and double the number in each square, until the grains are allotted to all 64 squares. So, one grain in the first square, two in the second square, four in the third square, eight in the fourth square and so on and so forth.

The sage's rather meagre expectations amused the king, who smirked and agreed to the bet. He lost the game and graciously called for a sack of grains. However, when the number of grains were calculated, he realised that a single sack of grains was not enough. In fact, all the grain in his kingdom was not enough to reward the sage!

A chessboard has 64 squares. If one grain is allotted to the first square and the amount is doubled in each succeeding square, the total amount the king needed was 18,446,744,073,709,551,615 grains. This is equivalent to 210 billion tonnes of rice, many times more than the world production of rice in 2019.[1] The king finally realised that the sage had conned him because he was made to believe that the sage needed some rice, not an infinite amount of it.

This story highlights the power of geometric progressions. Geometric progressions increase in leaps and bounds and often people find it difficult to comprehend such patterns.

Consider a series in which a club member gets a laptop if he enlists six persons for the club membership. The scheme is equally open to the newly-enlisted club members and is actually the key attraction for joining the club. They try to enlist more club members and the circle goes on and on. Mathematically, the number of club members in each round are as under:

1, 6, 36, 216, 1,296, 7,776, 46,656, 279,936
1,679,616 10,077,696 60,466,176 362,797,056
2,176,782,336 13,060,694,016...

Every number in the above series is equal to the previous number multiplied by the number 6. The series increases exponentially, much like an unravelling pyramid. Note that the last number in the above series is more than the population of the entire world! This round cannot be completed even if club members enlist the entire world population. Of course, not all in the world are foolish enough to enlist in the scheme. Thus, the scheme will fail in the first few rounds itself.

Such business models are called pyramid schemes and represent a class of financial frauds that are quite rampant from the pre-modern times itself. The scheme's promoter convinces gullible people that the model is workable, even though it is mathematically proven to be unsustainable. The promoter asks a fixed number of people (say *n*) to enrol for the scheme by paying a membership charge. These members are given some product that is much cheaper than the membership charge. So, why would the members pay for it? It is because there is scope to earn much more. Each member is eligible to get hefty commissions if they enrol *n* more members. Whenever new members in a chain enrol more members, all older members in the chain get a commission. Over time, each member recovers the membership charge and makes a windfall. Members buy into the scheme because they appear to be get-rich-quick schemes.

In reality, however, only the first few members profit from the scheme. They get commission every time new members pay to enrol for the scheme. The scheme goes bust after a few rounds (since the model is a mathematical impossibility) and most members incur losses. Only the promoter and first few members profit from the scheme.

Take, for example, the direct selling business of Frontier Trading in the late 1990s and early 2000s in India. The company was selling Japan Life mattresses worth no more than ₹5,000 at prices as high as ₹1 lakh. Customers weren't purchasing such overpriced products sold through retail shops. So, the company pushed the product directly to new customers through older customers.

This model is called 'direct selling', which could be a legal and legitimate business. However, it was found later that Frontier Trading was using Japan Life Mattress as a ruse to run a pyramid scheme. The business' primary focus was to acquire new customers rather than to sell mattresses. When an old customer becomes a distributor and pitches the mattress to a new customer, the new customer purchases the mattress because it is merely a ruse to sell dreams of quick riches. The payment of ₹1 lakh was a subscription charge for the scheme, while the mattress came free of cost with it. Once part of the scheme, the customer could help acquire other customers. He would receive commission from the subscription paid by new customers.

The scheme was convenient for Frontier Trading in more ways than one. It openly and aggressively advertised the benefits of Japan Life mattresses, thus seeding a sense of familiarity in the minds of the target population.

The scheme being unfeasible from a mathematical standpoint, the business soon defaulted in giving the promised commissions. Many people who had been cheated lodged complaints and law enforcement officials started investigations in 2002. The reality of the scheme was soon apparent, but the company had garnered collections worth ₹800 crores by then, according to one estimate. Investigators found that victims in a small town like Hubli in Karnataka had purchased beds worth ₹82 crores in a single month. The scheme had about

3,000 members in Hubli, which included doctors and other highly qualified professionals.[2]

Economic Risks of Pyramid Schemes

Pyramid schemes are widely prevalent. A note by the Andhra Pradesh police to the state government in early 2010, estimated that more than 2,000 pyramid schemes were running in Hyderabad alone and there were more than 10,000 in the state of Andhra Pradesh.[3] Pyramid schemes have remained more or less the same in substance, but in form, they have changed substantially. While earlier they used to tap affinity groups such as cults, temple communities, caste groups, etc., now they are targeting customers through social networking sites. Some pyramid schemes have assumed huge proportions after escaping the long arm of the law, even when some customers have accused them of fraud. A few people have even committed suicides after losing money in such schemes.

Unfortunately, this kind of financial fraud affects the poor more than the rich. While every fraud plays on OPM, this one typically preys on the poor. Their frontline customers (or recruits) are usually local community leaders and enterprising housewives in low-income groups. These are people that the local community trusts and looks up to. They bring in new members from among the community. Many instances have been reported where members have taken loans to enrol into these schemes. When the scheme fails, all of them lose money. Relations within the community rupture, level of trust in the neighbourhood takes a dip and some get cornered by loan sharks.

While most members lose money when the scheme goes bust, early members do manage to recover their investment. However, driven by greed, they often plough back their money into the scheme. So, they too, more often than not, end up losing money.

Journalist Sucheta Dalal believes that women are especially vulnerable to pyramid schemes. Dalal said: 'Women, particularly homemakers with no independent income, are especially susceptible to the lures of pyramid schemes because of the promise of easy returns and independent income. Women are also more effective in persuading new enrolment within family-and-friends circle. It is not without reason that many pyramid companies market themselves as an opportunity to: "Work from home"; "Work four hours and earn ₹50,000 per month" or with slogans such as "U R the boss of your business, so enrol immediately"; "Earn up to ₹35,000+ Monthly by just working 2 hours at home"; "Do u want to earn extra by sitting at Home? Then contact us".'[4]

Creating awareness against such get-rich-quick schemes often does not help because the 'fraudsters assiduously work at creating a cult-like selling environment wherein their members begin to view all criticism as a personal attack on their personal road to prosperity. Since the returns for early members are extremely high, they flatly refuse to listen to reason and have no qualms on using blatant lies about the prospects of the scheme, in order to ensnare and enrol new members.'[5]

This is one area in which law enforcement also cannot be used to prevent the incidence of fraud. India did introduce a law banning pyramid schemes as early as 1978. The Prize Chits and Money Circulation Schemes (Banning) Act of 1978 explicitly bans money circulation schemes, which are defined as:

> Money circulation scheme means any scheme, by whatever name called, for the making of quick or easy money, or for the receipt of any money or valuable thing as the consideration for a promise to pay money, on any event or contingency relative or applicable to the enrolment of members into the scheme, whether or not such money or thing is derived from the entrance money of the members of such scheme or periodical subscriptions.[6]

Courts said the cryptic language in the above definition includes pyramid schemes, but these schemes do not market themselves as pyramid schemes. They colour their business operations as legitimate multi-level marketing (MLM). MLM or direct selling can be a legitimate way of pushing sales. The primary focus of a legitimate MLM company is to sell the company's products through referrals from existing customers, who introduce the product to new customers and get a commission for it. This is a completely legitimate marketing strategy. In fact, many mobile apps use referral marketing to increase their user base.

For instance, in their initial years of operation in India, Uber and Ola would offer attractive commissions and cashback to an existing customer for referring their apps to new customers. Some customers managed to travel free of cost in Ola cabs for more than a year after they managed to rope in enough number of friends in their network to use the Ola app.

Pyramid schemes are different from legitimate referral schemes. They focus on getting more and more customers so that the promoters can make more money. They use a product though, such as health supplements or travel vouchers or kitchenware, as a front in their transactions. On paper, the money they collect from a new member is not subscription charge or membership charge, but consideration for the product. Therefore, it is difficult for law enforcement agencies to legally prove a pyramid scheme until it goes bust.

Victims lodge complaints when the scheme goes bust and it is only then that law enforcement agencies can register a case of cheating and fraud.

On the other side of the spectrum lie genuine MLM companies that may be unfairly targeted by a begrudged customer as a pyramid scheme. Law enforcement agencies often take cognisance of such complaints and initiate enforcement action against such companies.

Take, for instance, the case of MNCs such as Amway, Herbalife, Tupperware and Oriflame. Journalist Aruna Ravikumar has claimed to have identified the Amway business model as a pyramid scheme.[7] Amway, short for the American Way, is an American MLM company that sells health, beauty and home care products. Allegations of running pyramid schemes have often been levelled against the company. The US Federal Trade Commission (FTC) initiated investigated against Amway in the 1970s, and concluded in 1979 that it was not running a pyramid scheme.

At the time, Amway manufactured and sold cleaning supplies and other household products. Under the Amway Plan, each distributor purchased household products at wholesale from the person who 'recruited' or 'sponsored' her. The top distributors purchased from Amway itself. A distributor earned money from retail sales by pocketing the difference between the wholesale price at which she purchased the product and the retail price at which she sold it. She also received a monthly bonus based on the total amount of Amway products that she purchased for resale to both consumers and her sponsored distributors.[8] FTC ruled that Amway did not run a pyramid scheme because distributors were not paid to 'recruit' more customers. Neither were distributors forced to purchase excess stock. If a distributor could not sell inventories to customers, they could return the stock to Amway.[9]

In India, the company has faced law enforcement action from time to time. In 2006, the Andhra Pradesh police conducted raids and seizures on Amway distributors under the Prize Chits and Money Circulation Schemes (Banning) Act. In 2011, the Kerala police sealed Amway offices in various parts of the state and seized products worth more than ₹2 crore. In 2013, the Kerala police arrested William Pinckney, Managing Director of Amway India, along with two other directors. It took him more than two months to get bail. Despite these regional setbacks, Amway India clocked a compound annual growth rate (CAGR) of 20 per cent in the first 19 years of its operation in India. It invested ₹600 crore in a new manufacturing plant in

Madurai in 2015. Today, it is the largest direct selling company in India and one of the bigger players in the FMCG segment.[10]

Ravikumar is unrelenting in her criticism of Amway. She said Amway 'from its inception was more about marketing and sales technique than about its product'. She analysed the chain of Ashok Reddy, a 'diamond distributor' of Amway, and found that over 2,000 persons were below him in the pyramid. Two Americans were above him in the pyramid and were paid commissions for all 'recruitments' and purchases that Reddy and all the 2,000 persons under him in the pyramid made. These two Americans had no clue about all the people in India downline, but made commission out of money paid by anyone in the chain.[11]

While many more critics around the world have alleged Amway of running pyramid schemes, the company has been on a growth path. There is a thin line separating legitimate MLM businesses from pyramid schemes and, legally speaking, it is often difficult to differentiate between them. Many a time, it is not possible to prove a pyramid scheme beyond reasonable doubt until the scheme fails and the promoters default on a large number of customers.

Balance sheets of pyramid schemes sometimes give them away. For an MLM company, there are three key expenses: cost of goods sold, commissions paid and advertisement expenses. These expenses are deducted from sales in the profit and loss (P&L) statement to arrive at the firm's profits. For a genuine MLM business, the cost of goods is more than the commission payment, but for a fraudulent MLM business, commission payment may be more than the cost of goods sold.

Sales - Cost of Goods Sold - Commission - Advertisement & Marketing - Miscellaneous Expenses = Profit

In the case of Apple FMCG Marketing Pvt. Ltd vs Union of India, an MLM company by the name of Apple FMCG Marketing approached the Madras High Court on a writ, praying for a court declaration that it was not running an illegal scheme. The court noted that the company was paying 65 per cent of its sales proceeds as commission to distributors, which meant that the cost of the good was only 35 per cent of the sale price (actually, cost of the goods would be much lower in percentage terms, if one were to account for overhead expenses and profits of the company). The distributors in the chain were getting commission without doing any work as the chain expanded. This was nothing but 'easy money' and came within the definition of money circulation schemes in the Prize Chits & Money Circulation Schemes (Banning) Act.

On the thin dividing line between legal and illegal MLM businesses, the court ruled that:

> It is true that several companies including Multinational Companies carry on the business of the "Multilevel Marketing" and it is also true that the Executive and the law enforcing authorities keep a blind eye on such activities. This also does not make

> an illegal act legal. It is always a fact that the law enforcing authority would try to close the stable only after the horse had escaped. That is, the law enforcing authority would realise that this scheme would ultimately leave a large number of persons cheated. Thereafter, after losing their money, they would approach the executive complaining that they were cheated. Till such time, the law enforcing authorities do not act. They do not take preventive action to enforce the provisions of the existing law.[12]

The high court indicated that paying abnormally high commissions to distributors in a chain was an indication of running an unsustainable MLM business. In the same ruling, however, the high court clarified that law enforcing authorities could take remedial action only if there was proof the scheme had been used to cheat a large number of people. It appears that nothing can be said on the legality of Amway and other multinational MLM corporations conclusively.

The verdict on SpeakAsia and TVI Express, on the other hand, is however clear. These are the two large pyramid schemes that hit India in the late 2000s and early 2010. They went bust after duping millions of their hard-earned money. The story of Travel Ventures International Express (TVI Express) was both incredible and incredulous. It was started in 2009 by 25-year-old Tarun Trikha, a boy from Delhi. TVI Express ran a website through which it managed to reach customers around the world. The website offered membership to a travel club in exchange for a membership fee of ₹15,000. The money was supposed to double if the member managed to bring in two new members into the club, while the member would get a bonus of ₹5 lakh if she could enrol 64 new members.

Interestingly, the scheme was not even selling any product. Most pyramid schemes sell a product as a ruse to run pyramid scheme, but Trikha's style was more blatant and casual. Members did get travel vouchers upon paying membership fees, but the travel vouchers were meaningless. TVI Express' website promised accommodation in a 3-5-star hotel for seven days to anyone who redeemed the vouchers, but a majority did not redeem the vouchers. The customers TVI Express' website reached out to were more interested in getting rich quick. Many customers took out multiple memberships of the travel club in their quest to get rich sooner.

Trikha reached out to customers in Australia, the US, the UK, China and many other countries through his website. He did not bother to incorporate companies in these countries. Money paid by members (victims) went to Trikha and his family members' bank accounts.[13] The number of people he could sell his scheme to in a matter of two years was a stupendous 7 million!

Alexander the Great had conquered half the known world of his time by the time he was 28 years old. Trikha had succeeded in duping customers across the globe by the time he was 28 years old. So brazen was his scheme that he did not actually pay the monies he had promised to the members of his travel club, he just kept handing them more travel e-vouchers that did not carry any value. Since he could not fool all the people all the time, many people demanded payback. When he did not pay, they complained to their local authorities, who initiated criminal proceedings against him. Trikha was on the run from February 2011, but was finally nabbed at the Delhi Airport on 4 April 2013, where he was trying to board a flight to Nepal.

The model followed by SpeakAsia Online was very similar to that of TVI Express. SpeakAsia reached out to gullible investors from different corners of the world through their website. It promised ₹52,000 a year to a person who invested ₹11,000 annually and brought in a minimum number of members. However, SpeakAsia's storytelling was slightly different from other online pyramid schemes. Other schemes gave a cheap product (TVI Express sold travel vouchers) to the victim at a high membership fee and asked them to sell the product at high fees to others. SpeakAsia claimed on its website that it had been hired by MNCs to conduct online surveys. It required current 'members' to pay yearly fees and fill out online forms. They were promised fixed returns upon getting a minimum number of new 'recruits'.

SpeakAsia was introduced in India in mid-2010 by Ram Sumiran Pal and his brother, who duped 2.4 million investors of ₹2,200 crores in just one year. They could not pay the promised amount to their investors and quietly wrapped up when investors across the country complained against them. Pal went into hiding, but was eventually caught in November 2013.

The TVI Express and SpeakAsia scams show that it is quite easy to sell get-quick-rich schemes, especially through network marketing. These two organisations could reach out to a wide population and could easily drop the bait because they were running online scams. Their membership swelled to millions in just a year's time.

However, both schemes were unsuccessful. People like Trikha and Pal may be conmen, but they are not con artists. They had not planned their exit when running their scams. Neither did they run the schemes at a sustainable pace. They are like many other novices who scammed, shirked and got busted. They neither tried to exploit loopholes in the law, nor developed a business model that would insulate them from law enforcement action. Thus, they do not draw any respect from this book.

But then, is it even possible to keep fooling people and defaulting on promises without facing any action from law enforcement agencies? A 'perfect model' for running a pyramid scheme without eventually facing the brunt of law is yet to be devised. However, a genius by the name of Vijay Eswaran has developed a corporate structure to run an international MLM business, which may very well be a forerunner of the perfect model.

The Qnet Spiderweb

The November 2012 issue of *Forbes Asia* carried a special feature on Malaysian billionaire Vijay Eswaran, titled *Selling a Better Life*. The story drew more than 35,000 views online and 167 comments, while nearly 5,000 users had shared the story on Facebook in just four months after its release. A majority of the comments were positive and adulatory.

However, some people were scandalised that by featuring Eswaran, *Forbes* was promoting a fraud. One reader opined that Qnet Ltd, the company run by Eswaran, was openly using the *Forbes* article to mislead people. Sucheta Dalal did not mince words when she stated in her *MoneyLife* blog that Qnet was a fraud and she even suggested that *Forbes* was bribed to run the story.[14]

Eswaran figured at Rank 25 on *Forbes*' list of richest Malaysians that year. He remains one of the wealthiest men of Malaysia even though his companies and Independent Representatives (IRs), a designation given to MLM distributors, have been accused of running fraudulent pyramid schemes in more than two dozen countries. They have even been convicted of fraud in some of these countries.

Eswaran's Qnet Group of companies (later rebranded as QI group) has substantial business presence in more than 30 countries despite pugnacious action against its MLM companies by numerous countries. In India, action was taken against the group, its franchisees as well as many IRs. It changed both its brand and business model in India after the country's law enforcement authorities acted against it, leading to the imprisonment of IRs and promoters of its business franchises. Telecom Regulatory Authority of India (TRAI) blocked the websites it was using to conduct businesses in India. Café Coffee Day (CCD) outlets were directed to ban meetings of Qnet's IRs after it was found that the IRs indoctrinated new IRs at CCD outlets.[15] Despite all this, Qnet still has vast operations in India. It enrolled new IRs through a new website, https://www.qnetindia.in/login, as on 22 March 2020. The story of Eswaran's rise and persistence is both stunning and disturbing.

Eswaran was born in Penang, Malaysia, to Malaysian Hindu parents in October 1960. It is said he financed his higher education in the UK by working as a cab driver and managed to get a degree in Socio-economics from London School of Economics in 1984. After spending some years in the UK and the US, he returned to Malaysia and started GoldQuest in 1998. GoldQuest was incorporated in Hong Kong, even though the company has never operated in Hong Kong or China Mainland.[16]

GoldQuest's MLM scheme was a sale of limited-edition coins through binary recruitment. Under binary recruitment, each member was required to 'recruit' two new members. New members had to pay a sign-in fee for coins plus membership. A part of the sign-in fee was paid to the 'recruiter' and others above her in the chain as commission. On paper, the sign-in fee appeared as the purchase price of the limited-edition coins, but in reality, the cost of these limited-edition coins was much lower than the fee a new member had to pay.[17]

GoldQuest faced retaliation from law enforcement authorities in most countries it was operating in. Nepal declared GoldQuest illegal and banned it in February 2003, alleging that it dupes unsuspecting people that results in huge outflow of money from the country.[18] The huge outflow might be payments to the headquarters in Hong Kong out of the money collected from members in Nepal. In 2005, it was banned in both Sri Lanka and Iran, primarily because of the huge outflow of money from these countries as well to GoldQuest's headquarters.

In India, action was initiated against GoldQuest after police received multiple complaints of cheating and fraud. The Chennai police took legal action against the company in mid-2008 for cheating various customers. They jailed seven employees of GoldQuest and seized all consumer goods from its Chennai warehouse. The company, however, maintained that there was a 'mix-up' that led to the police action.[19]

The SFIO conducted a detailed forensic investigation and concluded it was a fraudulent pyramid scheme. Based on the data provided by the company, the SFIO report said it 'sold products for a price of ₹806.15 crore to 2.39 lakh individuals. Out of these, (only) about 50,000 people ever received any amount of commissions. Only about 20,000 were able to get more commission than ₹30,000, the initial amount of investment. So even though people were sold the (concept, and they) bought the products as a business opportunity, about (2.19 lakh) people have actually lost money.'[20] SFIO went on to conclude that GoldQuest and QuestNet (another group company) 'indulged in a lot of deception to circumvent the eye of the law enforcement agencies and the courts'.[21]

Many other countries took stringent action against GoldQuest around this time. Rwanda banned the company in 2009 after the National bank of Rwanda described it as a pyramid scheme. Sudan and Syria, too, banned the company on similar grounds.

The Chennai police's action was, however, a watershed moment for GoldQuest, for India was its largest market. The police action triggered a restructuring of both its business process and business model. The MLM business was renamed Qnet. Instead of gold coins, Qnet sells travel packages (like TVI Express), health and beauty products and watches. This is also the time, I believe, when the group developed a model that substantially mitigated law enforcement (LE) risks.

Qnet was not just a new name, but a new business model altogether. The new model involved use of franchises on the ground to run the MLM business. Qnet opened separate websites for each market jurisdiction, through which new IRs could register. The websites contained e-learning modules to train IRs. Information technology can help you operate your business only to an extent. You still need evangelists on the ground to identify new customers and convince them to join the company, Qnet in this case. To remove this problem, Qnet gave business franchises to local companies.

This is how Qnet controlled its business interests remotely from Hong Kong. It did not do any business in Hong Kong or Mainland China. So, it did not face any LE risks there. Hong Kong being an offshore finance centre was open to seamless transfer of money to its bank accounts. Qnet's major markets were India and some African countries. In these markets, business was conducted by franchisees. Qnet maintained absolute control over the business because IRs had to be registered on its website and funds were transferred as per its directions. Franchisees remitted profits to Qnet Hong Kong in the form of royalty or license fees, for using Qnet's brand and website.

LE authorities could bring criminal charges against a person for either guilty mind or guilty act or both. By establishing a franchisee model, Qnet kept itself at an arm's length from action in the field. It ring-fenced itself from any 'guilty act' that led to fraud and cheating charges. LE authorities could still bring charges against Qnet for possessing a guilty mind, or *mens rea*, but this is more difficult to prove.

Implementing this model is not as easy as it sounds. Rise in digitalisation enabled many businesses to operate remotely. Many e-commerce companies were registered in tax havens such as Hong Kong, Ireland and the Netherlands, so that they did not have to pay taxes in markets in which they operated. These companies provided services digitally and did not need to maintain any physical office in the host country. However, these companies still needed men on the ground to conduct marketing activities. Pitching products to clients and selling services cannot happen remotely.

To obviate this bottleneck, digitalised companies would incorporate a subsidiary to provide sales support in the market where they sold their services. Employees formally worked for the subsidiary, but actually reported to managers running the parent company. As with all modern day MNCs, the subsidiary's activities were firmly integrated with the parent company's activities.

This model itself is challenging for a company like Qnet because marketing and distribution are not a peripheral work of the company. It is their core work. Binary recruitment is the core business function of Qnet. Company managers need to regularly interact with IRs and train them to increase business. On top of it, the company cannot ring-fence itself from LE action if it operates through a subsidiary in India. A natural solution is to outsource the mundane work to a willing franchisee, but franchisees come with their own set of problems. A business franchise is owned by third parties and can ditch the business at any point. Worse, a franchise may take all business and conduct its own MLM independently.

Apparently, Qnet has successfully handled these challenges. Many complaints have been lodged against the MLM schemes of Qnet in different jurisdictions over the decade of 2010s. Many persons claimed they lost money due to Qnet's schemes, some even committed suicides.[22] Police and other law enforcement agencies took stringent action against franchisees and senior IRs, but Qnet kept going at it. It has become a platform for enterprising persons to start their own boutique MLM scheme. Qnet provides the platform, the brand, e-learning and physical training, merchandise and readymade packages and also takes a part of the profit in the form of royalty. Justice Mridula Bhatkar aptly summarised the model in an order in May 2016,[23] when she observed that Qnet is 'a chain where a person is fooled and then he is trained to fool others to earn money. For that purpose, workshops are conducted where study and business material are provided with a jugglery of words, promises and dreams. Thus, the deceit and fraud are camouflaged under the name of e-marketing and business.'

When the chain created by a particular IR defaults, that chain is accused of fraud and IRs in that chain are charged with cheating. The local franchise is also charged because the franchise has officially floated the scheme.

LE officials levelled charges against Qnet and Eswaran for fraud and criminal conspiracy, but those did not stick. Qnet can be tried only in a court of law in Hong Kong for its business activities. LE officials find it difficult to muster enough evidence of abetment to prove charges against Qnet in Hong Kong.

Therein lies the ingenuity of Eswaran. He has developed a successful model to manage LE risks in a business that is open to significant such risks. In a way, Qnet now operates like a global marketplace of network marketing. In recent years, Eswaran has rebranded it as the QI Group and runs it from a high-rise tower in Kuala Lumpur called the QI Tower.

The master franchisee of Qnet in India is Vihaan Direct Selling (India) Private Limited, which was incorporated in October 2011. It has two shareholders, who own 80 per cent and 20 per cent, respectively, of the company. It got tangled with LE problems within a couple of years of starting operations in India. In 2014, the EOW of the Mumbai police froze bank accounts of many IRs following multiple complaints of cheating. EOW Mumbai filed a FIR against Qnet and Vihaan and barred them from holding workshops and training sessions in its jurisdiction.[24] EOW conducted a thorough investigation and filed a 55,000-page charge sheet in December 2016 against Vihaan and Qnet. One of the accused in the charge sheet was Vihaan's majority shareholder Michael Ferreira, a former World Amateur Billiards champion and a Padma Bhushan awardee.[25]

The Hyderabad police and the Delhi police initiated action against Vihaan in the same year, on charges of running fraudulent pyramid schemes. Many other states in India took action against it in 2018. On 14 August 2019, the Department of Consumer Affairs of India released a public notice highlighting various violations found during an inspection of the company. The inspection concluded that Vihaan was running a 'product-based pyramid scheme business' and the products are 'merely a means of disguising or laundering investments in the pyramid schemes'.

On analysing Vihaan's accounts, the inspection team found that the total cost of products sold in FY 2016–17 was ₹47.26 crore, while the company had paid commission of ₹304.12 crore in the same period. The inspection team felt that the commission payment was 'highly disproportionate to normal business transactions' and 'clearly shows that the products sold by the company are immaterial and the company is running (an) illegal product-based pyramid scheme and offering huge commission to its IRs'.[26]

The commission payout in FY 2014–15 was 61 per cent of total revenue, which increased to 65 per cent in FY 2015–16, and 71.56 per cent in FY 2016–17. This was expected. As chains grow longer, more people in the chain have to be paid commissions for every sale. This continues until the commission becomes so high that new revenue earned cannot pay the commission anymore. At that point, the chain defaults.

The inspection team also found that most of the goods sold by Vihaan were spurious, but were claimed to be genuine. The company and its IRs had used 'misleading, deceptive and unfair recruiting practices, including misrepresentation of actual or potential sales or earnings, in their interaction with the prospective or existing direct sellers'.

Internationally, more than a dozen-odd countries have accused Qnet of running fraudulent pyramid schemes, including Egypt, Saudi Arabia, Indonesia, Iran, Mali, Tajikistan, Azerbaijan, Moldova, Burkina Paso, Sri Lanka and Nepal. Hundreds of innocent people have gone bankrupt after being convinced by IRs, who they knew intimately, to invest in Qnet. However, the game between Qnet and the LE authorities seems to be never ending.

The Wizard of Malgudi

R.K. Narayan's *The Financial Expert* was first published in 1952. The book is about Margayya, a petty money lender in the fictional town of Malgudi (inspired by Mysore, Narayan's home town), who did his business under a Banyan tree in front of the Central Co-operative Land Mortgage Bank. He used to get loans from the bank's shareholders at low interest rates and further advanced them to needy people at a high rate. The difference was his profit: enough for an honest living in Malgudi.

In a turn of events, however, the bank's secretary and peon seize Margayya's customer details and drive him away. Later, he teams up with a shrewd character, Dr Pal, to collect deposits from black marketeers with a promise to pay interest at 29 per cent per annum (as against banks that were offering a rate of 4.5 per cent annually). Margayya's venture becomes an instant hit and hordes of depositors put in their money with Margayya.

So, how could Margayya generate such high returns? Apparently, he worked hard with his accounts books and money bags. Now, how can accounts books generate such high returns? He has to invest the public deposits in a business venture and get at least 29 per cent returns in order to pay back. Margayya did no such thing. And this is where lies the wizardry of the foremost financial expert of Malgudi. Margayya reasoned that on any given day, if he receives deposits of ₹20,000 and has to pay interest of ₹15,000, then he is still left with ₹5,000 that day. He has to ensure, for all days to come, that his 'cash in' remains more than his 'cash out.' Since he was offering interest rates much higher than banks, the depositors would plough back their interest in Margayya's venture.

Margayya becomes rich. Every nook and corner of his house is now stocked with sacks full of currency notes. He owns a car and generously contributed to the War Fund and other community initiatives.

And then appears a twist in the tale. While Margayya was toiling along on his account books day and night, Dr Pal was exposing his son Balu to bad influences. Margayya visited his son's house one day and found from Balu's wife that he was frequenting the quarters of Malgudi's infamous theatre girls. On his way back, Margayya found Balu coming out of a car with Dr Pal and two women. Margayya dismissed the women in disgust and beat up Dr Pal.

FIGURE 1: *Narayan's Novel* The Financial Expert *Was First Released in 1952*

Source: Shared under Creative Commons License by John Rambow on Flickr.com

FIGURE 2: Banker Margayya *Is a Kannada Movie Based on Narayan's Book*

Source: National Film Archives of India

A bandaged and bruised Dr Pal descended upon the bazaar the next day and whispered to all and sundry that Margayya will soon go bankrupt. People panicked and rushed to Margayya asking for their money. This time they were asking for the principal amount, not the interest. Of course, he did not have that much money. He was paying older customers from the money collected from newer customers. His business model worked only when 'cash flow in' was more than 'cash flow out'.

Margayya emptied his wealth, but still could not pay back all his depositors. Margayya was left a disgraced man in all of Malgudi. Narayan does not reveal to us if Margayya siphoned off some funds from his venture and hid them away, but tries to convince us that Margayya was back to square one. *Banker Margayya*, a Kannada movie based on Narayan's novel, also does not dwell into this question.

Scamsters running such schemes in real life often hide away wealth in *benami* properties or tax havens for they know that the scheme would go bust eventually. You do not need to be a financial wizard to understand that such schemes do not work indefinitely. To give returns of 29 per cent and run your expenses, you have to make profit of at least 30 per cent. No business gives consistent returns of 30 per cent. You may advance the money collected from customers to desperate businessmen for 30 per cent or so, but a businessman agreeing to pay interest at 30 per cent rate is not in a good shape and will most probably default. So, the only possibility of running this kind of scheme is to loot newer customers to pay older customers. In short, it is a mathematical impossibility to pay such high interest rates and sustain business. Scamsters know this and try to siphon off money when they can.

These schemes are termed as Unregulated Collective Investment Schemes (UCIS). Not all collective investment schemes are fraudulent. Mutual funds, for example, are collective investment schemes. They raise funds from the public and invest in share or bond markets. They distribute the profit they make from their investment among investors. Real Estate Investment Trusts (REITs) are collective investments schemes that use funds collected from the public to own real estate assets. A REIT distributes rents and profits it receives among the people who invested in the REIT. These are regulated by the SEBI. SEBI has put in place checks and balances to ensure investors' interests are protected and funds are not misused. In comparison, UCIS operate outside the regulatory purview and, thus, can exercise opacity in their working. They offer higher interest rates to entice customers who would otherwise invest their money in a bank or mutual fund. They can afford to offer unsustainably high interest rates because there is no regulation on them.

Colloquially, UCIS are called ponzi schemes, after an Italian swindler by the name of Charles Ponzi ran such a scheme in 1920s North America. Neither was he the first to design the scheme, nor was his scheme unique. Ponzi schemes are so elementary that they have been happening since time immemorial. It does not need a financial expert to run these schemes. It feeds on greed of people, but Ponzi's scheme became so famous that the name ponzi scheme stuck.

R.K. Narayan's novel, published in 1952, shows that localised ponzi schemes were prevalent in small towns of India in pre-independence India. Large ponzi schemes were rampant in India in the 1960s and 1970s, primarily because of two reasons: low spread of formal banking and high tax rates. Low penetration of banks and long, acrimonious queues in the few branches in rural areas prompted people to invest in these alternative schemes. Ponzi schemes usually recruit agents who are paid anywhere between 10 per cent to 20 per cent of the initial capital they bring. These agents tap social groups they are a part of. They approach people during panchayat gatherings, festivals and temple prayers. They deliver their schemes at the customer's doorstep, thus easing the investment process. Low income groups naturally turned to these schemes. The unusually low interest rates offered by national banks pushed people further into the ponzi web.

Income tax rates in India throughout the 1960s and 1970s were stiff. This prompted rampant tax evasion and the black economy was thriving. People with black money could not invest their money in formal banking channels. They invested either in traditional instruments such as land and gold or in collective investment schemes. Since these schemes were unregulated, they took money from Peter to pay Paul and ultimately went bust.

Concerned by loss of investor money in such frauds, the central government passed the Prize Chits & Money Circulation Schemes (Banning) Act of 1978. This Act banned money circulation schemes, but its operation was effectively post facto. That is, the Act could be applied to a ponzi scheme only when such a scheme had been bust and customers had complained about being duped. It was curative in nature, rather than preventive.

The Act of 1978 was followed by a major default in 1980. The Sanchayita Chit Fund was a ponzi scheme that collected more than ₹120 crore in the 1970s from people in West Bengal before it went bust in 1980. The government set up a mechanism to liquidate assets of the chit fund and refund money of investors. However, many investors are still waiting for their refund.[27]

This was followed in the 1990s by scams in states of South India promising high returns on teak bonds, agro bonds and even potato bonds. Anubhav Plantations, one of the larger ponzi schemes of the period, started operations in 1992 in Chennai, and promised absurdly high returns from exploitation of teak plantations. Its Director C. Natesan said teak plants provided extraordinary returns because teak was cheap to plant and grow. Each tree yields 10–15 cubic feet of wood after 14 years of growth, which can yield huge returns. Anubhav Plantation was considered a success story in monetising plantations and Natesan had quite a reputation as an entrepreneur of the post-liberalisation era.

Anubhav Plantations promised yearly interests and a bumper return after 20 years of investment. However, the scheme started defaulting in 1998. The money going out as interest on old investments (which had bloated) became more than fresh investment coming in. When the company could not pay interests, investors panicked and went to Chennai to recover both interest and the principal amount. Natesan had, by then, gone underground.

Most investors of Anubhav Plantations were retired salaried-class people, essentially those from the middle-class. Many of them had invested their entire life savings in Anubhav and had to go bankrupt. Many people were shocked to find Anubhav Plantations was a ponzi scheme. A government enquiry established that the company did not make any profit from teak plantations. It used money received from new investors to pay back old investors, in the process duping gullible investors of some ₹400 crore!

The teak plantation scams of 1990s, included many other Collective Investment Schemes (CIS) that operated in Chennai, Bangalore and Hyderabad areas. Many entities running CIS started defaulting in making their payment to investors in the mid-90s. 'This not only caused huge losses to the investors who lost their life savings to such unscrupulous entities, but also eroded the confidence of the general public in financial savings.'[28] While the promoters of such entities had themselves invested minimal amounts, they 'raised a majority of the funds for the plans/ schemes from ordinary small investors'.[29] As a result, 'the Government of India felt that it was necessary to regulate such financial schemes and set up an appropriate regulatory framework' to regulate these entities. Consequently, Section 12 of SEBI Act of 1992 was amended in 1995 and a ban was imposed on a person carrying CIS unless the scheme was registered with SEBI.

This new law was meant to act as a preventive measure. Since the Prize Chits & Money Circulation Schemes (Banning) Act of 1978 was only curative and could not prevent ponzi schemes from cheating investors, this new law was brought to prevent ponzi schemes from approaching investors. This banned any entity from collecting deposits from the public without prior approval of SEBI, including all ponzi schemes. Theoretically.

Theoretically, large ponzi schemes cannot survive in the current regulatory environment because they are banned. Only way they can operate a large CIS is by taking registration from SEBI, which imposes numerous checks. If an entity does not take SEBI approval and yet runs a large CIS, SEBI would come for it and prosecute its directors. In practice, ponzi schemes survived and prospered. Of special concern are large ponzi schemes that have tumbled out of the cupboard many times in the last two decades. Larger the scheme, more the number of investors and more the number of victims when the scheme goes bust. So, how could they survive despite the ban? The culprit is, quite ironically, a legal idea called the Rule of Law.

Rule of Law restricts arbitrary exercise of power by subordinating it to well-defined and established laws.[30] If a regulator exercises its power arbitrarily, one can take judicial recourse. Judicial recourse can be taken in high courts and the Supreme Court. Interestingly, this judicial recourse can also be used to delay and prolong a regulator's act. A look at the case of PACL Limited aptly demonstrates this point.

PACL Limited was started by Nirmal Singh Bhangoo in 1996. It is said that Bhangoo was earlier a milk seller near Attari border of Punjab, but he did have experience in raising investments prior to starting PACL Limited. He had worked as an agent for the Peerless General

Finance Company,[31] a Kolkata-based savings company that has been accused of duping millions of depositors.[32] PACL was collecting deposits from the public by promising them high returns or plots of agricultural land.

SEBI sent a notice to PACL as early as in March 1998 to stop its operations and not to launch any new scheme. PACL replied the same month that its transactions were in the nature of sale and purchase of agricultural land and, thus, were outside the purview of SEBI.

SEBI audited the operations of PACL and found that the company was running a collective investment scheme in the garb of a real estate company. In its scheme, an investor was asked for a down payment for a piece of land that would be handed over to her after five years (or so) in some part of the country. The investor had the option of taking back her down payment along with hefty interest instead of taking the land. No land was identified at the time of taking investment, neither was any land detail provided. All land parcels seemed to have fixed prices. Land was provided to investors from one corner of the country in another part of the country.

This is not how a real estate company functions. Real estate companies allocate a plot of land or a flat at the time of taking advance. PACL did not even own land parcels when it took money from investors. In short, it was a collective investment scheme run under the garb of real estate business.

SEBI sent another letter on 10 December 1999, requesting PACL to register itself with SEBI if it wanted to continue its operations. If it had chosen to register, it had to follow the SEBI (Collective Investment Schemes) Regulations 1999, and had to get a license to raise money from the public. The regulations, however, placed many transparency conditions and checks against misuse of funds.

PACL refused to register and claimed that SEBI had no jurisdiction to scrutinise its transactions because it mainly dealt in sale and purchase of agricultural land. It then filed a writ petition against SEBI in the Jaipur High Court in December 1999.

While the writ petition was pending, SEBI passed an order on 24 June 2002, stating that PACL's schemes were clearly CIS and so PACL needed to comply with SEBI's regulations.[33] However, the Rajasthan High Court passed an order on 28 November 2003, ruling that the PACL schemes were not CIS and quashed the SEBI notices.

SEBI appealed against the decision of the Rajasthan High Court in the Supreme Court of India. The Supreme Court heard both sides and passed an order on 26 February 2013, overruling the high court's order. It directed SEBI to investigate the affairs of PACL afresh and take a decision. It directed PACL to allow SEBI to inspect, investigate and verify its accounts and other records.

The unregistered CIS that SEBI had detected in March 1998, came back to it in March 2013, after exhausting all judicial remedy. PACL had grown into an elephantine corporation by then. SEBI took more than a year to complete its investigation and adjudication, primarily because of delay on PACL's part. PACL collected thousands of crores from the public in this short period. It mobilised ₹4,069.60 crore between the date of the Supreme Court order and 30 April 2014. It collected another ₹295.17 crore in just 45 days after 30 April 2014![34] In a way, the delay helped PACL survive a bit more, but caused monumental damage to the people of India.

The SEBI investigation that followed the Supreme Court order was impeded due to repeated adjournments that PACL sought. The company claimed that its records were voluminous and took good time to furnish documents. Sample application forms that PACL furnished were not legible, show cause notices to various directors were returned unserved.

Nirmal Singh Bhangoo, who was generally known to be the promoter of PACL, stumped everyone by deposing that he was only an advisor to the company on the real estate sector of India. He said he was a director in the company for a short period between June 1996 and February 1998. He had ceased to be director of PACL just before the SEBI notice. Hence, SEBI's show cause notices were wrongly issued to him.

Many individuals running questionable schemes appoint people of repute as directors of their companies, while they themselves do not take up any official role. This helps them run their scheme from behind the screens and insulates them from any legal action. Qnet went a step further and appointed a franchise in India to run its MLM scheme. The franchise had a limited role to play in running the scheme, but it was the first entity in the LE line of fire.

In PACL's case, Bhangoo indeed was not a director of the company. However, PACL was owned by investment companies, not individuals. Two of the three main shareholding companies of PACL were owned by Bhangoo and his relatives,[35] which made Bhangoo and his relatives the beneficial owners of the company.

The SEBI investigation revealed the inside story of how PACL worked. The company did not advertise any scheme asking for deposits. Rather, it gave a rule book to its agents that was used by the agents to scout for deposits. The rule book made tall claims of high returns on investments and higher returns if deposits were maintained for longer periods.

Agents were paid mind-boggling amounts for bringing in investment. PACL said in its submissions that agents were paid between 6.6 per cent and 12.50 per cent of money taken from customers, but SEBI's calculation from accounts revealed that agents were paid 19.83 per cent of deposits from customers, on average.[36] Brokers in real estate business are paid 1 per cent to 2 per cent of sale consideration. PACL was paying about 20 per cent of deposits as commission to agents.

The agreements that PACL and its agents drew with customers did not mention details of the plot that the customer was promised. Sample agreements submitted with SEBI merely mentioned that PACL was in the process of 'making arrangements for purchasing/procuring the land'.

SEBI's whole-time member Prashant Saran said in his ruling:

> I find that the schemes operated by PACL give a picture that the land is being sold as a homogeneous

"3. METHODOLOGY

(a) Agro Farm

The Company generally acquires land on long term lease or on ownership basis for and on behalf of unit holders. Preference is given for waste land development ... . The company applies hightech means to retrieve and develop the waste lands at a very faster pace.

... ...

(d) Security

Ownership of land unit is transferred in the name of the unit holder on the completion of payment schedule as per the applicable scheme. The necessary paper work, legal documents will be completed within a short span of time. Since the unit holder is the owner of the land unit, the investment is fully secured.

... ...

7. HIGHLIGHTS OF THE SCHEMES OFFERED BY PEARLS

(a) Higher Returns

A unique features of these schemes are that the longer you invest/ wait the better higher benefits you get from these schemes i.e. your income grows in higher proportions as every year passes.

(b) Fully Secured

The land ownership is transferred in your name within a reasonable period generally not exceeding 270 days. It safeguards your interests and as such the investment is fully secured.

... .

(e) Buy Back Option

The Company offers buy back option at the end of the term opted by the unit holders on the prices notified under the aggregate expected return column under various tables which are subject to change without prior notice by the Company under the relevant scheme(s). ... . The unit holder has the option to sell off his unit holdings back to the Company on expiry of the term. However, it is not obligatory for the unit holder to sell the units to the Company. ... ...

Unitholder has to notify 180 days before the expiry of the agreement date for exercising the buy back option.

... ...

(g) Joint Holding

FIGURE 3: *An Extract of PACL Rule Book. Extract Reproduced from SEBI (2014)*

Source: SEBI (2014)

commodity at a fixed price, which is possible only if the land transactions are a sham and a cover for running a CIS scheme and not a genuine sale of agricultural land. At this juncture, I would also like to examine whether the schemes promoted by PACL passes the credulity test. It is difficult for me to believe that a person in Uttar Pradesh will purchase 100–150 yds of agricultural land 2,000 kilometers away. The lack of maintenance of proper records/ data is a clear indication that the activities of PACL are in the nature of ponzi scheme.[37]

Having established that PACL was a ponzi scheme, SEBI ordered it to stop all operations and refund money to depositors in August 2014. The process it started in March 1998 reached a logical conclusion after 16 years.

Quite expectedly, PACL defaulted. It had collected over ₹49,100 crore from investors across India. CBI arrested Bhangoo and three other company officials in January 2016, on charges of running a ponzi scheme. In February 2016, the Supreme Court directed SEBI to constitute a committee to recover assets siphoned off from PACL and to refund investors. SEBI constituted a committee under Justice R.M. Lodha and this committee helped refund some of the investors. The committee was still making efforts to recover funds and refund investors when this book was being penned down.

The PACL case throws some crucial insights on how large ponzi schemes operate. They run front businesses such as real estate, jewellery retail, pharmaceuticals, etc., to hoodwink SEBI and other regulators. By running multiple and diversified front businesses, they create a perception that they are big conglomerates.

Ponzi schemes are perilous for employees and agents alike. In order to ring-fence themselves from law enforcement authorities, ponzi schemers appoint employees as directors in their companies. Schemers often target unemployed youth with low expectation levels and lower understanding of business for the posts of directors and managers in their companies. Agents, who are part of the criminal conspiracy and abetment process, pitch the schemers' products to members of their community. Many a time, they themselves are deeply invested in these schemes and become victims when the scheme goes bust. And they, of course, have to face the risks of customer allegations as well. When caught, they take advantage of the rule of law to stall closure proceedings. They intentionally delay proceedings by taking adjournments, approaching higher courts on writ and by not providing proper accounts for inspection.

Take the case of the Saradha ponzi scam that left the state of West Bengal in complete shock in 2013. This group collected most of its funds after SEBI initiated investigations against it. It went bust weeks before SEBI gave its final verdict and drove many people to bankruptcy.

SEBI first confronted the Saradha Group in 2009. To confound SEBI, Saradha opened about 200 new companies to create more cross-holdings, which created an extremely complex multi-tiered corporate structure for the regulator to grapple with and hindered their ability to consolidate blame. SEBI, however, continued with its investigation through 2010. The group adapted by camouflaging its methods of raising capital. It began operating variations of collective investment schemes involving tourism packages, hotel booking, real estate, infrastructure finance etc. Middlemen rarely informed investors about the true nature of their investments, although the investors were promised high returns after a fixed period.[38]

In May 2012, SEBI called for specific documents pertaining to Saradha Realty India Limited, to understand if it was into real estate or simply collecting money from the public. Saradha Group submitted 16 boxes of voluminous documents in September 2012, which had all but the information specifically asked for.[39] After a few days, it submitted another 19 boxes of voluminous but irrelevant documents. SEBI's whole-time director Rajeev Kumar Agarwal observed that Saradha Group had 'sent 35 cartons as a strategy to avoid submitting the specific information' called for.

On 19 December 2012, Saradha Group's legal representative appeared in the Kolkata office of SEBI with 28 more such cartons. Since none of the information in these cartons was relevant, they were returned and Saradha was clearly advised not to furnish irrelevant documents. The group sought time until March 2013, to furnish the documents asked for. In March 2013, the Group came up with a bizarre reply: its data was stored in a server in Boston, which was under the control of a few brokers who had apparently defrauded the company.

Based on whatever information was available with it, SEBI built a case that Saradha Realty was taking deposits from customers by promising them returns of 12 per cent to 24 per cent. Agarwal said 'at the time of making the initial contribution/payment, the investor only gets a promise to be allotted a piece of land/plot in the properties developed and managed by (Saradha Realty) or to get repaid along with promised benefits. At this stage, the land unit is not identified as it is non-distinguishable.' Agarwal passed an order on 23 April 2013, asking Saradha Realty to desist from raising any further capital and refund all deposits within three months.

Unfortunately, the SEBI order came a little late. In January 2013, for the first time, Saradha Group's cash inflow was less than the cash outflow. This was a clear sign for any ponzi scheme that its days were up. The group failed in paying some depositors and agents. This raised suspicion in the market that all may not be good with them. This prompted many depositors to withdraw their principal amount. This further aggravated the situation. The kingpin of the scam wrote an 18-page confessional letter to CBI on 6 April 2013, in which he blamed some politicians of West Bengal for the debacle and then he fled on 10 April 2013. The SEBI order came after two weeks.

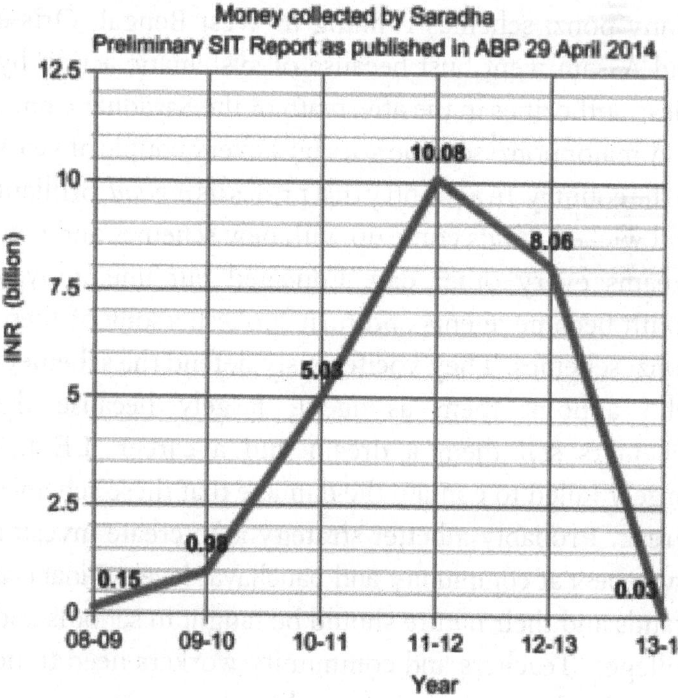

FIGURE 4: *Money collected by Saradha Group*

Source: Author

As can be seen from the graph, a major part of the collections was between FY 2010–11 and 2012–13.

Although already under the SEBI scanner by then, SEBI could do little to provisionally block it from collecting money. It could pass an injunction only after following the due process of law.

The Saradha scam snowballed into a major political controversy because the Group allegedly had significant business relations with local politicians. It also served to sensitise people of India to the vagaries of investing in unregulated schemes. The scam prompted authorities such as CBI, ED, the IT department, state EOWs and the local police to systematically target ponzi schemes. Many ponzi schemes running in West Bengal, Orissa and Assam went bust because of systematic action by these authorities in the aftermath of the Saradha scam.[40]

A major ponzi scheme goes bust every couple of years in the country. In a country that prides its *jugaad*, brilliant and wicked minds come up with new schemes and new dreams every other day. Educated but unemployed youth become agents and turn spokespersons of these ponzi schemes. They vociferously defend the schemers who appoint them as agent, largely because the schemers sell them a dream and a career. LE has largely failed to contain the damage that these schemes wreak. Probably a better strategy is to create investor awareness at community and panchayat levels. Financial frauds and their nature should be taught in schools and colleges. Teachers and community workers need to be trained to be anti-ponzi evangelists.

Unfortunately, ponzi schemes are fast mutating into new forms, which are hard to understand and even harder to punish. National law enforcement authorities are severely under-armed to deal with the new disruptive models of collective investment schemes that have emerged due to digitalisation.

Rise of Online Ponzi Brigade

As ponzi schemes migrate to the internet, they now have a wide array of models to choose from. These models are disruptive, in the sense that they allow scamsters to raise money anonymously, siphon off easily and move around the world in absolute opacity. Many online ponzi schemes are successfully fleecing innocent netizens on social networking sites for years now. Fraudsters typically register companies offshore in tax havens with strong secrecy laws and approach customers through social networking websites. Many a time, it is difficult to establish the real man behind the scheme.

By far, the most successful online ponzi scheme is the Mavrodi Mondial Money (MMM) scheme. MMM was a Russian company in the 1990s, and was once considered the largest ponzi scheme of the world. In 2011, MMM took advantage of the rapid penetration of the internet and new-age technology in developing countries to start an online ponzi scheme, targeting people from developing countries.

MMM has a dedicated website for each country it operates in. The website's URL is www.countryname-MMM.net. Its website for depositors from India is www.India-MMM.net. This website enlightens viewers that 'MMM is not a bank, MMM does not collect your MONEY, MMM is not an online business, investment or MLM program. MMM is a community where people help each other.' Consumers are encouraged to send money and are promised monetary support from the common fund with 30 per cent returns after a few years. MMM has its own Facebook page, its Twitter handle and its own e-learning module to teach people how to make money using MMM.

MMM has been extremely successful and is growing by the day. A study in Nigeria found that in a period of six months, starting from June 2016, more than $77.8 million was remitted by Nigerian residents to MMM as investment. This was 61 per cent more than Nigeria's annual education budget. MMM Nigeria crashed shortly after the study and customers lost money in millions of dollars. MMM reinstated its website shortly after the crash and is again back in business in Nigeria.[40]

The largest online ponzi scheme that has been detected so far is China's Ezubao. It projected itself as a start-up running peer-to-peer lending and collected massive funds from Chinese residents, promising them huge returns from peer-to-peer lending. It started operations in 2014, and within a short span amassed more than $9 billion from Chinese investors. It stopped its online facilities in December 2015, and went bust shortly thereafter.

The clear advantage of online ponzi schemes over the traditional ones is the number of customers they can reach out to in a short span of time. They do not require to maintain branches and agents to reach out to customers. They post advertisements online and use data analytics to target customers who are looking for opportunities. They engage large populations through

Facebook and WhatsApp groups, which helps them to convert customers fast.

For instance, Noida-based Anubhav Mittal devised a novel scheme in which he proposed netizens to invest money and click 'likes' on certain Facebook pages to earn huge returns. The idea he peddled was that companies make promotional expenses for hitting 'like' on their official pages on Facebook. These companies pay him for clicks, owing to which he makes huge profits.

Mittal's website www.socialtrade.biz and his Facebook page gained traction easily. He swindled about ₹3,700 crore in a short period before the Uttar Pradesh police shut it down. Compare Mittal with the Saradha Group, in which investors lost about ₹3,000 crore.

Operations of online ponzi schemes have become especially murky with the rise of cryptocurrencies. Cryptocurrencies are volatile, have no intrinsic value and so are naturally compatible with ponzi schemes. I have a theory that Bitcoin, the first ever cryptocurrency, is a financial fraud. Many techies have hotly contested my theory on Bitcoin, but promptly agree that cryptocurrencies open up many avenues for running ponzi schemes.

First, my theory on Bitcoin. Bitcoin was founded by Satoshi Nakamoto in 2008. It is a digital currency that is not administered by any central bank. All currencies before Bitcoin were administered by central banks. Bitcoin is administered by a decentralised system in which one user can send value to another user using Bitcoin as token. Each transaction is authenticated by six accountants on a ledger. Since there are no accountants in the payroll of a decentralised system, the system requires freelancers. Freelancers are paid in new Bitcoins for authenticating transactions. Freelancers are called miners because they literally mine new Bitcoins by authenticating transactions.

While other currencies are backed by sovereign guarantee of respective nations, Bitcoin is not backed by any country or asset. It has no intrinsic value; it derives value from two things. One, it is accepted as a medium of exchange by a wide array of users. And two, it has limited supply. Central banks regulate the exchange rate of their currencies by controlling the currency's supply in the market. Since there is no central control for Bitcoin, its exchange rate viz-a-viz the US dollar is volatile. Speculations further increase its volatility.

Bitcoin is accepted as a medium of exchange because of multiple reasons. The primary one being the anonymity it brings. Each user is identified by a 36-digit public key, consisting of letters and numbers. A user's identity never gets revealed, even when s/he is purchasing contraband or drugs on the dark web.

No one knows who Satoshi Nakamoto is. His identity remains one of the biggest mysteries. He had kept 1 million Bitcoins for himself at the time of the currency's launch. These Bitcoins, called the founder's coins, were worthless when he launched the currency. However, over time, Bitcoin has become valuable viz-a-viz paper currencies. Today, the founder's coins of Nakamoto are worth about $15 billion! How did that happen?

Like any ponzi scheme, Nakamoto sold an idea. Nakamoto questioned the US government and US

Federal Reserve. Referring to the 2008 sub-prime crisis, he claimed that the US government could not be trusted. He argued that the US Federal Reserve indiscriminately printed dollars, which left the common man in doubt about the real value of a dollar. Hence, the dollar could not be a reliable store of value. His new currency worked on a reliable technology that maintained integrity of a decentralised system. It could not be manipulated by any government.

Nakamoto's idea attracted the heart of socialists and the mind of capitalists. In his scheme, he appointed miners as agents. Miners toiled by running codes and got remunerated in Bitcoins. Since a Bitcoin has no intrinsic value, the miners were forced to sell Bitcoins or exchange them for goods and services. Miners marketed the currency and worked as evangelists in spreading the currency. Once the currency picked traction, many gullible investors poured in their money. Few circumstantial factors helped the currency. Economic fugitives and loan defaulters found it to be an anonymous means of investment. No creditor, no authority, no court can freeze your bitcoins because no one has control over the system and no one can establish that a public key belongs to you. Black marketeers trading on the dark web prefer to transact in Bitcoins due to the anonymity it provides.

And thus, Nakamoto's wealth increased from naught in 2008 to a whopping $15 billion in 2019. No government knows his identity, no authority can punish him, no taxman can rob him, no police can catch him. He may very well be the greatest of fraudsters of our times.

Success of Bitcoin opened a Pandora's Box. Bitcoin and other early cryptocurrencies provided the proof of concept that decentralised digital currencies can work. And, thus, many other cryptocurrencies followed. The website www.coinmarketcap.com listed 2,477 cryptocurrencies as on 25 March 2020. Just a handful of top cryptocurrencies are recognised as a medium of exchange by the average internet user, rest are merely tokens. Coin founders, however, sell them as investment vehicles that would yield huge returns. Fraudsters often raise money from gullible investors by releasing an Initial Coin Offering (ICO) after creating a hype on social networking sites and then run away with the money.

So, it is not surprising that ponzi schemers saw them as potential avenues to sell their schemes. Amit Bhardwaj, infamously nicked as the Bitcoin Ponzi King, ran one such scheme that promised high returns to anyone who invested in Bitcoins through his website www.gainbitcoin.com. Bharadwaj posed as an expert in cryptocurrencies at a time when the concept was still new in India. He reached out to a wide array of people through social networking websites and increased their awareness about the 'benefits' of investing in cryptocurrencies. He did not peddle his scheme himself. For that, he set up an MLM network. Customers who had invested in his venture were asked to bring in more customers.

Each customer was promised returns as high as 10 per cent per month for making investments in his venture, which started in 2016. Additionally, a customer got commission from investments made by downline customers in her chain.

Customers were required to make their investment in Bitcoins. Bhardwaj opened multiple Bitcoin wallets to which customers were asked to send their Bitcoins. By doing this, he managed to collect a stately sum of 9,736 Bitcoins in the entire duration of his venture. In Indian currency, these Bitcoins were worth ₹500–₹1,000 crore, depending on the date on which the valuation was made (exchange rate of Bitcoins and the Indian currency varies dynamically).

When Bhardwaj was offering returns of 10 per cent per month, some early investors must have benefited from the scheme. Surely, Bhardwaj did not pocket all 9,736 Bitcoins? Unfortunately, though, even early investors lost their money. Bhardwaj turned out to be a brilliant innovator. He understood that if he offered 10 per cent returns per month, his ponzi scheme would go bust sooner than expected. Ponzi schemes survive only when cash inflow is more than cash outflow. A return of 10 per cent per month plus commission to topline members of the distribution network would mean heavy cash outflow. And this meant, cash outflow would exceed cash inflow in a short time, making the scheme go bust.

To tide over this problem, Bhardwaj did not make any real payments. He kept adding figures to the investments made. When an investor logged into his website, they found a calculation of their current balance (initial investments plus profit of 10 per cent per month plus referral commissions) in Bitcoins. No bitcoin was actually paid.

Investors, however, soon became impatient. They asked for release of their Bitcoins. Bhardwaj's ponzi scheme could have gone bust at this point, but he wriggled out of the situation by starting his own cryptocurrency called MCAP. He offered to pay back investors in MCAP. He artificially pegged the price of MCAP against Bitcoin and transferred MCAPs to investors.

What Bhardwaj did can be better understood with an analogy. I take ₹100 from you, promising to pay you ₹200 after 10 months. After 10 months, I hand you a certificate that says the certificate is worth ₹200. I have prepared and printed the certificate. It has no real value. Sure, a ₹200 note also has no intrinsic value, but it is widely considered as a means of exchange. You can use a ₹200 note to purchase goods from the market, but what use is a certificate ? What can you do with it? Of course, you will not accept my certificates.

Forget drugs, no one will send you cannabis grass on the dark web even if you offer a billion MCAPs. Bhardwaj, however, managed to convince many of his investors to take MCAPs. These investors were new to the world of cryptocurrency and did not understand the conceptual difference between Bitcoin and a digital token. MCAP was just a digital token. Bharadwaj even managed to make money by issuing ICO of MCAP.

A B-school professor would tell you that Bhardwaj is a visionary leader. He turned adversity into an opportunity. The reality of MCAP soon came to the fore. Many of his investors were those who had put in their money to make a quick buck. They wanted their money back in hard notes, not MCAPs. They understood they had been cheated and complained to LE authorities. Bhardwaj dumped his scheme in November 2017 and went underground. The police issued a look-out notice for him, following which he was arrested in Bangkok on 31 March 2018, and brought back to India.

Bhardwaj's scam reveals many novel challenges posed by crypto-ponzi schemes. Bhardwaj did not deal in national currencies. He accepted deposits in Bitcoins, which can be easily and anonymously transferred across national borders. His investors sent Bitcoins to his wallets, which can be accessed anywhere in the world. He most likely converted the Bitcoins into Dirhams in Dubai's Bitcoin market[42] and used the money to purchase assets in Dubai.

Siphoning funds is easy with Bitcoins since they leave no money trail. Investigators could not reach out to the people to whose wallets Bhardwaj transferred the Bitcoins. Hence, a clear money trail linking his fraudulent income in India to his properties in Dubai could not be established. Funds have to be recovered to refund innocent investors, but in order to recover funds, Indian authorities have to convince courts in Dubai that the properties were purchased with money scammed from Indian investors. Without a clear money trail, this is not possible.

It is difficult to bring conviction in such cases. What is the proof that the investors transferred their Bitcoins to the accused? The wallet to which they transferred Bitcoins was known only by its public key. The wallet was not registered to the accused. Neither was it linked to the accused's PAN or Aadhar Card.

Bitcoins also make it easy to hide wealth from authorities. Bitcoins might still be lying in some wallet of Bhardwaj, but Indian authorities cannot freeze the wallet. Bhardwaj was granted an interim bail by the Supreme Court on health grounds on 3 April 2019. The apex court asked Bhardwaj to deposit a bail bond of ₹10 crore with its registry for getting bail. Apparently, he had the money to deposit his bail bond. His associates are in touch with investors for an out-of-court settlement. Given the difficulty in recovering funds, investors may ultimately accept whatever he offers and leave him with the riches he has gathered.

Crypto-ponzi schemes have become a social hazard. Many such schemes are being peddled on the internet today. Legal remedy to crypto-ponzi fraud is difficult and legal recourse is not even available to victims in countries where cryptocurrencies are banned. In such countries, investors do not even lodge complaints, fearing that authorities may charge them instead for transacting in cryptocurrencies. Such countries have become breeding grounds for crypto-ponzi scams.

The difficulty in regulating online ponzi and pyramid schemes reinforces the argument that law enforcement is not the right solution to the problem. Robust laws and proactive enforcement are necessary, but not sufficient conditions for eradicating these financial frauds. Individuals and communities have to be sensitised about the real nature of such frauds and the myth that one can get rich quickly must be busted.

6

Shells, Mailboxes and Islands: The Fraud Ecosystem

Shipping tycoon, nuclear physicist, musicologist, amateur versifier and financial wizard–these are some of the adjectives used to describe one of the earliest embezzlers of independent India. Jayanti Dharma Teja may very well be to the economic crimes industry of India what Dracula is to the genre to vampire fiction. Teja was a bundle of contradictions. He was, at the same time, an erudite academician and a slimy fugitive of the law. In a way, he is the figure most Indians of an earlier generation conjure up when you ask them about financial frauds.

Teja was son of Jayanti Venkat Narayan Teja, a missionary of the Brahmo Samaj and a freedom fighter. The father was instrumental in starting Congress units in Odisha and Andhra Pradesh and had been imprisoned six times by the British. Teja's mother, Surama, was the first woman in South India to be imprisoned as a nationalist–she went to jail five times.

Born to such illustrious parents, Teja managed to get fine tutelage in Purdue University in the United States. He went on to do research in nuclear physics under Enrico Fermi, the renowned Italian physicist, and got acquainted with the likes of Albert Einstein,

Robert Oppenheimer and Joseph Goldberger. So, when Teja landed in Delhi in 1960 with his American wife Betsy, he was welcomed with open arms by the then Prime Minister Jawaharlal Nehru. He was invited to a dinner at the Prime Minister's residence, where he professed his desire to come back and do something for the country. That was a time when just a handful of Indians had the kind of academic exposure and success in the West that Teja had. That one of them was willing to come back with nationalistic motives was indeed great news.

Nehru apparently had asked Teja to develop a strategy for India in one of the two sectors: Steel or shipping. Teja chose shipping and drafted a three-page note on how to develop India's shipping industry quickly.[1]

On their way back to Europe, Teja and his wife stopped at Rome and it is here that his American wife developed an infection of the nervous system. She died within a day. In just a few months, he married Ranjeet, an economist who he was acquainted with for years now. Teja came back to India with his new wife in 1961 and set up the Jayanti Shipping Corporation. He applied for a loan to purchase bulk carriers and oil tankers and got the application recommended by Nehru. He was granted a loan of ₹20 crore, a princely sum at the time. Jayanti Shipping grew by leaps and bounds and managed to acquire 26 ships in five years.

This was all a bubble though. Teja had invested just ₹200 in Jayanti Shipping. His acquisitions were entirely funded by the initial loan of ₹20 crore. He then hypothecated the ships he purchased with this loan to get more loan. The second tranche of loan was used to purchase more ships. These new ships were hypothecated to get more loans, which enabled him to purchase more ships. Teja managed to acquire an impressive fleet of ships by doing this financial trickery. The entire expansion was driven by loan funds or OPM.

While committing the fraud, Teja didn't forget to siphon off some of the OPM for himself. When acquiring ships for Jayanti Shipping from the Mitsubishi Heavy Industries of Tokyo, Teja asked them to add a 2 per cent commission for him. The commission was to be transferred to his private account in London. When Mitsubishi asked for confirmation from the company, he gave them a forged copy of the resolution of Jayanti Shipping's board of directors. It was the testimony of Fumiho Karaki, the VP of Mitsubishi, that later helped the CBI unravel the modus operandi.

Teja also kept for himself a shilling, as commission, for every tonne of freight carried by some vessels of Jayanti Shipping. He indulged in rampant falsification of the company's accounts, which the internal auditors frequently objected to. It can be concluded that Teja stashed for himself a good sum for a rainy day.

Teja knew that rainy days would come, for such bubbles rupture with a bang. That's why he acquired properties in many places around the world. Investigations were, however, initiated even before the bubble could burst. Multiple allegations of under-the-table dealings were levied against him due to which Indira Gandhi ordered an inquiry by the CBI in August 1966. The CBI found many irregularities in his company's accounts, news of which reached Teja while he was holidaying in Europe. Teja and his wife slipped away to New York and lay low.

Meanwhile, the Indian government was anxiously searching for Teja. They found that he had taken up a research post in Brookhaven National Laboratory and stayed in New York and Long Island (he had houses in both places). Teja still had an Indian passport and was already working in the US without a valid work permit. The Indian government managed to put enough diplomatic pressure on the US administration to arrest Teja and his wife for 'overstaying'.

Teja and Ranjeet were soon released on bail on paying a bond of $10,000 each (a huge amount at the time), while the Indian government initiated extradition proceedings against the couple. While the proceedings were underway, the Tejas jumped bail and flew away to San José, the capital of Costa Rica. Apparently, the President of Costa Rica, Jose Figueras, was an old friend of Teja.

It is not clear why, but Figueras went all out to shelter Teja and protect him from the Indian authorities. Sumit Mitra of *India Today* wrote: 'Indian authorities did their best to hound him out of his haven by carrying the extradition proceedings right up to the Costa Rican Supreme Court. But Figueras arranged elaborate legal defence.'[2] While Indian authorities hired a battery of lawyers from the US to fight their case in Costa Rican courts, Figueras helped Teja hire a former Chief Justice of their Supreme Court. Teja won the case.

According to Costa Rican laws, court rulings have to be upheld by the president. Teja's friend Figueras had lost elections by then and had been replaced by a new

President. Interestingly, the new President Fernando Tregos not only upheld the court ruling, but also allowed him to acquire a diplomatic passport of Costa Rica!

Teja was too big a character to remain in hiding. Armed with the new diplomatic passport from Costa Rica, he ventured out and hopped around the world. He was intercepted by the Scotland Yard in London during one such trip.

India moved an extradition plea in a London court. The hearings hogged headlines not just in India but world over. During the hearings, Teja claimed that he had run secret missions for India to the Soviet Union during the Chinese aggression and he negotiated a security pact of India and Japan against China. While his provocative claims were embarrassing for the country, India did win the extradition case in London and Teja was transferred to Tihar Jail in Delhi.

The CBI could prove eight separate charges of forgery and falsification of accounts and he was sentenced to three years in jail in October 1972. The story does not end here though. While Teja was on the run from Indian authorities, taxmen in India initiated income tax and wealth tax cases against him. Instances of his famed riches outside India had been reported in the national and the international media. Where did he get all that money from? Has he paid any tax on the income he siphoned off from Jayanti Shipping? Has he paid any wealth tax on his properties all over the world? His numerous assets around the world triggered income tax and wealth tax assessments in his absence, which led to a heavy tax demand.[3]

After Teja was brought back to India and did his jail time, he was a free bird. The taxmen did not, however, stop hounding him for the arrears. Teja again escaped from India in May 1977, purportedly using a fresh passport. A huge furore erupted at the time because as per Indian laws, a citizen was not entitled to a fresh passport within five years of a sentence (Teja was sentenced in October 1972).

In 1981, Teja was second on the list of largest individual tax defaulters in the country. With penalties and interest, his total income tax arrears stood at ₹7.17 crore, while his total wealth tax arrears stood at ₹1.76 crore. The only person above him on the list was Haridas Mundhra,[4] another legend in the area of financial irregularities, as discussed in one of the earlier chapters of this book.

The misadventures of Teja reveal many important clues about what motivates a person to indulge in serious economic offences. An evil mind is a necessary but not a sufficient condition for indulging in this kind of offence. Such schemes have to be patiently run over long periods of time. The offender is usually a qualified person and is in no way fatalistic. They know that the scheme may go bust anytime, hence the offender always needs an exit plan.

Exit plan is critical to any serious fraud. Serious frauds do not go unforgiven, for the simple reason that one fraudster escaping unscathed becomes a role model for many others. Jail time of even a few years hits people habituated to affluence harder than others. In today's time, serious frauds trigger multiple violations unlike Teja's time. The offender may face multiple actions from the ED, the CBI, the IT department, SEBI, the RBI and the SFIO for the same scam. With such deterrents in place, a secure exit plan is crucial for a hustler to venture into a serious fraud scheme. Serious frauds tend to proliferate when an exit plan is easily available, while they are rare when exit plans are difficult to make.

Exit plans more or less consist of plans to siphon funds, park stolen funds in assets, protect assets from the law and prepare a country to take shelter in. Exit strategies are costly, so also are the lawyers needed to fight extradition cases. Hence, siphoning off OPM is the first and most important plan that a hustler of serious frauds concentrates on.

Once funds are siphoned off, they need to be parked in bank accounts or assets that can be insulated from investigating agencies. For this, the fraudster needs to scout for jurisdictions that maintain high levels of secrecy. They may need help from professionals to structure their holding in a way that hides them as beneficial owners of their assets. They also need to scout for countries that do not have extradition treaties with India and can resist diplomatic pressure from India for a price. A country following the rule of law would never abet fraud. Hence, it has to be a country with weak laws.

Surprisingly, many easy options are available at the disposal of a hustler to execute exit plans. Shell companies of all hues are available off-the-shelf, both within and outside India, for falsifying accounts and siphoning off funds. It is not difficult to reach out to Hawala dealers ready to move cash across international borders for a commission. Tax havens compete with one another to protect the identity and anonymity of persons who park money in their area. Some small countries even grant citizenship to anyone who invests a minimum amount of money in assets in their territory. These facilities originally came up to aid and abet evaders in hiding their money from taxmen, but are of utility to fraudsters as well.

Such an ecosystem promotes the propensity to commit fraud. It is not that countries have not tried to clamp down on the industries aiding and abetting fraudsters. They have, but they cannot do away with a business that has a market. This chapter investigates the murky world of shell companies and tax havens, the syndicates who run them and the jurisdictions which promote them.

Where It's Their Berth Right

Tax havens are foreign jurisdictions that charge zero or nominal tax on funds that are parked in their territory. However, tax havens are much more than just low-tax jurisdictions. The name 'tax haven' is a misnomer, for these states are haven for all kinds of dirty money. It is a haven for the narco who seeks to launder his drug money. It is a haven for the sex trafficker who seeks to wash his blood money. It hides the wealth of a person undergoing a divorce from his/her spouse. It is the jurisdiction used by multinationals to secretly pay bribes to influence policies in weak countries. It is the jurisdiction of choice for the corrupt to park their bribe money. An economic offender knows that law enforcement agencies in hot pursuit can never get access to his wealth stashed in tax havens, let alone recover it. For those who have committed serious frauds and are on the run, havens are nothing short of heaven. The fact that most of them are exotic islands with pristine beaches and party culture adds to their lure.

The story of tax havens and how they have provided sanctuary to plunderers, dictators, fraudsters, rogues, drug lords, warlords, traffickers and tax evaders is a sad episode of globalisation. Low tax rate is not the key determinant of a tax haven. Many countries have low corporate tax rates but still are not termed as tax havens. The key determinant is secrecy. Tax havens have stringent banking secrecy laws that prohibit banks from revealing personal details of their clients. Some tax havens have laws that allow formation of companies, trusts and foundations without revealing the beneficiary's name. Tax havens intentionally formulate laws that attract the rich and the rogues to park their funds in these tax havens. Some tax havens have gone overboard and are now offering citizenship to the rich.

So, which tax havens have been the most successful in serving the evaders and the economic fugitives? Tax Justice Network (TJN), an international NGO, publishes a ranking of top corporate tax havens every year. All of these jurisdictions have low tax regimes and high secrecy intensity. The top 10 jurisdictions in 2020 are[5]:

1. British Virgin Islands (BVI)
2. Bermuda
3. Cayman Islands
4. The Netherlands

5. Switzerland
6. Luxembourg
7. Jersey
8. Singapore
9. Bahamas
10. Hong Kong

An independent study of tax havens that are preferred by economic fugitives has not been conducted. Such a list may include Panama, St Kitts & Nevis, Antigua and Dubai.

The Ministry of External Affairs of India has released a list of 28 fugitive economic offenders, which included the likes of Vijay Mallya, Nirav Modi, his uncle Mehul Choksi and the Sandesara brothers (Chetan and Diptiben) who had allegedly cheated Indian banks to the tune of ₹14,500 crore through their company Sterling Biotech Limited. These 28 offenders are now based out of different countries such as the UK, St Kitts & Nevis, Antigua, Dubai, Nigeria and Kenya. Chetan Sandesara and Diptiben Sandesara are based out of Nigeria, an unusual choice, probably because the country has no extradition treaty with India.

Where these economic offenders have parked their ill-gotten funds may give us a clue about preferred tax havens for fraudsters. These details have not been made public as the hunt for their stash is still on. It will not be easy for law enforcement agencies to trace their money as most tax havens have strict bank secrecy norms.

Take, for example, the case of Switzerland, which has been protecting innocent evaders from taxmen of other countries since 1815. I have heard fables of the 'numbered accounts' maintained by the rich and the powerful in Swiss bank accounts, when I was a kid. As per one report,[6] banks operating from Switzerland hold US $6.5 trillion in assets under management (AUM), of which 48 per cent originated from abroad.

Switzerland's bank secrecy laws are famous, primarily because the country got into the business quite early on. It was a haven of peace in the middle of a turbulent Europe in the 17th and 18th centuries. The Congress of Vienna formalised Swiss neutrality in 1815, which meant that it would not take sides in any European war. The relative peace and stability of Switzerland attracted nobles and businessmen to shift their wealth to Swiss bank accounts. Swiss banks prospered and so did the Swiss economy. Switzerland introduced tough laws to protect the identity of bank account holders.

The two world wars devastated Europe, but business boomed in Switzerland. After each world war, European nations endeavoured to rebuild their country and they needed revenue for doing that. These countries increased effective tax rates to gather more revenue. The rich in these countries clandestinely shifted their wealth to Switzerland to escape paying taxes. This is why there was a huge surge in investment in Swiss banks in the inter-war years.

Once Switzerland made a reputation for itself, more and more wealth poured in. Dictators, corrupt lawmakers from developing countries, drug lords, arms dealers, all queued up in Switzerland. There are other tax havens that provide similar facilities to the rogue, but they are less of a brand in the game than Switzerland is. Naturally, they don't have as much black money inflows as Switzerland.

Building this brand, however, has not been an easy task for Switzerland. Punishment for breach of bank secrecy laws is severe. There is a punishment even for asking about an account holder. And the Swiss take this law very seriously. One French computer engineer, Hervé Falciani, still tried his luck. He worked in the Swiss branch of HSBC for eight years from 2001 to 2008. While working for the bank, he realised that the way data was managed at HSBC fostered tax evasion and proposed a new system, which was rejected by his superiors. After this, he collected evidence of potential tax fraud, involving some 13,000 account holders. Account holders were citizens of America, France, the UK, Brazil, Venezuela, Belgium and many other countries.

Falciani tried to make the information available to the Swiss judicial authorities, but was unsuccessful. In 2008, he travelled to Beirut and tried to sell the data there, but Swiss authorities got wind of this and initiated legal action against him. Falciani fled to France. The Swiss judiciary issued an international arrest warrant against him, following which France arrested him in January 2009.

Switzerland pleaded with France to mount a search on Falciani's house and seize the laptop containing the data he had stolen from HSBC Switzerland. The prosecutor did mount a search, but was scandalised upon seeing the data. He initiated investigation against the tax evaders appearing in the data. The list of tax evaders is famously called the 'Falciani list' and this leak is touted to be the biggest banking leak in history.

France collaborated with other countries in taking action against the evaders in the Falciani list. France, meanwhile, released Falciani.

The Swiss authorities were fuming. How could Falciani do this to the innocent evaders! We don't know if they were planning anything serious, but Falciani claimed that the US government advised him to flee from France as it would be easy for someone to pay to try and kill him in France.[7] He fled to Spain, where he was arrested upon his arrival due to the international arrest warrant issued by Swiss judiciary. Spain debated over whether or not to extradite him to Switzerland and finally, in 2013, decided not to.

In 2014, the Swiss federal government indicted Falciani in absentia for violating the country's bank secrecy laws and for industrial espionage. He was again arrested in Spain in April 2018, and again released in September 2018 after a Spanish high court rejected the extradition request from Switzerland.

Another country with stringent banking secrecy laws is Dubai. This country stubbornly maintains opacity of its banking transactions despite pressure from the FATF. Many international agencies have accused it of being a money laundering paradise. The anti-corruption advocacy group, Transparency International, said in its Corruption Perception Index of 2019: 'Dubai has become an active global hub for money laundering... where the corrupt and other criminals can go to buy luxurious property with no restrictions.'

Possibly, Dubai wants to position itself as a laundering paradise and such comments augur well for it. According to the TJN, Dubai is:

> One of the world's best known tax havens or secrecy jurisdictions, built on an increasingly complex array of offshore facilities: free-trade zones; a low-tax environment; multiple secrecy facilities and lax enforcement. In addition, Dubai has an ask-no-questions, see-no-evil approach to commercial and financial regulation as well as foreign financial crimes. It has consequently attracted large financial flows and some of the world's most high-profile criminals. A significant slice of the inbound money comes in the form of cash or gold.[8]

Dubai's journey as a tax haven started after Sheikh Rashid took over the city as Emir (or ruler) in 1958. He established lax banking and customs laws that encouraged traders to use it as a trading hub. He was famously tolerant to smuggling and tacitly encouraged smugglers operating out of India to use Dubai as their base. So much so that India had, at one time, put Sheikh Rashid on its list of most wanted smugglers.[9]

Haji Mastan, Vardha Bhai (Varadarajan Mudaliar) and Karim Lala, the dreaded gangsters of Mumbai in 1960s and 1970s, made their riches by smuggling gold and electronics items from Dubai to India. Most of the contraband was imported through the sea route, taking advantage of the long western coastline of India.

Smuggling operations were later taken over by the D-Company (led by Dawood Ibrahim) and Byculla Company (led by Arun Gawli). These gangsters continued smuggling through the Dubai route till 1992. Dawood took refuge in Dubai when law enforcers in India went after him. Smuggling reduced substantially after the liberalisation of international trade in India in 1992.

Dubai's haven business spiked in 1979. Two important events had occurred in the region in the year: the Iranian revolution and invasion of the USSR (or the Soviet Union) into Afghanistan. Rich businessmen from Iran as well as Afghanistan moved their wealth to Dubai, apprehending political and legal instability in their own country. Dubai then realised that strife and unrest in its neighbourhood is good for the city. Dubai prospered whenever a country in its vicinity suffered from civil war or unrest.

The indispensability of Dubai for financial dealings became even more important with the rise of Islamic terrorism. Dubai already had a *laissez faire* attitude towards terror financing. The entire conspiracy behind the 1992 Bombay bomb blasts involving Tiger Menon, the ISI and Dawood Ibrahim was hatched in Dubai. Funds for organising the blasts were routed by the ISI through Dubai. Pakistan's nuclear trafficking kingpin, Abdul Qadeer Khan, used Dubai as a hub to move funds that were used in trafficking nuclear materials. Large sums of money were wired from Dubai to finance the 9/11 terror attacks on the US.

The rise of Islamic terrorism across the Middle East and American invasion of Iraq and Afghanistan accorded an aura of indispensability to Dubai. Misha Glenny observed in his book *McMafia* that 'Dubai had become so useful for terrorists, the superrich, the United States, dictators, Russian oligarchs, celebrities, Europe, and gangsters that if it did not exist, the global élites would have to invent it'.[10]

Dubai has also succeeded in becoming the world's hawala capital. Hawala trade developed as a by-product of the smuggling racket run from Dubai. Today, hawaladars based in Dubai move money for poppy traders of Afghanistan, government of Iran (which faces hurdles in its international transactions due to US sanctions), insurgency groups in Syria, terrorists infesting the entire middle east region and the Islamic State.

Switzerland and Dubai are two ends of a spectrum of island nations that have opened shops to cater to a range of nefarious clients. Each tax haven has its own unique selling proposition (USP) that targets a specific kind of client. One country that peddles its wares to all kinds of clients, those at the left, right and centre of the spectrum, is the UK, which runs the largest offshore finance network in the world through its crown dependencies (Jersey, Guernsey and the Isle of Man). They together handle the largest volume of illicit financial flows. On adding seven overseas territories of the UK, namely Cayman Islands, British Virgin Islands, Bermuda, Gibraltar, Montserrat, Anguilla and Turks and Caicos, one sees a global spiderweb of tax haven network.[11]

Various limbs of this global spiderweb services clients from different geographies. British author Nicholas Shaxson explains in his book *Treasure Islands* that the overseas territories in the Caribbean help American clients evade tax in America, while the crown dependencies service clients from Europe. We also know that the City of London is the favourite place for Russian oligarchs and mafiosi to park funds.

Cayman Islands and the City of London are also blamed for precipitating the 2008 recession by running opaque shadow banking facilities for Wall Street bankers.

The Offshore Advantage

Tax havens offer a variety of packages to help hide the wealth, from the government, from the ex-wife and from creditors. Chiefly, the offerings are of four types: personal bank accounts, mailbox companies, foundation and trust. Personal bank accounts are the simplest offering. Many tax havens have liberal Know Your Customer (KYC) requirements and have laws against revealing account holder data. These are ideal locations to open personal bank accounts.

Many tax havens are buckling under international pressure and FATF requirements and have started following international KYC norms. To hide the identity of account holders, now consultants are advising their clients not to directly hold bank accounts in tax havens. So, now customers are opening a bunch of shell companies in a chain, that is, one shell company is held by another, which is again held by another. Accounts are opened by shell companies down in the chain. Most tax havens do not maintain any registry of beneficial owners.

Shell companies that operate out of a mailbox are called mailbox companies. Companies have to give some address of business to the registry at the time of incorporation. Mailbox companies give the mailbox number as the address of business. This further enhances privacy and secrecy.

Foundations and trusts are more popular than companies when it comes to protecting wealth. A trust has no owner since it is not a legal entity. It is merely a legal arrangement (like a contract). A typical trust is a three-way arrangement. The original owner (the 'settlor') transfers his wealth into a trust and asks a 'trustee' (or trustees) to manage the wealth, for the benefit of 'beneficiaries'. The beneficiaries are usually family members of the settlor. Genuine trusts help a person plan inheritance and manage his estate, but trust structures have a high scope of misuse. Trusts run in tax havens are often misused for hiding illicit gains.

Trusts are prone to misuse because they turn personal wealth into ownerless assets. From a legal perspective, the settlor no longer owns the assets. He has transferred the assets into a trust. The beneficiaries don't own the assets either. They benefit from the trust, but they do not own it. The trustees are required to manage the assets under precise instructions of the settlor. Hence, the trustees do not own the assets. Then who owns the asset?

No one. Trusts convert assets with clear ownership into ownerless assets. According to Andres Knobel of TJN: 'Trusts slice and dice up the concept of "ownership" into different rights and duties. The settlor has rights to give instructions on the management and future ownership of assets, the trustee has rights to hold and manage those assets under the trust instructions, and beneficiaries have the right to obtain distributions from the trust or otherwise enjoy trust assets, but only under trust instructions or the discretion of the trustee.'[12]

This feature is oft misused by fugitives. A person who has defaulted on loans and is on the run from creditors can use trusts to legally transfer ownership of their wealth. Creditors cannot recover their money from the trust as the fugitive is no longer the owner.

Criminals and terrorists also find the trust structure convenient. Law enforcement agencies often try to freeze assets owned by criminals and their family members, but they cannot touch assets legally not owned by the criminal. In fact, trusts introduce so many veils in ownership that law enforcers and creditors would not even be aware of the nexus between the settlor and the trust's assets.

After Nirav Modi and members of his family were declared as economic fugitives for fleeing the country after allegedly duping PNB, the ED requested Singapore to freeze ₹44 crore kept in a bank account in Singapore owned by Maiank Mehta and Purvi Modi (brother-in-law and sister, respectively, of Modi). The Singapore High Court froze the bank accounts in July 2019, after conducting a fair hearing. This action took place in less than one-and-a-half years of the fraud being detected. Compare this with the offshore assets of Robert Allen Stanford, former financier and sponsor of professional sports-turned-financial fraudster. Stanford was arrested in June 2009 for running a $7 billion ponzi scheme and was sentenced to 110 years in jail. He had created a Cook Islands trust called the 'Baby Mama Trust', whose beneficiary is a mistress with whom he had two children. The trust owns funds kept in Swiss and Isle of Man accounts. A court in the US issued an order for the forfeiture of this asset to give back to the ponzi scheme's victims. It has been more than 10 years, but the assets under the trust's management have still not been recovered.[13]

In fact, Cook Islands is famous for its robust asset protection trusts. The island disregards foreign court orders, even US court orders. Creditors of persons who have established trusts in the Islands have filed lawsuits in the island multiple times and lost. So, there is a trove of case laws that can be quoted in a new lawsuit to strike it down.

Knobel noted that trusts 'manipulate ownership rights so that individuals can control and enjoy trust assets while legally distancing themselves far enough from them, so that the assets cannot be reached or even known about by creditors, tax authorities, law enforcement, or public scrutiny... These legal barriers can become impenetrable secrecy barriers shielding those people who enjoy and control the assets from scrutiny.'[14]

Foundations perform functions similar to trusts but there are key differences between them. A foundation is a legal entity upon registration. It can, therefore, open bank accounts. It can enter into agreements or contracts and can legally undertake business activity. The founder of a foundation (akin to the 'settlor' of a trust) transfers his assets to the foundation for a specific purpose. The assets are managed by a council (akin to the 'trustees' of a trust) in favour of specified beneficiaries.

Since differences between trusts and foundations are minor, foundations are also susceptible to misuse like trusts. If a person merely wants to park his/her wealth, trust is his instrument of choice. If the person wants to run a business activity without revealing his ownership, foundation is his instrument of choice.

Other than these standard packages to hide and ring-fence wealth, some tax havens offer innovative instruments to park funds anonymously. For instance, Seychelles offers the facility of bearer shares. Bearer shares are shares of a company, but do not mention the owner's name. Whoever produces the share certificates is the owner of these shares. All that a fugitive from law needs to do is park money under a company name and get its bearer shares. They can come back another time, produce the share certificates and take back their money. No questions asked, no names recorded.

While tax havens indulge a client with many options, the client needs assistance from intermediaries to park his/her funds safely. These intermediaries are usually hawala agents, accountants, lawyers and consultants. These professionals assist clients in hiding their wealth, knowing fully well that this is ill-gotten wealth, raised by evading taxes or, worse, money laundering. Hence, it is not surprising that some of these intermediaries also con their clients. Since the client is mostly a financial fraud or tax fraud, such intermediaries actually defraud frauds. They generally run 'hot air business' scams, in which they promise confidentiality and good returns to clients and then con them. They naturally lie higher than others in the food chain of frauds.

Some experts speculate that Hasan Ali Khan, who is touted to be the biggest hawala dealer and tax evader of our times, may actually be a con artist running a hot air business.

The Hasan Ali Scam

The Hasan Ali Khan case hogged the limelight in India for over half a decade, primarily as it involved huge amounts of money parked in Swiss bank accounts, hawala transactions and, possibly, money laundering. He was the biggest individual tax defaulter of India for the FY 2008–09. At one point, a multi-disciplinary team of officers from the ED, IT department, Intelligence Bureau (IB), Mumbai police and the RBI were constituted to solve this case.

Genesis of the case can be traced to a Dubai-based informer named Mohammed Hussein. Hussein owned a jewellery showroom in Dubai, from which Hasan Ali and his associate Kashinath Tapuriah bought jewellery worth ₹2 crore on credit. However, they never paid him and kept assuring him that they had a vast amount of money stuck in Swiss bank deposits and would pay him as soon as the money was released.[15] Aggrieved by the alleged duplicity of Ali, Hussein approached the investigation wing of Mumbai's Income Tax department in late 2006.

The IT department started a covert inquiry into Ali's business on receiving this tip-off. They found that Ali owned expensive apartments in the posh Koregaon Park in Pune and Pedder Road in Mumbai, apart from a fleet of luxury vehicles. However, he had not filed IT returns since 2001. Both Ali and his associate, Tapuriah, had been accused of cheating and forgery in the past. The IT department found six old cases of fraud against Ali in Hyderabad, of which two were registered in 1990–91 for defrauding the State Bank of Hyderabad and ANZ Grindlays Bank. Rest of the cases were filed by different individuals for cheating and forgery in 1994. Interestingly, their allegation was that Ali had collected about a crore rupees from them and promised them foreign bank securities, but later handed over fake foreign bank cheques to them.

Tapuriah married Chandrika Mundhra, daughter of Haridas Mundhra (who we spoke about earlier in this book) in the early 1950s, and was involved in the management of Mundhra's businesses. However, Mundhra's business ventures went through rough weather after his fraud against LIC was exposed. In the 1960s, he worked as a broker for MNCs looking for government contracts in India. In 1972, he was accused of involvement in siphoning off funds of a company that was earlier acquired by Mundhra.

The sleuths investigating this case must have realised that while both Ali and Tapuriah had chequered backgrounds, Tapuriah had managed big business at some point but Ali had not. Ali positioned himself variously as a scrap dealer and stud farm owner, businesses that do not yield large revenues.

IT sleuths mounted a raid on the residences of Ali and Tapuriah on 5 January 2007. They seized ₹90 lakh cash and jewellery worth ₹10 lakh from Ali's residences. The real discovery, though, during this raid was a laptop belonging to one Philip Anandraj from Ali's residence and two pen drives from under Tapuriah's bed.

Anandraj, it appears, was another victim of Ali like Hussein. India-born Anandraj had settled in Switzerland and ran a chain of pubs. He had been declared bankrupt in 2004. According to his version, he had come to India to recover $500,000 that he had loaned to Ali. He was staying at Ali's residence, hoping to recover his money. IT sleuths recovered scanned documents of bank accounts in Ali's name from Anandraj's laptop. On being queried, Anandraj explained that Ali had given him these documents as proof of his wealth.

The laptop contained details of many bank accounts in Ali's name maintained with UBS Bank, Switzerland. An Indian businessman maintaining Swiss bank accounts is nothing to be surprised about, but what popped the balls out of the sleuths' eyes was a communication from UBS to Ali that said:

> UBS Ltd, hereby confirms, that as per telephonic discussions between our client Mr Khan (Hasan Ali Khan) and the Chairman's office today, UBS Ltd has agreed to the following: The client can withdraw a part of his assets deposited with UBS Ltd, to the tune of $6 billion of the total deposited $8,000,453,000. The client is free to invest this amount as and when he chooses to do so. The balance of $2,000,453,000 will remain bound with the UBS Ltd until 15 January 2007, after which the client may again freely pursue any mode of investment or deposit...[16]

Hasan Ali Khan had a bank balance of US $8 billion, which translates into ₹36,000 crores. Such wealth of a single person stashed in a Swiss bank account was unheard of. This made him a household name in India, overnight.

The pen drives recovered from Tapuriah contained details of numerous transactions of Ali's Swiss bank accounts with accounts of Tapuriah and his wife Chandrika in offshore bank accounts. For instance, one document contains instructions from Ali to the UBS for transferring $1.695 billion from his account number 206-794.786 to a Swiss account of Chandrika on 6 January 2006. Another document is a communication from the UBS to Ali, informing him that the balance in his bank account number ZA1-A1A was $976 million on 28 February 1999.[17]

The IT department went on to raise a tax demand of ₹34,000 crore on Ali on the basis of incriminating evidence gathered during the search. The ED started a parallel case of money laundering immediately after the IT raid was concluded. The ED's principal ground for launching a money laundering case was that Ali did not have any reasonable business source to explain such a high quantum of wealth. They alleged that Ali had laundered proceeds of crime (since he did not have any big business to justify the wealth) and placed them in Swiss banks using the hawala route.

Experts, laymen, media, card players, gossipers and other kinds of Indians discussed many theories on what could be the source of Ali's wealth. The most circulated theory was that Ali was a *benamidar* (name lender) of some powerful Indian politicians. Yet, others branded him as a banker keeping black money of his clients safe in Switzerland. One recovered document showed that international arms dealer, Adnan Khashoggi, had helped him open a bank account in Switzerland. This led to a theory that he was a front for Khashoggi and it were the clandestine arms deals that helped him make such huge amount of wealth.

Courts can write letters to foreign courts requesting some sort of judicial assistance. Such letters are called Letter Rogatory (LR). Immediately after registering a money laundering case, the ED managed to get a LR request from an Indian court served to a court in Switzerland, requesting it for details of the bank accounts. The IT sleuths mounted the raid on 5 January 2007, and the Swiss authorities informed the Indian embassy in Berne 10 days later, on 15 January, that the documents of Hasan Ali Khan shared with them appeared to be forged. However, they did not give any further information, on grounds that the ED had to first give evidence of the predicate offence.

Months later, UBS sent an internal investigation report and an external audit review by Deloitte to the ED in November 2007. The Deloitte report identified only three accounts that Ali had with UBS Switzerland. All three accounts were opened on 30 July 2001. Of these three, two accounts were in Ali's name and one was in his wife's name. All the three accounts were closed in October 2001. The two accounts in Ali's name had not recorded even a single transaction! The account in his wife's name bore the number 206-794.786. This account had just two transactions: a cash deposit of $61,031 on 15 August 2001 and an immediate transfer of $60,700 on the same day to a third party in the UAE.

UBS claimed in its report that this particular transaction was a fraud transaction. It opined: 'We believe (Hasan Ali) Khan had been in negotiations to purchase a property in Switzerland and had obtained approximately $60,000 from the vendors–though we now assume this to have been a kind of advance fee fraud transaction... The money was deposited into the account and immediately wired out so that the owners of the property could not recover the sums. The owners subsequently contacted UBS in an attempt to recover the funds and only at this point did UBS become aware of the suspect nature of this transaction.'

UBS clarified that there was no other transaction in this account. None of the high value transfers instructions to Kashinath or Chandrika or other beneficiaries, which were recovered from Tapuriah's pen drives, actually took place. UBS closed the three accounts opened in July 2001, within months because it suspected that Ali was committing a fraud.

The account number ZA1-A1A, referred to in some of the documents seized during the raid, did not even exist. UBS concluded:

> We remain convinced that Hasan Ali Khan targeted UBS for the purpose of practicing fraudulent activities on unsuspecting persons. Our investigations show that UBS wanted to do nothing with Mr Khan and on many occasions rejected his requests to open accounts. He was ultimately able to open some accounts, we did identify this and the accounts were quickly closed.[18]

Further investigation revealed many other details of Ali's fraudulent activities. For instance, the Mumbai police found that he maintained multiple passports, but the great riches stashed in Swiss bank accounts remained elusive. A multi-disciplinary team of officers comprising the ED, the IT department, the IB, the Mumbai police and the RBI was formed in 2010 to thoroughly investigate the case. He was jailed in 2012 and served jail time of four years before being released in 2015.

The IT department had raised a demand of ₹34,000 crore on Ali, of which the tax tribunal confirmed ₹3 crore in 2016 and remanded back the rest to the tax department for reconsideration. The tribunal discussed the evidentiary value of UBS internal investigation report and Deloitte's audit report at length and admitted them as additional evidence.[19]

So, what could be the true story of Hasan Ali Khan? Since we will never know the whole truth, we can but speculate. One theory is that UBS Switzerland was in cahoots with Ali and lied about his bank balance. It helped Ali by forging his bank account statements. Deloitte reviewed the forged bank account statements. Swiss banks can go to any extent to protect their clients' wealth from their national authorities and UBS is no different, but this is a highly improbable theory. The tax tribunal notes in its order that the tax department had parallelly confirmed bank balance of Ali through Foreign Tax Division of the Finance Ministry from Swiss government. The Swiss government had confirmed that the $8 billion balance in Ali's bank account was forged. Besides, the act of getting its accounts reviewed by Deloitte demonstrates UBS' intent of transparency.

A second, and more plausible, theory is that Ali had forged the documents to show that he is a big man with immense wealth. Such posture is often needed to defraud people. The first cases against Ali were bank fraud cases in 1990–91. This was followed by allegations of four individuals in Hyderabad that they were duped by Ali. Hussein was also allegedly duped by Ali. Anandraj came to India to recover the money he had loaned to Ali. These stray incidents of Ali's career indicate that he might have been a confidence man. Victims gained confidence in him due to his immense wealth and advanced money to him. He used the money to maintain a lavish lifestyle, which further increased his victims' confidence on his affluence. If this theory is true, then it means he got trapped in his own web of lies. His con was so convincing that the authorities investigated a small-time con artist like him with extraordinary vigour.

Shell Companies: The Layers Beneath

Shell companies originated primarily to abet and facilitate tax evasion. They act as vessels for converting black money into white money. In a typical scheme, black money is given to an agent in hard cash. The agent introduces cash in multiple bank accounts held under the name of multiple shell companies. These shell companies then send the funds to another group of shell companies. Shell companies in the second layer then send the funds to another group of shell companies in the same way. And so on and so forth. By doing this, the funds are layered.

The purpose of layering is to obscure the source of funds. When an investigator or an auditor tries to find the source of funds, she will be baffled by the layers through which the funds would have been rotated. It will take her months of effort to collect data from different bank branches and collate them to prove that the funds were originally deposited as cash.

It is this feature of shell companies that make them valuable resources for money laundering as well. Layering happens to be one of the three stages of laundering criminal money into legit money. Hence, shell companies can be (mis)used by drug smugglers, gold smugglers, flesh traders and terrorists. Income of these criminal elements is usually in the form of cash. It is called 'blood money', as the money is generated from proceeds of crime.

Although shell companies primarily serve evaders and launderers, they have significant utility for swindlers as well. Shell companies are handy in rotating funds and circular transactions. They can be used as fictitious vendors and contractors. Fraudulent managers and promoters siphon off funds from their company, using such fictitious vendors. Shells are useful for all seasons. Shell companies and the men who run them form a critical part of a conducive ecosystem for conducting frauds.

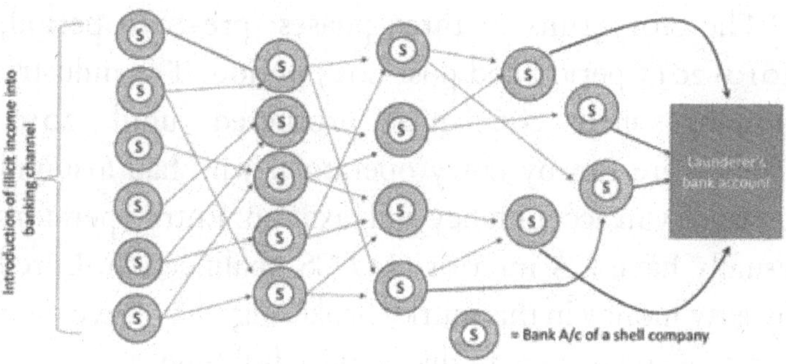

FIGURE 1: *Layers within Shell Companies*
Source: Author

Running shell companies used to be big business in India until a few years back, with major hubs in and around Chowringhee area in Kolkata, Kalbadevi in Mumbai and Patparganj in New Delhi. People who operate shell companies are called 'entry operators' because they provide accommodation entries to their clients' accounts. Accommodation entries are fictitious entries in a firm's books of account to accommodate its nefarious activities.

An entry operator used to operate 150–200 shell companies from a small office and launder hundreds of crores of rupees a year. Policymakers have taken note of the rampant laundering activities of these entry operators and have brought about specific anti-abuse provisions from time to time. A coordinated clampdown on shell companies by various law enforcement agencies has today brought this industry to ruins. However, the story of how this industry blossomed and provided accommodation entries for launderers and frauds is an exciting and interesting story. This story also helps us to understand why financial frauds were so rampant in India.

The story runs in three phases: pre-2010 period, 2010–2015 period and post-2015 period. The industry running shell companies prospered until 2010. They were run by entry operators, who had a sound pedagogy in accountancy and taxation. Entry operators usually have CA inter or CA/CS qualification. Lured by easy money in this murky brokering, they leave their practice and engage in this activity full time.

Entry operators offering accommodation entry services (a jargon for providing expert help in fudging accounts) had sprouted all over the country with a boom in economic activity after 1992. Over time, Kolkata became the biggest cluster of such shell companies. According to anecdotal narrations, rogue businessmen from all over the country would approach the Kolkata-based industry to get accommodation entries.

Why Kolkata? According to one theory, a vibrant Marwari community in Kolkata was the reason for the blossoming of this industry. The Marwari community has been active in Bengal for more than 400 years now. However, it is not a single community. It is a loose term for outsiders who were enterprising and maintained close business ties with extended family members. The greatest money lender during the time of Nawab Siraj-ud-Daulah was Murshidabad-based Jagat Seth. He was often referred to as 'banker of the world'. Roben Orme, official historian of the East India Company, had described him as the greatest shroff and banker of the world. Historians believe that he had conspired with Robert Clive to defeat Siraj-ud-Daulah in the battle of Plassey, which eventually resulted in the British rule over India.

Marwari migration to Kolkata increased perceptibly in the following centuries as Kolkata became the most important city of British India. In 1917, Kolkata was hit by the infamous Marwari *ghee* (clarified butter) scam. There were reports that certain *ghee* traders were adulterating the clarified butter with cow fat. This spread panic among the Brahmin community of Kolkata who had been using the *ghee* (Hinduism discourages consuming cow fat) and they lined up in Varanasi to purify themselves.

However, business deteriorated and stagnated in post-independence Kolkata. Many of the enterprising Marwari entrepreneurs moved out of Kolkata. Yet others dominated the CA profession. Some of them started *jama kharchi* (shell) companies to give accommodation entries to businessmen in their extended kin group. Since Marwari family networks span the entire country, they had a reach all over the country. Slowly, other entry operators moved to Kolkata and Kolkata became a specialised hub for this murky business.

Given the scale of operations in Kolkata, entry operators charged very competitive commission rates. They also benefited from the economies of scale. As a result, it was cheaper for a rogue businessman to convert black money in Kolkata than in Mumbai or Delhi.

The primary modus operandi that entry operators used was to route funds through balance sheets of various shell companies and introduce it into the balance sheet of their client. Say company Fraudwala Pvt. Ltd wants white capital of ₹100 crore but has only black money, it gives the money to the entry operator and promises a commission to him. The entry operator does three things. He introduces the cash in small amounts in many bank accounts, he consolidates the funds by RTGS transfer into a few bank accounts and he rotates the funds through many shell companies so that it is difficult to trace the source of the funds. Then the funds are infused into Fraudwala Pvt. Ltd as capital. This way, the black money comes back to Fraudwala Pvt. Ltd in white.

As business flourished, all kinds of customers landed in Kolkata. Customers started using this scheme for other purposes as well. Media has reported how the CBI has accused public servants of using shell companies to launder bribe money. Reports abound on how the CBI and the ED attached properties of shell companies on grounds that the properties have been purchased using bribe money. Nothing stops a launderer from using this scheme to launder other proceeds of crime. Customers can also use this scheme to commit bank frauds, as discussed in the chapter on bank frauds.

The most interesting feature of entry operators' syndicate was that it was happening in the open. It was apparently an open secret and anyone could travel to Kolkata to avail of the scheme. Naturally, income tax assessors declared capital infusion from shell companies as unaccounted income. Affected parties frequently challenged action of tax assessors in courts and even succeeded in stalling their effort due to lack of any conclusive evidence.

The wide prevalence of shell companies partly explains why accounting and bank frauds were so common in India until as late as the 2000s. A conducive ecosystem tempts not only the criminally minded person but also genuine entrepreneurs to take short cuts. In those days, if a genuine entrepreneur was not granted a loan due to low capital at her disposal, she could look for an entry operator to generate bogus capital. The entry operator was free to pitch her wares, all in the hope of a commission.

Shell companies had multi-purpose benefits. They were used by rogue brokers on the share market to do phantom trading, by artificially jacking up or pulling down the price of scrips. They were the easiest tools for siphoning off funds from a company. A manager could always pay for fictitious consultancy to a shell company from her employer's accounts and receive the money in cash from the entry operator. And when off-the-shelf shell companies were so readily available, entrepreneurs would naturally be tempted to commit frauds.

Organised clampdown on entry operators began in 2010, after shell companies were found to be misused in almost every major case of financial and tax fraud. A new section, Section 56 (2) (viia), was introduced in the Income Tax Act. The new law, which was just a paragraph long, brought down the entire industry in a matter of months.

The second phase in this history of shell companies started in mid-2010. The *jama kharchi* industry faced an existential crisis. It could never recover from the 2010 amendment blow. However, entry operators sprouted in a decentralised manner all over the country. This new breed of entry operators helped match parties. For instance, if a customer wanted to convert white money into black and another customer wanted to convert black money into white, the entry operator would bring the two together by matching their requirements. He would, of course, keep a fee for his services.

The entry operator kept a basket of shell companies at his disposal to be used for matching clients. Customer A would give a loan to the shell company in cheque. The shell company would give loan to Customer B in cheque. Customer B would give cash to the entry operator. The entry operator would give cash to Customer A.

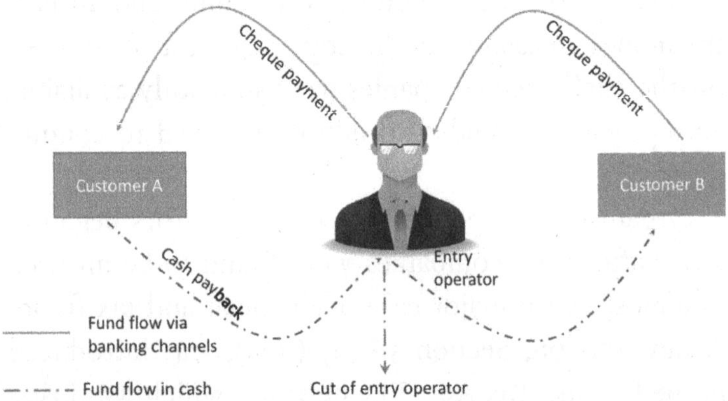

FIGURE 2: *Entry Operators' Modus Operandi for Customer Matching*

Source: Author

A new Companies Act was enacted in 2013, in the aftermath of the Satyam scandal. The SFIO had already highlighted how Raju had used a plethora of shell companies to fudge Satyam's accounts. The new Companies Act placed new restrictions on inter-corporate loans. It requires auditors to conduct an in-depth due diligence of inter-corporate deposits.

This brought further complications to the model. To avoid these requirements, entry operators started acquiring companies with an NBFC licence as NBFCs have an RBI authorisation to operate. The process to get an NBFC licence itself involves due diligence and verification by the RBI. So, entry operators found it easier to purchase an NBFC than incorporate one. After acquiring an NBFC, they freely used these firms to give accommodation entries. These NBFCs became the new highways through which money flowed from the formal economy to the parallel economy and vice versa.

This phase ended in 2015. Post-2015, various government agencies coordinated their attack on shell companies. Agencies under different ministries seemed to work in tandem with a vigour never seen before, to clamp down on shell companies. The MCA prepared a list of companies that do not have significant operations and struck off many of these companies. The MCA struck off as many as 2.25 lakh shell companies in the FY 2017–18 and another 2.25 lakh in FY 2018–19.

The SFIO conducted forensic audits and prepared a comprehensive list of shell companies. The Financial Intelligence Unit (FIU) used an analysis of bank accounts it had access to prepare a list of shell companies. The Income Tax department, too, prepared its own list. These agencies shared the lists of shell companies with each other and with other enforcement agencies. Based on lists shared with it, SEBI barred trading in shares of 331 suspected shell companies in August 2019.

To add insult to injury of entry operators, a stringent Benami Transactions (Prohibition) Act was introduced in 2015, which effectively termed shell companies as *benami* conduits. The post-2015 phase appears to be the swan song for shell companies.

EPILOGUE

I am writing this epilogue in the midst of a nationwide lockdown due to the COVID-19 pandemic. The pandemic presents new challenges for the world economy as a whole. Experts predict an economic slowdown, with the International Monetary Fund (IMF) saying this is the worst recession since the Great Depression and it is far worse than the global financial crisis of 2008. Crisis situations, somewhat similar to this, have been witness to many a serious fraud and it is likely that many will tumble out of the closet in the coming days.

While economic crises reveal some types of fraud, they catalyse other kinds of frauds. Pyramid schemes are especially attractive to the jobless youth and proliferate in times of slowdown. Slowdowns are characterised by low interest rates and low returns in equity markets. Therefore, ponzi schemes are often seen to burgeon in the aftermath of an economic crisis.

How do we then prepare for the next big fraud or how do we prevent these frauds from spreading like cancer in our economy? As has been demonstrated in each and every chapter of this book, serious frauds stick to a basic modus operandi that they have been following for years now. They cannot be completely stopped because they prey on areas where control does not exist.

Control and supervision in a system cannot be overdone, partly because control has its costs and partly because control slows down the system. Hence, control has to be optimised. It cannot be all encompassing. Systems that run on trust are the most efficient ones and produce maximum economic value. An ideal system runs without any control or supervision. It is based on trust. No cost is incurred on control. Neither is any time lost in checks and balances.

Hence, the most effective prevention strategy is to optimise control and expand control without letting the cost of control to escalate. The scope of control has definitely increased over the years and we are living in times when information technology has provided cheap solutions for expanding control. Neural networks and AI algorithms have managed to predict frauds from financial statements with reasonable accuracy. Financial institutions, corporate houses and government regulators should make extensive use of information technology in supervision and fraud prediction.

Effective deterrence also goes a long way in reducing the number and severity of frauds. India has invested significant diplomatic and legal resources in extradition of fugitive economic offenders cooling their heels in other countries. Extradition attempts are not always successful and the few successes come after protracted legal battles in foreign courts. However, such measures act as deterrence for others who harbour ill intentions for making a quick buck. Extradition efforts show that the government will keep chasing fraudsters their entire life and mete out justice.

International cooperation has gone a long way in clamping down on economic offenders. The Indian Prime Minister Narendra Modi called for joint action against fugitive economic offenders in the G20 summit in Buenos Aires in 2018. He offered a nine-point agenda to tackle economic offenders that included strong and active economic cooperation, cooperation in legal processes, extradition, exchange of information and stopping entry and safe haven to economic offenders.[1] He found strong support for his vision in the 2019 summit of the G20 group of countries in Osaka, Japan, from the host Shinzo Abe, the Japanese Prime Minister. In November 2019, Brazil, Russia, India, China and South Africa (BRICS) nations reaffirmed their commitment to denying safe haven to such fraudsters and economic offenders.

Clear laws and effective law enforcement are important for effective deterrence. However, law-making should be proactive, not reactive. Serious frauds often capture the imagination of the general public, which sways public opinion and that, in turn, pressurises lawmakers to make reactive laws. U.K. Sinha, former Chairman of the SEBI believes that internationally 'changes in the laws governing stock exchanges and share markets have been enacted only after major incidents of misconduct have taken place, and not pre-emptively or when these problems were still much smaller and more manageable'. Sinha argues that the US Securities and Exchange Commission (SEC) was set up only 'after numerous examples of misconduct were discovered during the Great Depression. Similarly, the 2001 crisis led to the Sarbanes-Oxley Act, and the 2008 crisis led to the Dodd-Frank Act. Many other countries followed suit and strengthened their laws governing the securities market after the crises.'[2]

However, reactive laws usually have unintended consequences. Many a time, such laws have an adverse impact on legitimate businesses. Some laws brought in response to serious frauds are so draconian that they throw the proverbial baby out with the bathwater.

In India, there are numerous law enforcement agencies for investigating frauds. While some agencies specialise in prosecution or asset recovery, others specialise in fraud detection. As a result, no one agency takes complete ownership of busting the scams. Some frauds manage to wriggle through the gaps in detection and enforcement. For instance, the Income Tax department investigates all kinds of financial frauds because frauds violate multiple provisions of tax laws, but they cannot take pre-emptive action when they detect a possible fraud. They can, however, report it to other agencies. SEBI can take pre-emptive action when the securities market is involved or when money is fraudulently raised from the public. EOW and CBI investigate bank frauds when the banks report possible frauds. The ED, on the other hand, can take action against money laundering, but ED's mandate is limited to enforcement of anti-money laundering laws. The SFIO takes up a case for investigation on receiving specific reference.

It is the same in other countries as well. Different financial regulators and law enforcing bodies have jurisdiction over different kinds of fraud. To solve this problem, international organisations such as the World Bank and Organisation for Economic Co-operation and Development (OECD) promote the 'whole-of-government approach (WGA)' to tackle financial crimes. The WGA advocates close coordination in work of tax and customs administrations, financial intelligence units, criminal law enforcement agencies, financial regulators and public prosecutors. At the moment, the Central Economic Intelligence Bureau (CEIB) plays the role of a coordinator for various agencies in India. However, joint investigations and coordinated actions, as envisaged by the WGA, have still not been institutionalised in India, as in most other countries. WGA is an idea that has merely germinated, but is yet to grow.

Another legion, probably of more importance than investigators, are the Chartered Accountants in Forensic Audit practice. Also referred to as Fraud Investigation and Dispute Services (FIDS), this unit works as the first line of defence against economic crimes. FIDS professionals are employed by companies and banks to detect embezzlement and fraud within their businesses. FIDS typically consists of six service areas: anti-bribery and corruption services, corporate intelligence services, digital forensics and e-discovery services, dispute advisory services, insolvency advisory and anti-money laundering services.

Leading the path of forensic audits in India are the Big 4 accounting firms. KPMG, for instance, started a forensic practice way back in 1985, in response to 'escalating white-collar crimes' at the time. Its stated goal is to help clients prevent, detect and mitigate the risk of fraud, misconduct and non-compliance. It also regularly shares insights on 'key industry concerns, trends as well as sector specific issues through whitepapers, surveys, point of view documents, events and articles'.[3] It releases two annual reports, namely India Fraud Survey report and the Anti-Money Laundering report.

Disruptive Technologies

Disruptive technologies disrupt conventional ways of doing business. They lead to new business models, which are either more efficient or provide better services. Developing control and supervision in any new business model takes time after the model is rolled out. New models also have hidden loopholes, which become apparent only after a fraud is committed. Hence, new business models based on disruptive technologies are always at a higher risk of being exposed to fraudulent activities than conventional models.

Innovations in the field of financial technology or fintech, that support or enable banking and financial services, are especially prone to fraudulent acts. As the technology is new, experts in the field of finance are often not aware of the issues that could crop up at the technological backend. The technology solution providers may have little knowledge and experience in the field of finance and this gives fraudsters an opportunity to exploit the fault lines that arise when technology weds finance.

Let us look at the co-location scam allegedly committed at the National Stock Exchange of India Limited (NSE). We have seen in the chapter on securities frauds how information asymmetry can be misused to manipulate markets. If I have price-sensitive information in my possession before everyone else in the market, I can use it to manipulate the market. Now, what if the information reaches my computer 0.001 seconds before it reaches my neighbour's computer (probably because I have a faster Wi-Fi network). Can I use it to manipulate the market? The time window available to me is so short that I cannot even blink in that time. I do not have the cognitive capacity to understand the information in a fraction of a second and take a decision. Interestingly, the mastermind of NSE co-location scam allegedly took advantage of information asymmetry of a fraction of a second arising out of a faster internet connection!

To understand the scam better, we need to understand a disruptive technology called algo-trading and the new stock trading model it pioneered. Traditionally, a trader in the stock market applies his mind and decides whether or not to buy or sell a stock. He then executes orders for buy or sell, as the case may be. Algo-trading automates this process. It is based on computer algorithms that assess whether the value of a stock will go up or down, based on various inputs, and executes orders without any human intervention. Algo-trading is not limited by cognitive and physical slowness of humans. Hence, algo-trading makes it possible to trade at fast speeds.

Algo-trading programmes are of many types. One type intends to take advantage of trends that are visible in small periods. Say the price of a stock on BSE shows an upward trend. Its price rises from time t to t + 1 second. The programme notes the upward trend. Then the price further increases at time t + 3 seconds. The programme predicts the price to rise further at time t + 5 seconds. The programme wants to take advantage of the price rise in these two seconds. So, it executes a buy order on the stock. Later, when the programme sees a downward trend at, say, t + 300 seconds, it immediately places a sell order. By doing this, it manages to buy at a low price and sell at the peak. Such programmes are called High Frequency Trading (HFT).

HFTs are characterised by complex algorithms, fast trades and very short-term investment horizons. HFTs' primary focus is on taking advantage of arbitrage that is possible on getting market information before others, even if the advantage is of only a fraction of a second. Hence, HFTs try to:

1. Get market trade data as fast as possible
2. Process the trade data and decide on a course of action at fastest possible speed
3. Execute trades at a high speed

For HFTs, time is money. Literally. They need fast internet connection and their computers need fast processing speed. To complicate matters, HFT programmes compete among themselves for making money. So, any HFT that has a marginally faster internet connection (say, the internet increases speed of data delivery by 0.001 seconds) has an edge over other HFT traders.

Now consider an HFT programme operating from a computer in Koramangala in Bengaluru. A second programme operates from a computer in Borivali in Mumbai. A third programme runs from Bandra, bang opposite the NSE office. Which of the three will first receive data that the exchange has just webcasted? The data will reach the three locations through fast optic fibres or satellite-based transponders. It will reach Bandra first, then Borivali and then Koramangala because the data will travel the least distance quickest. In their craze to get arbitrage of microseconds and picoseconds, most HFT traders are based around the NSE office. They install dedicated optic fibre networks to ensure that the data does not face any network logjam. The most optimal situation for them is when they can place their HFT programmes in the same location as the exchange's computer servers.

After HFTs started trading, the exchanges realised that they could rent out space in their building to these HFTs at premium because of their craze for saving microseconds and picoseconds. The phenomenon of stock exchanges renting out space in their office to HFT traders is called co-location.

In August 2015, SEBI got a pseudonymous complaint from someone called Ken Fong, alleging that NSE's co-location facilities were being misused for market manipulations. Fong claimed that NSE disseminated data on stock prices to traders using the Tick-by-Tick (TBT) data feed through Transmission Control Protocol/ Internet Protocol (TCP/IP). In this model of data dissemination, information is delivered one by one, unlike broadcast models in which 'everyone gets the price information at the same time (assuming they were at the same distance from the server). TBT data feed was disseminated sequentially'[4] on first-come-first-serve basis to the traders who logged into the server.

Hence, the first one to connect to the lowest load server got advantage in terms of receiving the data faster than others. NSE's servers were maintained by a company called Omnesys Technologies, in which NSE was a key shareholder. Fong alleged that employees of Omnesys and NSE's data centre were helping an HFT trader by the name of OPG Securities connect first and that too to the fastest servers. OPG got time arbitrage due to front running, which translated into profits for it in the market.

SEBI investigated the matter and found some merit in the allegations levied by Fong. It asked NSE to conduct a forensic investigation. NSE appointed Deloitte, one of the Big 4 audit firms, to conduct a detailed forensic analysis of its records. Deloitte submitted a report in December 2016, in which it observed that the TBT system architecture disseminated data to traders in a sequential manner. So, the trader who connected first to the server received ticks (market feed) before those who connected later. Hence, the system architecture was prone to manipulation.

Based on Deloitte's report, SEBI asked NSE to conduct a forensic audit to estimate the benefits/profits that traders got using this mechanism. NSE appointed EY, another Big 4 audit firm, this time. EY's report highlighted that some trading members were given preferential access to back-up servers at NSE. Back-up servers usually have lower load and are, therefore, faster. EY pointed out that the problem was not in the TBT architecture per se, but in the control mechanism. Traders were manually allocated to servers. Since the servers were not equally loaded, selective manual allocation of traders gave an unfair edge to preferred traders. Had NSE used a 'randomiser' to randomly allot traders to different servers, the system could not have been manipulated.

SEBI did not find any fault that would point towards NSE being involved in a scam, but it did penalise individual employees of NSE, Omnesys and OPG. The SEBI investigation showed how adoption of new technologies often leaves loopholes in the system and fraudsters can make the most of those loopholes. However, that is not necessarily a cause for concern. Fintech entrepreneurs should see fraud as a by-product of innovation and make conscious efforts to plug those. If loopholes are not plugged, frauds will happen. Hopefully whistle blowers like Ken Fong–most probably a pseudonym–will inform regulators about the frauds and those technology gaps will be plugged for good. Else, it may so happen that too many fraudsters will get involved in it, which will blow the cover.

Last Word

The purpose of this book is to raise an awareness about serious frauds, which are a threat to the economy, the society, and to you and me. The next major financial fraud may happen under your watch. Or you may already be a victim of an economic crime without even knowing about it. You will end up facing the brunt of law enforcement authorities. Hence, it is important for you, as a discerning citizen, to identify when you see a fraud and blow the whistle on it.

NOTES

PROLOGUE

1 Smith, Adams (1827) *The Wealth of Nations*, Book IV. New York NY: Bantam Classic.

2 Kelkar, V. and A. Shah (2019) *In Service of the Republic: The Art and Science of Economic Policy*, New Delhi: Penguin Allen Lane.

3 Reurink, A. (2016) 'Financial Fraud: A Literature Review', MPIfG Discussion Paper No. 16/5, Max Planck Institute for the Study of Societies, accessed on 6 May 2020 at: https://www.econstor.eu/bitstream/10419/141282/1/859161242.pdf

4 Reurink (2016), *supra*.

5 *Economist, The* (2020) 'Who's lost their trunks?' 18 April 2020 issue, p. 47.

6 Quoted in *The Economist* (2020), *supra*.

7 See Velikonja, U. (2013) 'The Cost of Securities Fraud', in *William and Mary Law Review* 54: 1887–1957.

8 *Economist, The* (2014) 'The Dozy Watchdogs'. 13 December 2014 issue, p. 24–26.

9 KPMG (2019) *Global Banking Fraud Survey*, May 2019, accessed on 6 May 2020 at: https://assets.kpmg/content/dam/kpmg/xx/pdf/2019/05/global-banking-fraud-survey.pdf

10 Frankel, T. (2012) *The Ponzi Scheme Puzzle: A History and Analysis of Con Artists and Victims*. New York: Oxford University Press.

11 Study cited in Reurink (2016), *supra*, p. 43.

12 Reurink (2016), *supra*, p. 79.

CHAPTER 1 THE PERFECT BANK HEIST: LOAN FRAUD

1 See the news report accessed online on 8 May 2020 at: https://www.businesstoday.in/current/corporate/vijay-mallya-london-mansion-golden-toilet/story/281231.html

2. As reported in *Economic Times* dated 21 December 2013, accessed on 17 October 2020 at: https://economictimes.indiatimes.com/industry/cons-products/liquor/karnataka-high-court-nixes-usl-share-sale-to-diageo/articleshow/27696559.cms?from=mdr
3 See the news report accessed online on 8 May 2020 at: https://www.businesstoday.in/current/corporate/vijay-mallya-london-mansion-golden-toilet/story/281231.html -offshore-accounts-116030900965_1.html
4 See news report accessed online on 8 May 2020 at: https://www.hindustantimes.com/business-news/npa-crisis-the-rise-and-fall-of-bhushan-steel-in-the-great-indian-debt-trap/story-GHrvRRFIBsMLXKJzbqvaFN.html
5 Mondal, D. (2019) 'How a web of shell companies helped Bhushan Steel promoters siphon off funds', accessed online on 8 May 2020 at: https://www.businesstoday.in/top-story/how-a-web-of-shell-companies-helped-bhushan-steel-promoters-siphon-off-funds/story/379460.html
6 For the sake of simplicity, all illustrations in this book will consider promoters' share at 30 per cent.
7 See, for example, reporting of *Livemint*, accessed on 8 May 2020 at: https://www.livemint.com/industry/banking/allahabad-bank-reports-rs-1-775-core-fraud-by-bhushan-power-steel-1563023976073.html
8 As reported by the *Mint*, accessed on 28 November 2019 at: https://www.livemint.com/industry/banking/surge-in-small-borrower-defaults-stokes-worries-11574789632515.html
9 See Walsh, J.P. and S. Nagaoka (2009) 'Who Invents?: Evidence from the Japan-US Inventor Survey', RIETI Discussion Paper, accessed on 13 November 2019 at: https://www.rieti.go.jp/jp/publications/dp/09e034.pdf
10 The software is worthless because the software is a dummy purchased from the 'conduit'. The conduit gives a dummy software asset and gets the entire capital. It then pays the capital back to the promoter.
11 Accessed on 15 November 2019: https://www2.deloitte.com/content/dam/Deloitte/in/Documents/finance/in-finance-DeloitteIndiaBankingFraudSurveyIII-noexp.pdf
12 As per credit rating agency ICRA, quoted in a news report in reuters. Accessed on 1 December 2019 at: https://

in.reuters.com/article/uk-india-autos-financing-insight/how-a-shadow-banking-crisis-sent-indias-autos-sector-into-a-tailspin-idINKCN1UU04W

13 Pai, T.V.M. (2019) 'NBFC crisis and its domino effect on Indian economy', accessed on 1 December 2019 at: https://www.businesstoday.in/opinion/columns/nbfc-crisis-domino-effect-on-indian-economy-ilfs-scam-gdp-growth/story/378109.html

14 Pai (2019), *supra.*

15 Pai (2019), *supra.*

16 As reported by *Financial Express* (2019), 'IL and FS Scam: Deals involving third party firms under scanner', accessed on 1 December 2019 at: https://www.financialexpress.com/industry/ilfs-scam-deals-involving-third-party-firms-under-scanner/1619140/

17 *Financial Express* (2019), *supra.*

18 See, for example, report of Livemint. (2019) titled 'Govt alleges 22 audit violations by Deloitte, KPMG arm in IL and FS fraud case', accessed on 9 May 2020 at: https://www.livemint.com/news/india/govt-alleges-22-audit-violations-by-deloitte-kpmg-arm-in-il-fs-fraud-case-1560436617469.html

19 Extracted from Criminal Complaint No. 20/2019 in the court of Addl Sessions Judge -cum- Special Judge (Companies Act) at Greater Mumbai, accessed on 1 December 2019 at: https://taxguru.in/wp-content/uploads/2019/06/ILFS-Charge-Sheet.pdf

20 Surendar, T. (2019) 'Satyam better managed than IL and FS: Vineet Nayyar', Fortune India, accessed on 1 December 2019 at: https://www.fortuneindia.com/enterprise/satyam-better-managed-that-ilfs-vineet-nayyar/103615

21 Extracted from Criminal Complaint No. 20/2019 in the court of Addl Sessions Judge -cum- Special Judge (Companies Act) at Greater Mumbai, *supra.*

22 The author has no access to the confidential investigation report of SFIO. Email extracts are sourced from a news report by *Outlook India* (2019) 'How devious IL and FS management bulldozed pliable rating agencies' *(IANS Exclusive)*, accessed on 9 May 2020 at: https://www.outlookindia.com/newsscroll/how-devious-ilampfs-management-bulldozed-pliable-rating-agencies-ians-exclusive/1567666

23 *Outlook India* (2019) 'How devious IL and FS management bulldozed pliable rating agencies' *(IANS Exclusive)*, ibid.

24 Gautam, P.S. (2019) 'A critical analysis of insolvency and bankruptcy reforms in India', dissertation submitted to The University of Manchester for the degree of MSc. International Development: Public Policy and Management.

25 Gautam (2019) *supra.*

26 Gautam (2019) *supra.*

27 In an answer to the Rajya Sabha, MoS Shiv Pratap Shukla revealed that 13,949 bank officials from 60 public and private banks were penalized for fraud between 2015 and 2017. A report of *Business Today* in this regard was accessed on 9 May 2020 at: https://www.businesstoday.in/sectors/banks/sbi-took-action-against-1287-officials-over-fraud-in-past-three-years/story/301649.html

28 Reported in *Economic Times* (11 July 2019). 'Bhushan Steel turns into a case bigger than anything Indian courts have ever seen.' accessed on 21 November 2019 at: https://economictimes.indiatimes.com/industry/indl-goods/svs/steel/bhushan-steel-case-70k-page-chargesheet-presents-a-mammoth-challenge-for-court/articleshow/70151597.cms

29 A news report cites a government source that Liberia or Albania may be the most probable refuge of Sandesara brothers. The news report, 'With kin's detention, ED likely to insist on exact address of Sandesara brothers' (*Economic Times*, 25 March 2019) was accessed on 28 November 2019 at: https://economictimes.indiatimes.com/news/politics-and-nation/with-kins-detention-ed-likely-to-insist-on-exact-address-of-sandesara-brothers/articleshow/68555066.cms?from=mdr

30 Yadav, R. (2019) 'PMC case shows why dual regulation doesn't work', the *Mint*, accessed on 5 December 2019 at: https://www.livemint.com/money/personal-finance/pmc-case-shows-why-dual-regulation-doesn-t-work-11575398109144.html

CHAPTER 2 TAKING STOCK: SECURITIES FRAUD

1 Neelakantan, M.S. (2017) 'Remembering Feroze, the forgotten Gandhi', *Deccan Chronicle*, 6 February 2017, accessed on 9 May 2020 at: https://www.deccanchronicle.com/lifestyle/books-and-art/060217/remembering-feroze-the-forgotten-gandhi.html

2 Shashi Bhushan, M.P. (1977) *Feroze Gandhi: A political Biography*. New Delhi: Progressive People's Sector Publications. Pg.75.

3 Guha, R. (2007) *India After Gandhi: The History Of The World's Largest Democracy*, New Delhi: Picador India.

4 Remark made in a Wikipedia page, accessed on 7 December 2019 at: https://en.wikipedia.org/wiki/Haridas_Mundhra

5 See RBI (1970) 'The Bank and the Mundhra' *Affair*, in *History of the Reserve Bank of India, Vol II*, accessed on 7 December 2019 at: https://rbidocs.rbi.org.in/rdocs/content/PDFs/90045.pdf

6 RBI (1970), *supra*.

7 RBI (1970), *supra*.

8 See RBI (1970), p. 800. Also see Desai, A.H. (1959) 'Afterthoughts on the Mundhra Affairs', the *Economic Weekly*, Special Number July 1959, accessed on 8 December 2019 at: https://www.epw.in/system/files/pdf/1959_11/28-29-30/afterthoughts_on_the_mundhra_affair.pdf

9 See p. 21 in Roy, T. (2016) 'Transfer of Economic Power in Corporate Calcutta 1950-1970', Economic History Working Paper No. 230/2016, LSE, accessed on 8 December 2019 at: http://www.lse.ac.uk/Economic-History/Assets/Documents/WorkingPapers/Economic-History/2016/WP230.pdf

10 From the Bombay High Court's ruling in the case of *Haridas Mundhra And Ors.* dated 21 October 1969, it appears that Mundhra was sentenced to imprisonment from 17 January 1961 to 1 June 1963. The ruling was accessed on 8 December 2019 at: https://indiankanoon.org/doc/1035987/?type=print

11 As per a report published in *India Today* on 31 March 1983, J. Dharma Teja was the second largest individual tax defaulter after Haridas Mundhra. See Mitra, S. (1983) 'Jayanti Dharma Teja: An unheralded comeback', *India Today*, accessed on 10 December 2019 at: https://www.indiatoday.in/magazine/special-report/story/19830331-jayanti-dharma-teja-an-unheralded-comeback-770561-2013-07-24

12 In response to a question in Rajya Sabha in March 1970, the minister of state for finance revealed to the Rajya Sabha that all known assets of Haridas Mundhra, both movable and immovable, have been attached by the income tax department for tax recovery purpose. Transcript of the speech was accessed on 9 December 2019 at: http://rsdebate.nic.in/rsdebate56/

bitstream/123456789/489962/2/IQ_71_17031970_S469_p30_p31.pdf

13. As reported in *Times of India* dated 10 March 2011, accessed on 17 October 2020 at: https://timesofindia.indiatimes.com/india/Tax-demand-on-Hasan-Ali-and-associates-pegged-at-Rs-71845-crore/articleshow/7667407.cms

14. As reported in a news article in *DNA India*, accessed on 17 October 2020 at:https://www.dnaindia.com/business/report-top-100-tax-defaulters-owe-rs-14-lakh-crore-1279773; Also see, Outlook dated 16 December 2011, accessed on 17 October 2020 at: https://www.outlookindia.com/newswire/story/govt-has-tax-demand-of-rs-196-lakh-cr-cag/744660

15 In *Re: MOH Ltd*, SEBI Order dated 18 May 2007.

16 See Parekh, S. (2018) *Fraud, Manipulation and Insider Trading in the Indian Securities Markets*, 55, Gurugram: Wolters Kluwer India.

17 Parekh (2018), *supra*. p. 56.

18 Observations of Securities Appellate Tribunal (SAT) in ruling in the case of *E. Sudhir Reddy v SEBI*, Appeal No. 138 of 2011, 16 December 2011.

19 Gadgil, M. and Menon, M.K. (2017) 'Dilip Pendse's unlikely journey', *Mumbai Mirror*, accessed on 13 December 2019 at: https://mumbaimirror.indiatimes.com/others/sunday-read/dilip-pendses-unlikely-journey/articleshow/59614923.cms

20 Gadgil and Menon (2017), *supra*.

21 Gadgil and Menon (2017), *supra*.

22 K-10 are a group of stocks of new economy companies that star speculator Ketan Parekh invested in.

23 A jargon used in the finance domain for losses.

24 *Re: Shri D.S. Pendse And Ors*.; SAT judgment dated 11 January 2008.

25 *Re: Shri D.S. Pendse And Ors.;* SAT judgment dated 11 January 2008.

26 News reported in *Business Standard*, accessed on 11 December 2019 at: https://www.business-standard.com/article/markets/sebi-discards-insider-trading-case-against-ex-tata-finance-md-dilip-pendse-117072801259_1.html

27 Khanna, S. (2017) 'The Tragedy of Dilip Pendse's Malfeasance', accessed on 11 December 2019 at: https://www.livemint.

com/Companies/TavQfafenFaCshqavT73XL/The-tragedy-of-Dilip-Pendses-malfeasance.html

28 SEBI Adjudication Order No. Order/BD/NR/2020-21/7591-7592, accessed on 10 May 2020 at: https://www.sebi.gov.in/enforcement/orders/apr-2020/adjudication-order-in-respect-of-neeraj-kumar-agarwal-and-shruti-vishal-vora-in-the-matter-of-circulation-of-upsi-through-whatsapp-messages-in-the-scrip-of-ambuja-cements-ltd-_46613.html

29 H. R. Rep. No. 1383/11, quoted in Parekh (2018), p. 25.

30 At its core, manipulation is also a case of information asymmetry. The person manipulating the stock market does not reveal the manipulation to others. Other traders in the stock market are not aware of the manipulation, and fall into the manipulator's trap.

31 As per Black's Law Dictionary, quoted in Parekh (2018).

32 *MoneyLife* (2017) 'Obvious Penny stocks manipulation that SEBI can't seem to pin down', 9 August 2017, accessed on 14 December 2019 at: https://www.moneylife.in/article/obvious-penny-stocks-manipulation-that-sebi-cant-seem-to-pin-down/51309.html

33 Bhadra, S. and P. Khan (2014) *RED HANDED: 20 Criminal Cases That Shook India*, New Delhi: Rupa Publications.

34 As per news reported in *The Telegraph* and extracted on 16 December 2019 at: https://www.telegraphindia.com/india/mystery-deaths-in-scandals/cid/1667829

35 Menon, S. and M. Vyas (2016) 'The Harshad Mehta case: Where time has overtaken justice by a mile', accessed on 16 December 2019 at: https://economictimes.indiatimes.com/news/politics-and-nation/the-harshad-mehta-case-where-time-has-overtaken-justice-by-a-mile/articleshow/53052771.cms

36 Value of shares held in benami names was ₹453 crore as on June 1995, as mentioned in a court submission. See Menon and Vyas (2016), *supra*.

37 Pramod Kumar Manocha vs Central Bureau of Investigation, Appeal No. 1117 of 1999, judgment of the Supreme Court dated 14 January 2003. Justice Pasayat quotes another decision of the Supreme Court when making this observation, viz. State of Gujarat vs Mohanlal Jitamalji Porwal and Anr. [Jt 1987(1) SC 783], Para. 84.

39 Thomas, P.J. (1948) 'Report on the Regulation of The Stock Market in India', accessed on 16 December 2019 at: https://www.sebi.gov.in/sebi_data/commondocs/may-2019/HistoryReport1948_p.pdf

39 The National Planning Committee on Industrial Finance (1948) headed by Pandit Jawaharlal Nehru had observed that the share market is 'the most respectable institution offering open facilities for daylight gambling. We cannot trust such social sores to find the necessary finance for an expanding industrialisation. If a sound system of industrial financing is to come in to being, if our national economy is to be forever rid of this most dangerous plague spot, if the available surplus for investment is to be instantaneously mobilised and scientifically reinvested, the most urgent task before the Indian Planning authority is to reorganise fundamentally the structure and working of these honourable asylums for gamblers, parasites and incurable reactionaries - called the stock exchanges or share bazars.' Quoted in Puranik, A. (1991) 'The role of stock exchange(s) in financing the private corporate sector and investment activity in India', Working Paper No. 016, Institute for Studies in Industrial Development, accessed on 10 May 2020 at: http://isid.org.in/pdf/stex.PDF. Puranik observes that: 'In brief, this can be stated that due to general distrust by the public of private business and closed circle character of industrial entrepreneurship, the role of new issues and stock exchanges remained on the periphery of private corporate sector financing and with the absence of any meaningful role in industrial financing, the functioning and structure of the institution of stock exchange became speculative activity oriented serving little the saving and investment activity of community.'

40 N. Narayanan vs Adjudicating Officer, SEBI (decision dated 26 April 2013 – MANU/SC/0426/2013).

41 N. Narayanan vs Adjudicating Officer, SEBI, *supra*.

42 Low float means the number of shares readily available for trading in the stock market is low. It is easier to manipulate prices of stocks with low float.

43 Joshi runs the popular fraud awareness website https://indiaforensic.com.

44 Joshi, M. (2017) *Stock Market and Accounting Frauds*, Kindle: Riskpro Publication.

45 Para. 2.4.2 in SEBI order No. WTM/SR/SEBI/ISD/18/03/2017.

46 Silverman, E. (2016) 'Former FDA official charged with securities fraud for tipping off hedge fund', 15 June 2016, STAT, accessed on 10 May 2020 at: https://www.statnews.com/pharmalot/2016/06/15/former-fda-official-securities-fraud/

47 As per a news report in *Daily Mail*, accessed on 3 January 2020 at: https://www.dailymail.co.uk/news/article-3652510/Hedge-fund-Visiums-Valvani-dead-apparent-suicide-police.html

48 See Levy, R. (2016) Behind the life and death of a star money manager accused of insider trading, accessed on 3 January 2020 at: https://www.businessinsider.in/finance/behind-the-life-and-death-of-a-star-money-manager-accused-of-insider-trading/articleshow/54588425.cms

49 See Levy (2016), *supra*.

CHAPTER 3 HUSTLERS OF HIGH SEAS: EXIM FRAUD

1 Although the chargesheets filed by ED and CBI are not in the public domain, they are discussed in detail in the report of John Carney (2018), examiner appointed by the US Bankruptcy Court, Southern District of New York, accessed on 12 January 2020 at: http://omnimgt.com/CMSVol2/pub_47243/686797_394.pdf

2 FATF report accessed on 12 January 2020 at: http://www.fatf-gafi.org/media/fatf/documents/reports/ML-TF-through-trade-in-diamonds.pdf

3 p. 27, Carney (2018), *supra*.

4 Lall, P.C. (2019) *Flawed*, New Delhi: Hachette India. p. 149

5 As per a news report accessed on 15 January 2020 at: https://economictimes.indiatimes.com/news/politics-and-nation/cbi-registers-da-case-against-retired-pnb-official-accused-in-nirav-modi-case/articleshow/66653251.cms?from=mdr

6 Carney (2018), *supra*.

7 Carney (2018), *supra*.

8 p. 73, Carney (2018), *supra*.

9 p. 73, Carney (2018), *supra*.

10 See, for example, Chaki, D. (2020) '"Pudiya Ghumao": How the diamond industry uses bogus trading to inflate balance' sheets accessed on 15 January 2020 at: https://www.livemint.com/Companies/qK6xxGDhJusoZiAGfVyWDK/Pudiya-Ghumao-How-the-diamond-industry-uses-bogus-trading.html

11 See the *Business Today* feature accessed on 15 January 2020 at: https://www.businesstoday.in/current/corporate/pnb-scam-bank-fraud-diamond-traders-nirav-modi-mehul-choksi/story/271807.html

12 Sarma, N. (2019) 'What will happen to Chinese steel after Trump tariff?' ORF, accessed on 18 January 2020 at: https://www.orfonline.org/expert-speak/what-will-happen-to-chinese-steel-after-trump-tariff-54842/

13 Interview of Pahuja to SMEFutures, accessed on 19 January 2020 at: https://smefutures.com/stainless-steel-industry-expecting-trade-remedial-measures/

14 Report in *Business Standard* titled 'Overseas stainless steel exporters, local importers misusing ASEAN-India FTA: ISSDA', accessed on 18 January 2020 at: https://www.business-standard.com/article/pti-stories/overseas-stainless-steel-exporters-local-importers-misusing-asean-india-fta-issda-119020501242_1.html

15 Report No. 145 of the Rajya Sabha, accessed on 19 January 2020 at: http://164.100.47.5/committee_web/ReportFile/13/97/145_2018_7_13.pdf

16 145th Report of the Rajya Sabha, *supra*.

17 As reported in RIS Policy Brief No. 66, February 2015, accessed on 19 January 2020 at: https://www.ris.org.in/sites/default/files/RIS%20Policy%20Brief-66.pdf

18 145th Report of the Rajya Sabha, *supra*.

19 Taillard, M. (2012) *Economics and Modern Warfare: The Invisible Fist of the Market*, New York, NY: Palgrave Macmillan, p. 15.

20 See press release of PIB dated 9 May 2018, accessed on 19 January 2020 at: https://pib.gov.in/newsite/PrintRelease.aspx?relid=179195

21 As per press release of Department of Revenue dated 20 November 2019, accessed on 19 January 2020 at: https://commerce.gov.in/PressRelease.aspx?Id=6739

22 Sud, Juhi Dion (2016) 'Circumvention of Anti-Dumping Measures: Law and Practice of India', 11 *Global Trade and Customs Journal*, Issue 11/12, pp. 508–514.

23 See Ram, J.R. (2018) Anti-circumvention investigation concerning Glass Fibre: Resolving inconsistencies in practice and interpretation', *International Trade Amicus*, issue 86, August 2018, accessed on 21 January 2020 at: https://www.lakshmisri.com/insights/articles/anti-circumvention-investigation-concerning-glass-fibre-resolving-inconsistencies-in-practice-and-interpretation/

24 Para. 5.50 of report no. 145 of Rajya Sabha, *supra*.

25 As claimed by the domestic industry to the Parliamentary Standing Committee on Commerce. See Para. 5.50 of report no .145 of Rajya Sabha, *supra*.

26 Thul, P.C. (2019) 'U.S. fines firms transhipping via Cambodia to dodge Trump's China tariffs', report accessed on 19 January 2020 at: https://www.reuters.com/article/usa-trade-china-cambodia/u-s-fines-firms-transhipping-via-cambodia-to-dodge-trumps-china-tariffs-idUSL4N23Q0XU

27 As per a Bloomberg news report, accessed on 26 January 2020 at: https://www.business-standard.com/article/international/vietnam-cracks-down-on-exporters-using-them-to-bypass-higher-us-tariffs-119112100602_1.html

28 Conway, P. (2018) 'How transshipment may undercut Trump's tariffs', *The Conversation*, accessed on 26 January 2020 at: https://theconversation.com/how-transshipment-may-undercut-trumps-tariffs-95487

29 See news report in *Financial Express* dated 25 September 2019, accessed on 26 January 2020 at: https://www.financialexpress.com/economy/rs-1000-crore-fraud-fake-gst-invoice-racket-unearthed-in-kandla/1716514/

30 See judgment of High Court of Delhi in the case of *Innovative Cargo Services v Commissioner of Customs (General)*, MANU/DE/1464/2017.

31 Khan, A. (2016) 'Rags bring riches in export subsidy scam', 15 June 2016, *India Today*.

32 Khan, A. (2016), *supra*.

33 Prasad, G.C. (2020) All GST refund claims on products with imperfect tax structure under scrutiny, 13 January 2020, the

Mint, accessed on 26 January 2020 at: https://www.livemint.com/news/india/all-gst-refund-claims-on-products-with-imperfect-tax-structure-under-scrutiny-11578935091757.html

34 As per a news report in *Financial Express* dated 25 September 2019, accessed on 26 January 2020 at: https://www.financialexpress.com/economy/rs-1000-crore-fraud-fake-gst-invoice-racket-unearthed-in-kandla/1716514/

35 See press release of Ministry of Finance dated 27 November 2019, accessed on 29 January 2020 at: https://pib.gov.in/newsite/PrintRelease.aspx?relid=195038

36 As reported by *Economic Times* on 15 January 2020, accessed on 29 January 2020 at: https://economictimes.indiatimes.com/news/economy/finance/over-1200-exporters-untraceable-government-saves-rs-350-crore-fake-igst-refund/articleshow/73274446.cms?from=mdr

37 See the news report '931 GST fraud cases identified through data analytics' of *Business Standard* dated 13 January 2020, accessed on 29 January 2020 at: https://www.business-standard.com/article/news-ani/931-gst-fraud-cases-identified-through-data-analytics-120011301028_1.html

CHAPTER 4 CHEFS WHO COOK BOOKS: ACCOUNTING FRAUD

1 See Bhasin, M.L. (2016) 'Creative Accounting Scam at Satyam Computer Limited: How the Fraud Story Unfolded?' *Open Journal of Accounting*, Vol 5, pp. 57-81.

2 Nag, K. (2012) *The Double Life of Ramalinga Raju: The Story of India's Biggest Corporate Fraud*, New Delhi: HarperCollins.

3 Nag, K. (2012) *supra*.

4 Nag (2012), *supra*.

5 See Nag (2012), *supra*.

6 See, for example, the views of Dinesh Kanabar, founder, Dhruva Advisors, in the *Mint* report 'The Fight to Fix The Fault in Our Audits', dated 24 February 2020, accessed on 24 February 2020 at: https://www.livemint.com/companies/news/the-fight-to-fix-the-fault-in-our-audits-11582473207517.html

7 See Nag (2012), *supra*.

8 This incident is narrated by Nag (2012), *supra*.

9 As reported in *Business Today*; report accessed on 22 February 2020 at: https://www.businesstoday.in/current/corporate/india-

among-worst-in-corporate-fraud-bribery-corruption-shows-survey/story/226408.html

10 As reported in *The Hindu BusinessLine* on 13 July 2016; news report accessed on 24 February 2020 at: https://www.thehindubusinessline.com/companies/usl-funds-diversion-not-covered-by-scope-of-diageos-due-diligence/article8845063.ece

11 Data quoted from the *Mint* report 'The Fight to Fix The Fault in Our Audits', dated 24 February 2020, accessed on 24 February 2020 at: https://www.livemint.com/companies/news/the-fight-to-fix-the-fault-in-our-audits-11582473207517.html

12 Order of Whole Time Member of SEBI in WTM/MPB/EFD-1-DRA-III/46/2018.

13 Mukherjea, S. (2014) *Gurus of Chaos*, New Delhi: Bloomsbury.

14 See, for example, Sherman, H.D. and S.D. Young(2016) 'Where Financial Reporting Still Falls Short', *Harvard Business Review* July-August 2016 issue. In this essay, the authors observe that: 'In a perfect world, investors, board members, and executives would have full confidence in companies' financial statements. They could rely on the numbers to make intelligent estimates of the magnitude, timing, and uncertainty of future cash flows and to judge whether the resulting estimate of value was fairly represented in the current stock price... Unfortunately, that's not what happens in the real world, for several reasons. First, corporate financial statements necessarily depend on estimates and judgment calls that can be widely off the mark, even when made in good faith. Second, standard financial metrics intended to enable comparisons between companies may not be the most accurate way to judge the value of any particular company—this is especially the case for innovative firms in fast-moving economies—giving rise to unofficial measures that come with their own problems. Finally, managers and executives routinely encounter strong incentives to deliberately inject error into financial statements.'

15 Berman, B. (2008) *IP Investing: Catalyst for Return or Recipe for Pain?* In Berman, B. (ed.), *From Assets to profits: Competing for IP Value and Return*. New York, NY: John Wiley and Inc.

16 Barkan, R. (2019) 'WeWork and Adam Neumann represent all that is wrong with the business world', *The Guardian*, 23 November 2019, accessed on 11 May 2020 at: https://

www.theguardian.com/commentisfree/2019/nov/23/wework-adam-neumann-business-world

17 Campbell, D. (2019) 'The WeWork S-1t Show: How the co-working giant went from a $47 billion valuation to talk of bankruptcy in just 6 weeks', *Business Insider*, India.

18. Please refer news article accessed on 17 October 2020 at: https://linkprotect.cudasvc.com/url?a=https%3a%2f%2fwww.cpaaustralia.com.au%2f~%2fmedia%2fcorporate%2fallfiles%2f-document%2fprofessional-resources%2fethics%2fcg-vol-7.pdf&c=E,1,zY2dpa7Re3uodw30omyq7x2i6rt3NVJudgGKd2XhEs-BVimncllvHtMpsl3JQtzO28Tb_DfjW2ggNtI6JaLxkryk6s-GYZmLqOw-HPfEC6tP9XggoogiExNJI26A, &typo=1, pp. 235–242.

CHAPTER 5 MERCHANTS OF DELUSIVE DREAMS: PYRAMID AND PONZI SCHEMES

1 For details, see the calculation accessed on 21 March 2020 at: https://www.techzim.co.zw/2016/08/pyramid-schemes-doomed-fail-mathematical-proof/

2 See Ravikumar, A. (2019) *Marauders of Hope*, The Write Place.

3 See the *Business Standard* news report 'The Biggest Ongoing Financial Scam', accessed on 21 March 2020 at: https://www.business-standard.com/article/opinion/debashis-basu-the-biggest-ongoing-financial-scam-112120300115_1.html

4 Quoted from Dalal, S. (2011) *Chain Game*, accessed on 21 March 2020 at: http://www.suchetadalal.com/?id=89a7c242-cc8f-712e-4e316c37c98f&base=sections&f&t=Chain+game

5 Dalal (2011), *supra*.

6 *S*ub-section (c) of Section 2 of The Prize Chits and Money Circulation Schemes (Banning) Act, 1978.

7 Ravikumar (2019), *supra*.

8 Quoted from Valentine, D.A. (1998) *Pyramid Schemes*, Federal Trade Commission, accessed on 21 March 2020 at: https://www.ftc.gov/public-statements/1998/05/pyramid-schemes

9 See Valentine (1998), *supra*.

10 As reported in 'Amway, art of direct selling', 22 August 2018, available at (accessed on 21 March 2020): https://www.financialexpress.com/industry/amway-plans-to-invest-rs-

1000-cr-in-india-over-a-period-of-2-3-years-aims-to-bolster-its-position-and-product-line/1285617/

11 Ravikumar (2019), *supra*.

12 Ruling in W.P.NO.22674 OF 2004 AND W.P.M.P.NO.27411 OF 2004, accessed on 21 March 2020 at: https://indiankanoon.org/doc/642280/

13 As reported by the *Daily Mail* on 20 April 2013, accessed on 21 March 2020 at: https://www.dailymail.co.uk/indiahome/indianews/article-2311810/Online-venture-TVI-Express-promoter-Tarun-Trikha-arrested-duping-lakh-subscribers-India.html

14 *Forbes Asia* ran a follow up article on the reaction to its story on Vijay Eswaran in its March 2013 issue. The follow up article was accessed on 22 March 2020 at: https://www.forbes.com/sites/donaldfrazier/2013/02/27/qnet-founder-eswaran-extolled-vilified-as-readers-weigh-in/#1f96d22c6c0b

15 As reported by *Financial Express* on 25 September 2014, report accessed on 22 March 2020 at: https://www.financialexpress.com/archive/cafe-coffee-day-ordered-to-slam-doors-on-qnet/1301775/

16 A feature on *MoneyLife* titled 'Who is helping Qnet thrive in India?' dated 28 December 2017 has quoted a reputed blog BehindMLM that claims that Qnet has been very careful not to conduct business in either Hong Kong or Mainland China.

17 Ravikumar (2019), *supra*.

18 Reported in *Nepali Times*, and accessed on 22 March 2020 at: http://archive.nepalitimes.com/news.php?id=4625#.Xne74pMzaqA

19 The company's version of things has been reported in brief in the much reviled *Forbes* article, accessed on 22 March 2020 here: https://www.forbes.com/sites/donaldfrazier/2012/10/24/selling-a-better-life/#694bb8a75fe5. The article states that, in one instance, an unscrupulous operator in Chennai set up a scam gold coin operation claiming he was with GoldQuest; then the reporter goes on to state that there was a 'mix-up' that led to police action, but does not give any specifics.

20 SFIO report, quoted in *MoneyLife*; accessed on 22 March 2020 at: https://www.moneylife.in/article/qnet-it-is-a-chain-where-a-person-is-fooled-and-then-he-is-trained-to-fool-others-to-earn-money-says-bombay-hc-order/46857.html

21 SFIO report, quoted in *MoneyLife*, supra.

22 A techie in Hyderabad committed suicide in August 2019, after incurring alleged losses from investments made in a Qnet scheme. But Qnet refuted the claim, stating that the deceased had earned substantial commission from Qnet over time (reporting accessed on 22 March 2020 at: https://timesofindia.indiatimes.com/city/hyderabad/andhra-techie-commits-suicide-post-qnet-losses-company-denies-wrongdoings/articleshow/70468795.cms). Dharmendra Lodha fell from his office building in Mumbai and died in July 2019. Police believe it to be a suicide, but his family members contest it. His friends had deposed to policemen that he was disturbed due to the losses he had incurred in a Qnet scheme (reporting accessed on 22 March 2020 at: https://www.mid-day.com/articles/airoli-office-death-alleging-police-inaction-kin-knocks-on-cps-door/21506500). A software engineer from Chennai also committed suicide allegedly due to losses incurred in a Qnet scheme (reporting accessed on 22.03.2020 at: https://gulfnews.com/uae/qnet-fires-over-400-represenatives-in-20-countries-1.70077493)

23 Reported by *Moneylife* on 9 May 2016; report accessed on 11 May 2020 at: https://www.moneylife.in/article/qnet-it-is-a-chain-where-a-person-is-fooled-and-then-he-is-trained-to-fool-others-to-earn-money-says-bombay-hc-order/46857.html

24 See the Wikipedia page of Qnet.

25 See *Times of India* news report dated 28 December 2016, accessed on 22 March 2020 at: https://timesofindia.indiatimes.com/city/mumbai/chargesheet-against-michael-ferreira-in-rs-425-crore-investor-scam/articleshow/56211982.cms

26 Public Notice of Department of Consumer Affairs dated 14 August 2019, accessed on 23 March 2020 at: https://consumeraffairs.nic.in/sites/default/files/file-uploads/latestnews/Public%20notice.pdf

27 See reporting dated 23 April 2013 in *Times of India*, accessed on 24 March 2020 at: https://timesofindia.indiatimes.com/city/kolkata/33-years-later-Sanchayita-payback-drags-on/articleshow/19686212.cms

28 SEBI (2014) Order in the case of PACL Limited vide WTM/PS/30/CIS/NRO/AUG/2014.

29 SEBI (2014), *supra*.
30 Definition as per Oxford dictionary.
31 See Para. 30 in SEBI (2014), *supra*.
32 See, for example, the news report in *India Today* dated 22 October 2013, 'Peerless faces charges of duping millions of depositors', accessed on 24 March 2020 at: https://www.indiatoday.in/magazine/economy/story/19830430-peerless-faces-charge-of-duping-millions-of-depositors-771322-2013-10-22
33 Para. 6 in SEBI (2014).
34 See Para. 25 and 27 of SEBI (2014).
35 See news report in *Business Standard* dated 27 August 2014, accessed on 25 March 2020 at: https://www.business-standard.com/article/markets/bhangoo-family-s-stake-in-pacls-parent-114082700797_1.html
36 p. 76 of SEBI (2014).
37 p. 81 of SEBI (2014).
38 See, for example, Para. 2 and 5 in SEBI's order in WTM/RKA/ERO-CIS/19/2013, dated 23 April 2013.
39 See Para. 7 of SEBI (2013) Order of Whole Time Director in WTM/RKA/ERO-CIS/19/2013, accessed on 25 March 2020 at: https://www.sebi.gov.in/sebi_data/attachdocs/1366731012533.pdf
40 Notable ponzi schemes that went bust in the aftermath of Saradha scam were the Rose Valley scheme and iCore scam in West Bengal and Assam, and Seashore group scandal and Artha Tatwa scam in Odisha.
41 Study quoted in ITU (2020) 'Unlicensed Digital Investment Schemes' *(UDIS)*, accessed on 25 March 2020 at: https://www.itu.int/en/ITU-T/extcoop/figisymposium/Documents/ITU_SIT_WG_Unlicensed%20Digital%20Investment%20Schemes_f.pdf
42 This is an intelligent guess based on the findings of the Enforcement Directorate. ED found that Bhardwaj owns multiple properties in Dubai. He has no other source of income to explain the money he used to purchase these properties. For details, see the news report, accessed on 25 March 2020, at: https://timesofindia.indiatimes.com/business/india-business/ed-attaches-dubai-offices-of-bitcoin-fraud-mastermind-bhardwaj/articleshow/65905046.cms

CHAPTER 6 SHELLS, MAILBOXES AND ISLANDS: THE FRAUD ECOSYSTEM

1 Mitra, Sumit (1983) 'Jayanti Dharma Teja: An unheralded comeback', *India Today*, 31 March 1983.

2 Mitra (1983), *supra*.

3 As reported in the ruling in the case of *Dr. Jayanti Dharma Teja vs Income-Tax Officer*, accessed on 10 March 2020 at: https://www.casemine.com/judgement/in/5d4a60563321bc5fod3895a9

4 Mitra (1983), *supra*.

5 See the Tax Justice Network's website , accessed online on 10 March 2020 at: https://corporatetaxhavenindex.org/introduction/cthi-2019-results

6 As per a report of the Swiss Bankers' Association, quoted in the news portal swissinfo.ch, accessed on 12 May 2020 at: https://www.swissinfo.ch/eng/tax-justice-network_switzerland-ranked--global-capital-of-bank-secrecy-/43864986

7 As reported in 'Ex-HSBC worker Herve Falciani says US told him to flee to Spain', 22 April 2013, news.com.au, accessed on 12 May 2020 at: https://www.news.com.au/finance/business/ex-hsbc-worker-us-said-to-head-for-spain/news-story/3f8157c16743143 5523ae9ed8de893d2

8 TJN report on Dubai, accessed online on 1 December 2018 at: https://www.financialsecrecyindex.com/PDF/UnitedArabEmirates_Dubai.pdf

9 Ibid.

10 Glenny, *McMafia*, quoted in TJN, ibid.

11 The Tax Justice Network revealed in 2019 that UK and UK-linked jurisdictions accounted for a third of tax avoidance risk, four times more than the next highest contributor. See the Accountancy Daily report accessed online on 12 May 2020 at: https://www.accountancydaily.co/uk-overseas-territories-top-tax-haven-risk-list. Also see the Tax Justice Network Financial Secrecy Index 2020 Narrative Report on the United Kingdom, accessed on 12 May 2020 at: https://fsi.taxjustice.net/PDF/UnitedKingdom.pdf

12 Knobel, A, (2017) 'Trusts: Weapons of Mass Injustice?' Report released by Tax Justice Network.

13 See the CNBC news report available at the address (accessed on 8 March 2020): https://www.cnbc.com/2019/02/20/allen-

stanfords-ponzi-scheme-victims-say-they-have-been-short-changed.html

14 Ibid.

15 These facts are based on an investigative work by journalist Ashish Khetan (2011), published as 'Bluff Master Ali' in *Tehelka*, 16 April 2011; accessed on 14 March 2020 at: http://old.tehelka.com/bluff-master-ali/

16 As quoted in Khetan (2011).

17 See Khetan (2011).

18 As quoted in Khetan (2011).

19 Judgment in ITA No. 4156-4162/M/2010, accessed on 14 March 2020 at: https://indiankanoon.org/doc/181026658/

EPILOGUE

1 See news report in *Economic Times* dated 27 July 2019, accessed on 14 April 2020 at: https://economictimes.indiatimes.com/news/economy/policy/economic-offenders-serious-threat-to-global-stability-says-india-as-it-calls-for-joint-brics-action/articleshow/70411232.cms?from=mdr

2 See Sinha, U.K. (2020) *Going Public: My Time at SEBI*, New Delhi: Penguin Portfolio.

3 As mentioned in the webpage of KPMG's forensic practice division, accessed on 14 April 2020 at: https://home.kpmg/in/en/home/services/advisory/risk-consulting/forensic.html

4 SEBI Order No. WTM/GM/EFD/03/2018-19.

GLOSSARY

ADIA	Abu Dhabi Investment Authority
ADS	American Depository Shares
AI	Artificial Intelligence
API	Active Pharmaceutical Ingredient
ARCs	Asset Reconstruction Companies
ASEAN	Association of Southeast Asian Nations
BRICS	Brazil, Russia, India, China and South Africa
BRI	Belt and Road Initiative
BSE	Bombay Stock Exchange
BVI	British Virgin Islands
CAG	Comptroller and Auditor General
CAGR	Compound annual growth rate
CBI	Central Bureau of Investigation
CBIC	Central Board of Indirect Taxes and Customs
CCD	Café Coffee Day
CEIB	Central Economic Intelligence Bureau
CEO	Chief Executive Officer
CFO	Chief Financial Officer
CIS	Collective Investment Schemes
COO	Country of origin
CRO	Chief Risk Officer
CrPC	Code of Criminal Procedure
CSM	Chopped strand mats
DEPB	Duty Entitlement Pass Book
DCF	Discounted cash flows
DRT	Debt Recovery Tribunal
DGAD	Directorate General of Anti-dumping and Allied Duties
DGFT	Directorate General of Foreign Trade
DGGI	Directorate General of GST Intelligence
DGTR	Directorate General of Trade Remedies

DoS	Directorate of Safeguards
DRI	Directorate of Revenue Intelligence
ED	Enforcement Directorate
EOW	Economic Offences Wing
ERP	Enterprise resource planning
EU	European Union
EWS	Early Warning Signals
EXIM	Export Import
FATF	Financial Action Task Force
FBI	Federal Bureau of Investigation
FDA	Food and Drug Administration
FDF	Finished Dosage Formulation
FIDS	Fraud Investigation and Dispute Services
FIR	First Information Report
FIU	Financial Intelligence Unit
FTA	Free trade agreement
FTC	Federal Trade Commission
GST	Goods and Services Tax
HFCs	Housing finance companies
HFT	High Frequency Trading
HOS	Heard on Street
IB	Information Bureau
IBC	Insolvency and Bankruptcy Code
ICO	Initial Coin Offering
ICS	Indian Civil Service
IFIN	IL&FS Financial Services
IL&FS	Infrastructure Leasing & Financial Services Limited
IMF	International Monetary Fund
IPC	Indian Penal Code
IR	Independent Representative
IRS	Indian Revenue Service
ISSDA	Indian Stainless Steel Development Association
ITC	Input tax credit
ITNL	IL&FS Transport Network

ITS	Indian Trade Service
KSM	Key Standing Material
KYC	Know Your Customer
LAS	Loan Against Shares
LC	Letter of Credit
LE	Law enforcement
LIC	Life Insurance Corporation
LoU	Letters of Undertaking
LPG	Liberalisation, Privatisation and Globalisation
LR	Letter Rogatory
MCA	Ministry of Corporate Affairs
MD	Managing Director
MIS	Management Information System
MLM	Multi-level marketing
MMM	Mavrodi Mondial Money
MTBL	Masters in Taxation and Business Laws
NAV	Net Asset Value
NBFCs	Non-banking financial companies
NCR	National Capital Region
NDA	Non-disclosure agreement
NFRA	National Financial Reporting Authority
NHB	National Housing Bank
NLEM	National List of Essential Medicines
NSE	National Stock Exchange of India Limited
NYSE	New York Stock Exchange
OECD	Organisation for Economic Co-operation and Development
OPM	Other People's Money
P&L	Profit and loss
PMC (bank)	Punjab & Maharashtra Co-operative (bank)
PNB	Punjab National Bank
PSBs	Public sector banks
PwC	PricewaterhouseCoopers

QR	Quantitative Restriction
REITs	Real Estate Investment Trusts
RERA	Real Estate Regulatory Authority
RBI	Reserve Bank of India
R&D	Research and development
RIS	Research and Information System for Developing Countries
RPT	Related party transactions
SAIL	Steel Authority of India Limited
SAT	Securities Appellate Tribunal
SBG	Shadow Bank Group
SBI	State Bank of India
SC	Supreme Court
SEBI	Securities and Exchange Board of India
SEC	Securities and Exchange Commission
SEZ	Special Economic Zone
SFIO	Serious Fraud Investigation Office
SIDBI	Small Industries Development Bank of India
SPV	Special Purpose Vehicle
TBT	Tick-by-Tick
TCP/IP	Transmission Control Protocol/ Internet Protocol
TDS	Tax deducted at source
TJN	Tax Justice Network
TRAI	Telecom Regulatory Authority of India
UCIS	Unregulated Collective Investment Schemes
UPSI	Unpublished Price Sensitive Information
USL	United Spirits Limited
USP	Unique selling proposition
WGA	Whole-of-government approach

ABOUT THE AUTHOR

SMARAK SWAIN graduated in Electrical Engineering from the Indian Institute of Technology, Kharagpur, in 2006 and joined the Indian Revenue Service (IRS) in 2008. He has done his master's in Taxation and Business Laws (MTBL) from the Nalsar University of Law, Hyderabad.

Swain has authored the critically acclaimed guide to *Base Erosion and Profit Shifting, Tangible Guide to Intangibles: Identification, Valuation, Taxation and Transfer Pricing*. He is also the author of the bestselling book *Loophole Games: A Treatise on Tax Avoidance Strategies*. He has wide exposure in fields of audit, assessment, investigation, transfer pricing and international taxation. Through his writings, he tries to raise awareness about regulatory challenges in the fields of taxation, finance and technology.

Originally from Odisha, Swain currently lives in Delhi with his family. His articles have been published in *Nikkei Asian Review*, *the Mint*, *The Economic Times*, *Firstpost* and *Asia Times*.